From the Ganges to the Thames

A Memoir

Sonia Melchett

QUARTET

First published in 2016 by Quartet Books Limited
A member of the Namara Group
27 Goodge Street, London W1T 2LD
Copyright © Sonia Melchett 2016
The right of Sonia Melchett to be identified
as the author of this work has been asserted
by her in accordance with the
Copyright, Designs and Patents Act, 1988
A catalogue record for this book
is available from the British Library
ISBN 978 0 7043 7410 2
Typeset by Josh Bryson
Printed and bound in Great Britain by
T J International Ltd, Padstow, Cornwall

For Andrew and my family

One

I was born in September 1925 on the steps of the Ramsay Hospital in Nainital, high in the foothills of the Himalayas. Forgetful of my imminent birth, my mother was riding her large black mare, alongside a handsome subaltern when her waters broke. Luckily, she was near the hospital, but she didn't make the entrance. My father, an army doctor, was stationed at Agra, when he heard the news. It was the custom in those days that, in the hot weather, wives of officers were dispatched to the hill stations, while their husbands sweated it out on the plains. Years later, when my mother told me the story, I was shocked, but not disbelieving. My mother, Wendy, was disarmingly honest and would never have invented it.

Wendy had married my father in rather strange circumstances. He came from a strictly religious family. The youngest of eleven children, he was brought up in Dublin and was known as 'Rags' because his clothes were handed down by his elder brothers. By the time they reached him, they were in tatters. His family was descended from a line of Scottish Protestants named Graham, a Reiver clan from the Scots Borders, which had settled in Dublin in the eighteenth century. His father had been a Senior Wrangler at Cambridge, where five of his brothers had also been undergraduates. But scarcity of money made it necessary for my father to go to Trinity College, Dublin, where he read medicine, specialising in gynaecology. His great-grandfather had been Napoleon's doctor at St Helena, and he had an aunt who had been murdered in China, when working there as a missionary. Six of his brothers were either in holy orders, teaching or medicine. One, Uncle 'Togo', became famous as an Ear, Nose & Throat Specialist in Dublin. Another, Uncle Chris, a Senior Chaplain to the British Navy, was very clever at making money on the Stock Market. When he took the ceremony of my first wedding at St Paul's, Knightsbridge, he complained to the family that he had never been paid for it.

Soon after my father qualified, he joined the Royal Army Medical Corps and was immediately posted to India, but he felt he shouldn't leave without first getting married. He had not yet met my mother, Wendy, who was the second youngest of a family of eight brothers and sisters of Scottish descent called Dunbar. She lived in a large, gloomy house in Cardiff. Her father was head of the Welsh Railways, and her eldest brother also served in transport and ended his career as head of the British-run Sudanese Railways, where he became a famous Egyptologist and archaeologist, the author of the *The Rock Pictures of Lower Nubia*.

My mother trained as a nurse, getting her first job in a children's hospital in Edinburgh, where my father's sister was also working. When Rags visited her, he soon fell in love with the small, beautiful, dark-haired and vivacious Wendy. Without much persuasion, she agreed to marry the tall and handsome young army doctor. It was a whirlwind romance, and the wedding photograph shows his brother officers holding an arch of swords over their heads.

The honeymoon was spent in Istanbul, where apparently I was conceived. Then my parents sailed on to India via the Middle East where they stayed with my uncle. My father was first stationed in Agra, where my sister Daphne (known as Bunty) was born three years later. He had hoped for a boy and treated us as if we were boys. I came in for the harshest punishments because I was the naughtier one. Bunty was dark-haired, shy and delicate with a tendency to fly into rages, especially if she was made to wear a pretty dress for a social occasion. My parents found her difficult to manage, but she and I were very close, and it was usually left for me to persuade her to obey. "You cope with her, Sonia," Wendy used to say. Bunty preferred animals to people, so I would use bribery to bring her round and I'd let her play with my pet mongoose.

As a doctor, my father was not attached to a particular regiment, so we were always being posted to different stations. My first memory was of being carried on my father's shoulders through a swarm of locusts that had invaded our compound, and being thrown up in the air and caught just before reaching the ground. He had a rather sadistic sense of humour. I remember once, when we were living in the old fort in Madras and before I could swim, he took me into the rough sea and started tossing me up above the breakers.

My memories of India are rather haphazard, as we had to return to England when I was eight. That was the custom in those days. But some scenes are embedded in my mind. Once when I was about three, I undid a packet of cigarettes and gave Bunty all the tobacco to eat in her cot. This resulted in several whacks from the ivory hairbrushes that were kept on top of my father's chest-of-drawers. These were used either to give me a few hard smacks on the bottom or a hundred strokes on my long hair. One day I decided I didn't like the white plaster of our bedroom and persuaded Bunty that, if we got enough bottles of ink, we could paint it black. I received a very sore bottom that time. But I loved my father, as he was a fount of knowledge and would never disappoint me. If he didn't know the answer, he would look it up in his *Pear's Cyclopaedia*, which he felt had all the answers.

I was also fascinated by his little office, where he did his experiments and kept pickled snakes and scorpions in bottles. What he did with them, I shall never know, but he was always writing articles for the *British Medical Journal*, so perhaps he was contributing to clinical knowledge in some obscure way. Once our car ran over a cobra in the road that was too big for pickling, but the skin was made into handbags – our pride and joy. He also had a valuable collection of stamps, and he and I used to spend hours sticking them into albums, while he would tell me about the various countries. I think this first lesson in geography is what produced my love of travelling.

When I was old enough, he would put me on the handlebars of his bicycle and take me to the military hospital. There he did his daily rounds, wearing khaki shorts and tunic with a Sam Browne belt shining across his chest, and we'd both be in our hand-whitened *topees*. They made a great fuss of me at the hospital, and I think it was my first encounter with the real India outside the compound of our bungalow. I remember the sick Indians lying on their beds, their eyes lighting up at my father's approach. They truly believed he had the magic powers of a *swami*. And there were the beggars we passed on the road, with my father explaining to me how their parents mutilated them on purpose to secure an income. But I was told never to give them money, as I would be surrounded by hundreds of others. I once disobeyed him when I saw a creature dragging himself along on his stumps on the path outside our veranda, and immediately the bungalow was besieged. I never owned up, so I was spared the hairbrushes.

When our *sais* took us riding every morning after *chota hazri*, my father would put a rupee coin between our knees and the saddle to make us grip properly and we had to show the coins were there on our return. Although he couldn't afford to keep his own polo ponies, he was a keen player. One Christmas, he had special miniature polo sticks made so that we could learn to play the game.

We were looked after by a series of *ayahs*. One in particular was quite cruel, very ugly and chewed red betel, which she spat out onto the veranda. I loved knitting and was halfway through a dress for my china doll, Rosebud, when she decided I must finish it before I could go to bed. I knitted for hours into the night, tears mingling with the wool. One evening, when she was still very young, Bunty did the unmentionable in her cot and Ayah made me get up and wash the sheets in the tubs. We slept on the veranda under mosquito nets, and another night my parents arrived back late from a dance and saw a snake just about to wriggle into my sister's cot. Ayah had forgotten to tie the net underneath.

My father rushed for the gun and shot it dead. I expect he pickled it later.

He was a very good shot and sometimes went on tiger shoots. I still love a faded snapshot of myself clad in jodhpurs and *topee* standing on a large dead tiger with my father, rifle in hand, proudly at its side. Pig-sticking was another of his favourite sports and he would often join his fellow officers on a trip up-country to Poona and beyond.

In Nagpur in Central India, we had a bearer who was sometimes left in charge of us. He would make me sit with him under a rug and feel his cock. I just thought it a bit odd and boring, and eventually he would get up and pee milky stuff in front of me. I never said anything, but his little game must have been discovered and he was summarily sacked. Later, one day when we visited the bazaar, I saw him leer at me and then disappear. Going there was a big treat, with stalls full of brightly coloured glass bangles, snake charmers and monkeys for sale. We would gaze transfixed as the cobras rose and swayed from their baskets to the sound of the owner's flute.

Looking back, it seems that so much of life was full of drama and danger. We were always hearing stories of trains being derailed or damaged by violent landslides. Sometimes journeys lasted over three days, which meant we would see a lot of our parents, as our *ayah* and the bearer would have to travel in a different part of the train. I loved the passing beauty of the landscape as we wound round precipitous mountains and over raging torrents. And the nights when my imagination could fly to the sound of the wheels and all dreams seemed possible. Once, at a temporary stop, my father stepped down to the platform to buy some cigarettes and when the train started up, he hadn't reappeared. My mother cried hysterically, "Rags, where are you? Hurry up!" But there was no sign of him and so she immediately pulled the communication cord. After much discussion with the guard, the train started to reverse. Eventually we were back at the station to find my father waiting on the platform, calmly smoking a cigarette. Apparently an Indian had collapsed with a heart attack and my father had revived him with massage and resuscitation before organising an ambulance to take him to hospital.

When we travelled to Agra where my sister had been born, I remember the feeling of disappointment as we were taken round the Taj Mahal. Nothing inside but a lot of empty rooms, although I did think it romantic that a man should build such a vast monument to the memory of his wife. Our bungalow at Kamptee was close to the holy River Kanhan, and I remember the *dhobi wallah* beating our sheets on the wet grey stones – a primitive laundry, but it seemed to work.

The event which made the most impression on me as a child in India was when we were sleeping on the veranda of our bungalow, which faced the road looking down to the river. We didn't have a fence round the compound, but instead we had several watchmen patrolling with rifles. Often at night, funeral processions, which were very colourful affairs, used to pass by. Four bearers would carry the body on a bier, which would be decorated with bright silks and flowers. Many relations and friends would surround it, chanting songs and covering it with gifts and coins. A stream of beggars would follow, picking up anything that fell on the road. Our *ayah* told us that the body would be taken to the Holy River to place it in the water together with the food, money and clothing necessary for the journey to Heaven. In this part of India people believed that the river was their god.

One night there was an occurrence. The person on the bier wasn't dead. It was the body of a young woman dressed in white with flowers in her hair. She was completely still, praying to herself. I thought it must be a wedding, so as Ayah and Bunty were fast asleep, I decided to follow the procession. I slipped past the night watchman and kept a short way behind the crowd, which stopped before they came to the river. But where was the bridegroom?

Suddenly I realised there was no bridegroom, but the corpse of a dead man. By this time I was rigid with fear, but I couldn't move. The young woman stood in front of the body and raised her arms. Others gave her bunches of flowers. She took them and raised them above her head and then gave them back, turning round in a complete circle. She kissed the dead man and then, one by one, took off her rings. A big bonfire was being built and when it was burning furiously, the woman was tied to a sort of scaffolding and taken towards the flames. I wanted to run, but I was transfixed as in a nightmare. The woman looked as if she was in a trance, and there was music, and all the people were singing and shouting with joy. Suddenly there was a terrible scream, and I found I was running, cutting my feet on the stones, tearing my nightdress on the trees until I reached our veranda. I rushed to Ayah and started sobbing. "Oh dear, child," she wailed, "you've seen *suttee*!"

We were moving the next day to join yet another regiment, so I had no time to dwell on what I had witnessed. My father was strict about not becoming overfond of possessions. Bunty and I were only allowed what we could pack into one small suitcase – anything over was given to the children of the Indian servants. But somehow I always managed to smuggle Rosebud, my china doll – a present from Uncle Togo. He would send us a yearly Christmas present from Dublin. Usually, they were party dresses and, as my mother made our clothes on her Singer sewing machine, these were particularly appreciated. But Rosebud was special. I gave her a life of her own. I would take photographs of her with my Box Brownie and stick them in her own handmade albums. Once I stupidly fed some scraps of food into her half-opened mouth, which my father had to extract with surgical instruments. Some thirty years later, in the nursery of our home in Tite Street in Chelsea, one of my daughters accidentally dropped Rosebud, breaking her china face. It was difficult for me to control the anger and loss I felt. "It's only a doll, Mummy," said my daughter.

Once, travelling across central India in a convoy with the servants in a car behind us, followed by the large horsebox with our horses and ponies, we had to ford the Ganges upstream, where the flow was at its highest. We were told the crossing might be quite dangerous and we should wait. An Indian carrying a long pole was instructed to cross the river on foot to test the bottom. We were to follow, if he made it. But as the waters rose, my father thought we should chance it. I remember the noises of our horse in the trailer behind us neighing with fright, and we nearly were stuck halfway across. But we eventually arrived safely at the far bank.

At an early age, I was conscious of my femininity and my effect on the opposite sex. I was what my mother called 'the darling of the Regiment'. I can remember a good-looking subaltern stopping outside our bungalow one day, looking down at me from his large Bay horse and tapping me lightly with his cane. "Here, my beauty, I've got a bone to pick with you. You cut me dead at the polo yesterday. I was most upset." And he cantered away. It was my first introduction to grown-up teasing. Pick my bones, cut, what did he mean? I didn't even have a knife.

Our education was haphazard to say the least. My father used to read us stories by his favourite author, Rudyard Kipling, and I came to know most of them by heart. My mother loved poetry, particularly Rupert Brooke. I think she must have started secretly pining for English fields and honey for tea. But she also read the classics, and our only education came from reading, which we loved.

Later my mother persuaded her sister, a spinster, to come and stay, and we acquired a basic education of sorts. Aunty Doll was a gentle, serious person, well educated and deeply religious. My mother was always trying to 'get her off' and eventually a tea planter did propose marriage. My aunt turned him down, her reason being that she didn't think she could really stand the climate. But her gentleness was deceptive. At times she could be resourceful and on one occasion extremely courageous.

My parents were away. She was in sole charge of the bungalow, when suddenly we heard a weird sound of howling in the trees at the edge of the compound. Anid, the bearer, came rushing onto the veranda, screaming, "*Memsahib*, mad jackal. Very dangerous." The howling came nearer and Anid shouted at us to run away. "Go inside immediately," said Aunty Doll in the firm voice she used when not to be disobeyed. From the window we watched as she pulled down one of my father's rifles from the rack on the wall, loaded it and stood her guard as the wild animal advanced. The next thing we knew was that a shot had been fired and the jackal lay dead a few yards from the steps of the veranda. Aunty Doll stood very still, red in the face and shaking violently. She had never shot a gun before in her life.

My mother used to love going to parties and giving them herself. But she was socially insecure, which sometimes made her appear snobbish. The bearer was always being made to look into the box at the bottom of our drive to see if anyone had left their visiting card. If a boy came round with a chit from the Colonel's wife inviting them to drinks, it was a moment of great satisfaction. Chits were the only means of communication – a single sheet of paper with a message written on one side, folded in half, one corner turned over and the name written on the outside. When my mother gave a dinner, I always loved seeing the table laid out with all the best glass and silver, and then going into the cooking quarters in the special area behind the bungalow to see the cooks prepare the food, some of which was done with feet as well as hands. I don't think my mother ever saw the meals being prepared; she would just give the menu to the bearer.

Bunty and I lived mainly on curry and rice and, as Bunty hated curry, my father said she must just eat the rice. When my mother objected, he said, "All the Indians do, why shouldn't she?" But once a week for a treat we would have our favourite meal – fried fish, chips and tomato ketchup – and I have loved it ever since. Bunty was very slim with enormous brown eyes and dark hair. As a child she was almost plain, although later she grew into a beauty and was often taken for Elizabeth Taylor. Physically brave, she was painfully shy, particularly of men. If ever there was a male in a room, she would refuse to go in. I was equally thin with long legs, blue eyes and curly blonde hair. I had slightly protruding teeth caused by sucking my thumb – even coating it with quinine did not stop me. When my mother tried to persuade my father to get the dentist to fit me with a brace, he refused. "A waste of money, and pure vanity. Use an elastic band, quite good enough." He had no time for female vanity. Even when he gave us our vaccinations, he put them in a prominent place on our legs which left unsightly marks, moving my mother to tears.

She always seemed rather afraid of my father. Although not conscious of it at the time, I don't think their sex life was particularly satisfactory. I remember once – the wall between their room and ours must have been rather thin – her crying out as if in pain, "Please, Rags, don't," and then the noise of sobbing. But she adored us children and possibly, because of his harshness, she would spoil us behind his back. Little things remain in my mind. Whenever they went to a dinner or a ball, there would always be a present under our pillows when we woke up – a sweet or a dance card with a tassled pencil.

The first time I fell in love was when I was seven with a boy called Peter. For his eighth birthday, his parents gave an enormous party for him, inviting children and their parents from up to thirty miles away. Even for India, this was quite a distance. They must have been in a grand regiment or rich or both, because it was the most sumptuous party we'd ever been to. It all took place in tents in the grounds in front of their bungalow. First we were told to go into the biggest marquee. At the far end, there was an enormous rainbow with hundreds of bags of gold coins at its foot. We all took one and were told we could spend them in all the other tents. Some had puppet shows, some snake charmers, some toys for sale. I bought two goldfish in a bowl. Peter thought the games we were meant to play were very childish. We played one where we were divided into two rows and skipped towards each other, singing. Peter was between me and a little Indian Princess. Suddenly she cried out, "You're holding my hand too tightly – I don't like it." I remember a feeling of violent jealousy. I told Peter he could hold my hand as hard as he liked.

After the game, he took me off to show me his birthday presents. One of them was a bicycle, but he said he wished it had been a motorbike like his elder brother's. He asked me if I'd like a ride on the motorbike. Soon we were hurtling through the tents and round the compound. All the parents came out of the bungalow and started screaming, because he was completely out of control and couldn't stop. I loved it and hung on to him very tightly. Eventually, his elder brother saved the day by grabbing hold of the handlebars. Returning home along bumpy roads, I was hanging on to my goldfish bowl, trying to keep it full of water. I don't think I ever saw Peter again, but it was the first time I remember feeling both jealousy and sexual attraction.

Another children's party was given by the Viceroy for one of his elephants' hundredth birthday. My mother was very excited, because we were going to the Viceregal Lodge, and she made us especially pretty dresses. At the party, we had to queue up for rides on the old elephant, but he was very friendly. He knelt down for Ayah to put us in the *howdah* on his back. It was very wobbly getting up, and we all screamed with delight.

At eight years old, white children were meant to leave India, as it was considered dangerous for their health to stay on. Parents had to make a difficult choice: either to remain together and send their children to boarding schools 'at home' or to separate, the mother travelling back with the children. My parents chose the parting.

As we pressed against the rail on the deck of the P&O troopship taking us to England and waved to my father standing on the fast-disappearing jetty, I felt an emptiness in the pit of my tummy. He stood very upright in his khaki uniform, his white *topee* showing over the heads of the crowd, and he lifted his cane to us in a final salute. I was eight years old and Bunty five. "Don't cry," my mother said, "I'm taking you home." But mixed with the emptiness was rage. This was our home and we were deserting my father; how could my mother do this to him?

That must have been a difficult journey for her. The three of us shared a cabin and it was a rough voyage, which in those days took six weeks. Bunty was seasick most of the time and I was sulky, withdrawn and full of resentment against my mother. I refused to play with the other children on board and spent most of the time hiding behind one of the lifebuoys on the top deck, either buried in a book or watching critically the antics of the passengers. Deck quoits was the popular game, and one day I saw my mother playing with animation and obviously enjoying herself. She looked very pretty in a white dress with a red sash and her dark brown eyes flashed with a liveliness that was new to me. Her partner was a young officer I didn't know. As the days went by I started following her stealthily, keeping my distance. As always on board ship, the passengers were beginning to divide into groups, but my mother's lot seemed to be the most active. They played bridge, deck games, drank, danced, and Wendy's partner was always the same young officer.

"Why don't you go and play with the other children?" she asked in desperation one day as she saw me lying behind my lifebuoy.

I gave her what I hoped was a deeply disapproving look. "Because I don't feel like playing and never will again."

"I can't understand it," I heard her say to her new friend. "She has never been tiresome like this before."

During the daytime, I never recalled the terrible incident I had witnessed by the banks of the Kanhan, but in the course of the voyage, I suffered from nightmares and would wake up sobbing and sweating with fear. My mother would take me in her arms and comfort me, believing that it was the separation from my father that was the cause of my tears. I didn't disillusion her, hoping it might add to her guilt.

One night, a few days before we were due to arrive in England, there was to be a fancy dress ball. My mother decided to go as a gypsy. For days beforehand our cabin was strewn with curtain rings being sewn onto coloured scarves and a fringed bedspread was miraculously transformed into a twirling skirt. My fury knew no bounds as I watched her giggling with self-appreciation as she made up her face in front of the tiny mirror. "Well, what do you think, girls?" Bunty, still looking faintly green, murmured her approval and I remained scowling and silent. "Oh, you are a spoilsport, Sonia." But she didn't really care about our reaction as she dashed from the cabin. While the throbbing music filled the ship and the hours slipped slowly by, my resentment grew until I could stand it no longer. My cotton nightdress was trailing to the ground as I crept out leaving Bunty asleep. I reached the crowded saloon and soon spotted my mother dancing in the arms of my enemy. Couples parted in alarm as I rushed towards her. "Come away, you must come away. How can you be dancing when Daddy is all alone in India?" My mother, deeply embarrassed and upset, pulled me by the arm out of the saloon and back to our cabin. My job done, I was soon fast asleep. Whether she returned to the dance, I never knew. I have no further memories of that journey but, thinking back, I feel sorry for my mother. It was probably the first time she had enjoyed herself for years and God knows what my father was getting up to in India.

My mother had always been vague, but I had never realised quite how vague until, as the gangplank was lowered at Southampton, I asked, "Where are we going to stay?"

"Oh, I expect we'll find some digs somewhere."

"But which town?" I asked.

She looked a little embarrassed. "Well, I hadn't really thought. Perhaps we'll just stay here for a while until we decide what to do."

After a friendly taxi driver had loaded our luggage, she asked if he knew of a good small hotel or guest house. "As near to the sea as possible," I added. I think I felt that if I was able to see the sea, I would somehow feel closer to my father.

Everywhere we tried was booked up, but eventually we found someone who was prepared to find a place for us. Our digs were on the front and consisted of a living-room with a small kitchen at one end, a bathroom and one bedroom with a double and a single bed.

My memory of the months we spent at Southampton is decidedly hazy except for two events. The first occurred a few days after our arrival. Rummaging amongst my mother's possessions in the desk – I was always a very nosy child – I came across a small snapshot of the officer she had flirted with on board ship. I was overcome with such a violent fit of jealousy that I tore it into as many pieces as possible and scattered them all over the floor. My mother was most upset when she discovered them. "You silly girl, he was only a friend. What on earth's the matter with you?" I suppose it was jealousy once removed on behalf of my father. I only know it is one of the fiercest and basest of emotions, and impossible to control.

The other memory was when I discovered that my mother had only half the second finger on her left hand. When I asked her about it, she turned scarlet and said she had lost it in an accident with a mangle when she was a girl. She had always been clever at hiding it, and when she played bridge she always held a pretty chiffon handkerchief in her left hand. When I told Bunty about it, she was horrified and refused to share the double bed with my mother for several nights. My father later told me that she had even hidden it from him until years after they were married. How sad to be ashamed of so small a deformity.

The next thing I recall is that we were living in a flat in Worthing. My mother's parents had retired there after leaving 'the Railways' and were living with Aunty Doll, who had returned from India a year before with no regrets in spite of her rejected tea-planter. Money was extremely short, and to pay for the fees of our day school, my mother took a job in a children's hospital. She had odd ideas of economy. She still made all our clothes, and Bunty and I were always well-dressed. When I met someone years later who was at the same school, she said that one of her earliest memories was of me in a smart-belted camelhair coat. But loo paper was considered a luxury, and we had to make do with newspaper brought back from the hospital. Her ideas on morality were also ambivalent. Certain items of 'Railways' cutlery seemed to find their way to the flat, as did towels marked 'Worthing General Hospital'. But if either of us said or repeated an unkind word about anyone, we would be severely ticked off. Punishment was a thing of the past, and the ivory hairbrushes became a distant memory, as did my father.

We didn't seem to have many friends. There was a red-headed boy, the son of one of my mother's bridge four, who told me he was going to be a famous photographer. He would make me sit for hours in different poses and then wait in his dark-room while he developed his masterpieces. But I didn't like him much and was always trying to avoid accepting invitations to his house. My mother considered his family rather grand and tried to encourage our friendship. "You must make an effort, Sonia, pull your weight in life and keep your end up. Not just for your sake but for Bunty, too," adding mysteriously, "I don't want you to go through what I did as a girl." I was to hear this theme repeated all too often in the years to come. Bunty was being just as difficult as ever and hated the day school so much that a small local weekly boarding school was thought to be the answer. This was to prove a mistake, and every Sunday evening when she was due to return, there would be terrible scenes which went on until my mother's soft heart weakened and she was allowed to stay at home.

Bunty was my only confidante and I would pour out to her everything of interest that happened to me. She was a willing listener and sat silently looking at me with her large brown eyes staring from her pale face. She enjoyed living vicariously the life that she was too frightened and too shy to live herself. I would tell her about the red-haired boy and about the man who always followed me back from school. When no one was looking, he would undo his trousers and pull out his cock and show it to me. I never thought of telling my mother as, even then, I had a subconscious knowledge that she needed protecting from the unpleasant side of life. She should only be told good news, never anything bad.

Suddenly our fortunes changed. My father had been posted home and was to be Head Medical Officer of the Duke of York's Cadet School at Dover. We found ourselves in a large furnished Victorian house, from which we could see Dover Castle. We had a maid and my mother felt it was almost like being back in India. We were sent as day girls to a convent in the town, but both Bunty and I disliked the nuns intensely. Apart from one who always seemed to be in as much trouble as the pupils and was performing constant acts of penance, the nuns appeared to us as a sadistic group of black crows. We were endlessly being punished for some minor misdemeanour and were either doing seven compulsory runs round the playground or writing out a hundred times, "I must show more respect for Mother Superior."

One day I conceived a plan that we would run away to the castle to frighten everyone, including our parents, and show how miserable we were. Food and water were smuggled to school in satchels and during the morning break we made our escape. We had been to the castle before, in a group, and more or less knew our way around. The first day we spent happily exploring the drawbridges, moat and dungeons. Although I was the leader, Bunty was the braver and would always take the first leap across a ditch into the unknown beyond. Of course, we had no idea how cold and miserable it would become during the night, but, when Bunty implored me to return, I stubbornly refused and insisted on sticking it out. In fact it was a great relief when we were discovered the following day by a search party sent out by our frantic and worried parents. My father's fury knew no bounds. We were too old for beating, but were banished to our room for three days on a diet of bread and water and no books. Naturally, my mother smuggled up extra rations and my copy of *Gone with the Wind*, which I managed to read by torchlight under the bedclothes. It turned out to be a happy end to our adventure, though a failure of our bid for independence. We were immediately dispatched back to the convent.

At Dover, we heard Neville Chamberlain's announcement on the wireless that German armed forces had invaded Polish territory and, as a consequence, we were now in a state of war with Germany. My father immediately joined the British Expeditionary Force. He would soon leave for the field hospitals of France to take part in what was to be known as the Phoney War. I was being sent to the Royal School at Bath, a semi-charitable institution for the children of poor Army officers, where the fees were subsidised but the education was said to be excellent. My mother said she couldn't stand the thought of returning to Worthing, but would take a flat in London. She later found one off the Cromwell Road, where she worked in a club for Polish officers by day and as an air raid warden by night. Bunty was to go to a small boarding school where she, at last, seemed fairly happy. The idea was that she would eventually join me at Bath, if I didn't find the life there too hard for her.

TWO

The Royal School for Daughters of Officers of the Army was certainly spartan, and I was soon writing to my parents that on no account should they submit Bunty to such an ordeal; she wouldn't stand it for twenty-four hours. Run on Army lines, the discipline was ferocious. I shall never forget the first day, sitting at the long refectory table for tea and having to eat unrefined bread without butter or jam. With our knowledge of diet now, we would all be consuming it dutifully, but then it seemed awful. The girl sitting next to me said she would throw up if she had to eat it. I managed to smuggle out her piece of bread under the elastic of my navy blue woollen knickers. She subsequently became my best friend until, later in my school career, I deserted her for the large spotty-faced captain of lacrosse, on whom I'd had a crush for some time.

Over our knickers and white woollen vests, we wore cream Viyella shirts, the striped school tie and dark blue pleated gymslips tied at the waist by a cotton sash. After we had been at school a year, we were allowed to change into mufti on Sunday evenings. We still used certain Army expressions and slang, and were all very conscious of our military backgrounds.

"What regiment is your father in?" asked the girl in the bed next to mine in the dormitory our first night.

"He's in the RAMC," I answered proudly.

"What on earth is that? Oh, you mean he's just a doctor."

I blushed violently, which was something I did until late in my teens, and then I foolishly asked what her father's regiment was.

"Oh, he's in the Green Jackets," she replied.

I soon realised there was just as much snobbery amongst the girls about their fathers' regiments as among the officers themselves. It had never occurred to me that my father wasn't a member of one of the noblest of professions. I still kept this belief fiercely to myself, and didn't dare announce it publicly in case of ridicule. That night I cried silently into my pillow.

The school was on top of a hill overlooking the splendid city of Bath, but, as far as I can remember, we were never shown the beautiful crescents or the Roman baths. But I do remember the Abbey where we went every Sunday, and the stone man falling off Jacob's Ladder on the façade. It seemed to me that I had fallen off a ladder into an enormous, dark, damp prison from which I would never escape. Visiting the school years later, it appeared to be a rather pleasant, not very large building with a good view over the city. It only proves how our memories can play tricks on us, especially when we are miserable.

In our case, however, we were to have a lucky reprieve. The Marquess of Bath, who was one of the governors of the school, offered his home, Longleat, to the authority for the duration of the war so that we could escape Hitler's bombs. We were to go there the following term. The great long galleries were turned into dormitories, temporary huts were built in the garden for classrooms and we were allowed the use of the magnificent grounds. I can't say that we girls really appreciated our surroundings, but they were certainly an improvement on Bath. I remember the labyrinth of stone chimneys and statues on the lead roof, the great staircase, and the family portraits looking down on our rows of narrow beds. Some of the atmosphere must have seeped into our subconscious minds, but I don't believe at the time we were fully aware that we were at a boarding school in one of the most historic Elizabethan mansions in England.

I came to know and love the grounds and the descending lakes designed by Capability Brown. We were allowed to ride and I was able to escape by myself and roam with my pony through the woods and fields, jumping the fallen trees. The days at Longleat seemed to be forever sunny with hours spent lying in the long grass, sucking the juice from the broken stalks and reading, reading, reading. Of course, my favourite hero was Heathcliffe and, as I hugged my hot-water bottle close to me in bed at night, my erotic fancies knew no bounds. I would one day be loved by a tall, dark, brooding man who would put me through every kind of torment until I eventually won his love. Actually hot-water bottles were essential, as there was no heating in the house except for the enormous log fire in the hall. We had jugs of cold water and basins in which to wash ourselves in the dormitories, and these were constantly spilling and spoiling the ceilings below. Lord Bath, an old-world figure with his high, white wing collar and formal clothes, still lived in the house and used to appear at speech days, sitting on the platform with our Head Mistress. I remember him best standing on the top of the steps at Longleat, flanked by his enormous Great Danes. We all adored him and I'm sure our Head Mistress was in love with him.

I was lazy at school, or so said my reports. I know I never did much work until just before exams, when I crammed like mad and managed to pass the vital grades. But I was good at games, a demon with the lacrosse stick – "Cradle, girls, cradle," sang out the beloved spotty captain – which I must say hasn't helped me greatly up the snakes and ladders of life. Nor did becoming captain of cricket promote my chance of future employment, although I was a formidable fast bowler. Winning the long jump and high jump, however, and being clapped by my friends' parents, gave me a taste for audience appreciation – probably a dubious asset. But I excelled in one sphere which has certainly enhanced my life, and that was in drama. I was quite a good actress, but a better director, which is what I enjoyed doing most. Putting on the school play or pageant at the end of term was a thrill unlike any other I'd known. Unfortunately, my parents never seemed to be watching me.

My father was with the Army in France and my mother was working in London. The one time I do remember her appearing at school, I would rather forget. It was at the time of my confirmation and I was passing through a deeply holy phase and taking my religious instruction extremely seriously. I couldn't wait for the ceremony and First Communion, which was to be conducted by the Bishop of Bath and Wells. I love Wells Cathedral with its great curving stone scissor arches holding up the central spire, and the medieval clock with its revolving figures and the small Lucifer-like creature of Jack Blandifer striking the bell on the hour. My mother had promised to attend, but she wasn't among the other parents, who had congregated for a glass of sweet sherry before boarding the coach with us. I was bitterly disappointed, but just as we were halfway down the long tree-lined avenue, a small lady was spotted running after us waving a book. Much to my deep shame it was my mother, carrying an ivory-covered prayer book, a gift from Aunty Doll. The coach was stopped and she joined the rest of the parents. My poor mother, she always let me down at the most important moments in my life.

During the holidays my father appeared on leave in London. The war had taken its toll on him. Three years earlier he had been involved in the evacuation from Dunkirk. As the doctors had to stay on the beaches until the end to see their wounded safely on to the boats, they took the fiercest shelling. He was also torpedoed twice on the short journey home across the Channel and had been on sick leave for months before returning to the fighting. At the end of the war, he was invalided out of the Army and suffered from bouts of illness until his death at the age of sixty-seven. During one brief reunion I persuaded him that, if I could pass my school certificate a year earlier than the normal age of sixteen, I should be allowed to leave school. He accepted the idea, having always disliked paying the school fees and being impatient for me to start earning my own living. My higher education was to be learnt by living my life.

I was a year younger than the average age in my form, so, although lazy, I must have been somewhat precocious. That year at Longleat, I decided to apply myself to work and gained my school certificate at the age of fifteen. In my final report the Head Mistress wrote, "Sonia has a good brain and should do well in life if she doesn't decide to become a social butterfly."

My mother's grand friend in Worthing had told her that the chicest secretarial college was called Queen's and was at a place called Englefield Green, near Eton. This appealed to my mother's snobbery and, as my father was abroad fighting in the final stages of the war, he was unable to voice his disapproval. By taking an extra job in London and making endless personal sacrifices, she scraped together the fees to send me for a year's finishing at Queen's. Apart from acquiring the necessary qualifications as a secretary, we learnt bookkeeping, a foreign language of our choice, housekeeping and flower arrangement. As we increased our speeds at shorthand and our fingers flew over the keys of our typewriters to imaginative phrases like "Now is the time to come to the aid of the party", our minds plotted trips to Eton and parties in London.

I shared a room with the daughter of an Earl, who had never before left the stately home where she had been privately educated and protected from everyday life. She was an exquisite, shy, doll-like creature with a porcelain complexion, who was terrified of the rough world in which she now found herself. I became fascinated by her. She was so vulnerable and mystified by the everyday things around her. I was also fascinated by the way she folded her sweaters, carefully turning in the sleeves and then rolling them into long sausage shapes. Apparently, that was how her lady's maid folded them. In turn, she was amazed by my practical worldliness and we became bosom friends. When I first took her to London to my mother's flat, she was terrified of the city and admitted to me that she had never crossed a main road by herself before.

Our flat became her second home and later, when she was ordered by her parents to join the Wrens, she used to appear looking immaculate in her Able Seawoman's uniform. But I trembled to think of how working in a barracks at Portsmouth contrasted with her previous existence.

Most of my contemporaries at the secretarial college had gone into one of the services or the Foreign Office, but I decided to apply for a job as an assistant to a BBC producer. We put out a programme for hospitals called *Here's Wishing You Well Again*, and I was sometimes allowed to introduce the stars. At home we were shorter of money than ever and I took an evening job working in a watch factory. We would sit on benches in front of an enormous moving conveyor belt and place our tiny pieces of metal in the appropriate spots. I quite enjoyed it as a part-time job and can never go along completely with those who raise their hands in horror at the monotony and soul-destroying quality of factory work. Of course, it is mindless and there is no job satisfaction, but there is a comradeship, my thoughts were free to wander, and there was the consolation of a pay packet at the end of the week.

The war in Europe was drawing to a close and the young men who took us out dancing in various clubs like The 400 were old for their years: they had seen too many of their contemporaries maimed or killed. Although they were still only boys, their eyes were those of old men. When they were on leave from the front, they crammed every moment with pleasure and the girls lucky enough to be working in London were not short of escorts or admirers. As my mother was still working at the Polish Club, there was always plenty of drink at the flat, which she sometimes took in lieu of salary: my mother's time spent in India drinking *chota* pegs on the veranda had given her a taste for gin. In later years I had to persuade her to change to whisky, which made her more benign. This was after there had been several disasters, when she started falling about and breaking bones. She also smoked heavily and on two occasions set her bed alight. But while she still had us with her, she kept herself under control. She was a great favourite with my boyfriends and they loved her for her generosity and for the light-hearted atmosphere she created. But she was very puritanical and always insisted on staying awake until I returned from a party or a nightclub, and I had to pop into her room for a final kiss.

There wasn't the pressure in those days for girls to sleep with the man with whom they were having a flirtation. It seemed we were much more romantic. Although as sexually aware as the present generation, we were all told that our virginity was something precious to be preserved for 'the real thing'. In my mother's eyes, 'the real thing' was any eligible young man, preferably with a title, who proposed to me. She was longing to 'get me off'. It is not being conceited to say that proposals were fairly frequent; I think the young men who had experienced the horrors of war longed to establish a permanent relationship as soon as the war ended. My new friend's brother had fallen in love with me. He was stationed at Portsmouth in the Navy and we used to gather at my mother's flat before going out on the town. If the bombs started, we went straight to The 400, which became our air raid shelter. My mother was over the moon that I had the chance of marrying into one of the grandest families in England and was furious when I told her I had refused him. A few months later he died tragically when he fell into a manhole in Portsmouth dockyard, and some members of his family blamed me for what they felt had been suicide. This was the first time in my life that someone close to me had died. It seemed impossible to comprehend that a boy so young and carefree should have his life suddenly ended. How could I believe in a God who removed one of His creatures in so arbitrary a fashion? His sister and I comforted each other and remained lifelong friends.

During this time Bunty was learning to be an actress at RADA, which was a drain on the family purse and turned out to be an emotional strain on her, resulting in a near breakdown. She was sent over to Ireland to stay with an aunt whose husband was trainer to the Aga Khan. There she rode the racehorses on their early morning gallops and eventually made a slow recovery.

The European war at last drew to an end. On VE night, we all gathered outside Buckingham Palace and swayed with the joyous crowds, singing and shouting. Later we went dancing at The 400 and in our party was a young Fleet Air Arm pilot with crinkly fair hair. Julian had just completed his training as a pilot in South Africa and was due to continue the war in the Far East. That night he took me home in his car, an old drop-head yellow Rolls-Royce. Before we said goodbye at the door of the flat, he asked for my telephone number.

Three

The young Fleet Air Arm pilot was the younger son of an industrial peer, Lord Melchett, whose Mond ancestors had come to England from Germany in the 1870s. At the time of our meeting his father was seriously ill with heart problems. The elder son, a brilliant scientist, who was to have followed in the family tradition, was killed a few weeks before the end of the war. With a friend as the pilot, he went for a joyride in a plane, which crashed into a Scottish loch. His body was never recovered. Inconsolable at the death of her elder and favourite son, their mother had been unable to tell her sick husband and was determined that her younger boy Julian should be brought back from South Africa to break the news. Using her influence with Winston Churchill and Lord Cherwell, she arranged that he should be flown back to England on indefinite compassionate leave. She didn't seem to realise or care that he, brought up in his brother's shadow and dazed by his death, was being given an impossible task. He assumed only that his parents would never forgive him the fact that he and not his brother had been allowed to live. But when he entered the sickroom there was no need for words. His father read the tragic truth in his eyes.

He was only twenty at the time, and later told me he bitterly resented leaving the Forces and being made to take over the responsibility of running the family estates, but eventually he became reconciled to the idea. He had done an agricultural course while training to be a pilot and knew a little about farming, but he wasn't ready to step into his brother's shoes. He also had to abandon the thought of taking up the place at Oxford he had been offered when he was at Eton College.

Whenever he could escape from the farm, Julian would motor up to London and collect me from the BBC in his open yellow Rolls. He would pour out his heart about all his new responsibilities and hopes for the future. Undaunted by his youth and lack of experience, he believed that by finding new ways of growing certain crops, the future course of agriculture could be changed just as much as industry had been changed by the advent of plastics. "My great-grandfather, my grandfather and dad have all been great scientists and industrialists and politicians. They have all contributed in some way to the welfare of mankind. I want to make my own contribution in my own way."

Being totally unaware of his family and their history, I listened with fascination. One night, when we were dining at a fashionable restaurant called the Bagatelle, I looked around the room at the overdressed, jewelled women and their suave escorts and said unthinkingly, "This place is great except for the fact that it's mostly full of rich Jews." I suppose it was an expression I must have heard frequently and never questioned. A mild form of conventional anti-Semitism had been part of my colonial background.

"You could say I'm Jewish, except that I'm not rich," Julian remarked. Blushing and embarrassed by my stupidity, I started a stammering apology. "Don't worry," he said, "I'm used to it." He took my hand and continued, "I first became conscious that I was part Jewish at my prep school. My brother told me one day that he was being persecuted. I was mystified, but he explained that his life was being made intolerable by constant bullying and that mine soon would be. He insisted we run away to London to our parents' flat in Grosvenor Square. It was my first awareness of anti-Semitism." In later years I was to come across my early gaucheness in others and became adept at cutting them short to avoid their embarrassment. Later he gave me his father's book called *Thy Neighbour* about the persecution of the Jews in Europe before the war. It was the most moving account I have read of that vile period and it opened my eyes forever.

One day he drove me down to the beautiful Queen Anne house in Bedfordshire, where the family had moved after leaving a vast Victorian mansion in Hampshire. As we drove over the pretty humpback bridge and down the rhododendron-lined drive, I began to feel increasingly apprehensive. He had been quite explicit about his feelings towards me and I knew, instinctively, that today he would ask me to marry him.

The butler had laid out a cold lunch at one end of the long polished dining-room table, and he opened a bottle of champagne. Afterwards we went on a tour of the house. All the furniture was shrouded in dust sheets and gave me a strange ghostly feeling. The magnificent collection of

Italian Renaissance art, the Raphael and Bellini pictures of Christ on the Cross with saints and angels, the Guardi and Canaletto scenes of Venice, and the music-room full of Greek marble sculptures, all created the eerie atmosphere of a Cocteau film. We reached the small bedroom he had had since he was a boy. "I love this room," Julian said and led me to the window to see the enormous copper beech rising from the lawn below, its great branches supported by wooden poles. "That tree knows of all my dreams." He took me in his arms. "And now my only dream is that you will live with me forever as my wife." I drew gently away. I wasn't ready for all this – for love, for marriage. I wanted to live a little, to taste freedom on my own, to explore life by myself, outside my mother's all-enveloping demands. I wasn't in love with him; I loved him like the brother I'd never had. I admired him – his courage and his idealism – more than anyone except my father. Although younger in years, I felt so much older. He seemed unsophisticated and unworldly compared to some of the men in their late twenties I'd been going out with. I procrastinated and tried to tell him some of my thoughts without hurting his feelings. But I knew he would persist.

When we returned to London, I didn't tell my mother what had taken place, but I did tell her that I wanted to go abroad for a while. My close friend Fiona McNeill-Moss had decided to take a job in the Control Commission in Germany and suggested I join her. I wanted to join her. My mother was distraught. "You aren't even old enough to join as an officer – you'll be one of the 'other ranks'." She was right, but I was insistent and enrolled as a Private in the RDR (Reparations, Deliveries and Restitutions) division of the Control Commission. My new admirer was shattered at first, but accepted that I needed time to make a decision about the future and to be by myself, away from family ties and obligations. He was adamant that he would one day convince me that we should spend our lives together, but he was prepared to be patient. "I will wait for you, forever if necessary." He said he would consider us engaged.

I arrived at Minden, a small German town near Bad Oeynhausen, in my ill-fitting khaki uniform to take up my job as secretary to a Brigadier in charge of the Polish Division of the RDR organisation. My heart sank as we were shown our quarters: a dormitory of army bunks, reminiscent of my school days at Bath. Early the next morning, we were woken by a Sergeant-major shouting, "Come on, my lovelies, time to rise and shine. The sun'll soon be scorching your eyebrows." But after the first few days I grew accustomed to the physical discomfort and bad food, and I became intrigued by my new adventure.

RDR was set up to restore various properties, factories and goods looted by the Germans from the countries they had over-run. Our particular branch dealt with Poland, and a team of Polish officers was stationed at Minden to liaise and negotiate with us. They were charming men and, when we weren't working, they would take us riding and dancing. Sometimes, if we had a few days off, we would go skiing in the Harz mountains or sailing at Travemünde, north of Hamburg. It was a carefree life for those in the occupying powers but, even at that age, I became very critical of how some members of the Commission misused their power and authority. I was also extremely sorry for the German civilians in whose home we were living in.

Cigarettes and coffee were the black market currency and a few packets of cigarettes could get you a suit made by the best tailor in Minden. I still have a pair of jodhpurs, which cost one pound of coffee, of slightly Germanic cut made by a man who used to make riding breeches for the German cavalry. Some high-ranking officers even abused their positions to furnish their homes in England with carpets and pictures taken from German houses. Many Germans were living in appalling conditions in the rubble of cities, and highly qualified people were performing menial tasks for the Allied Forces.

One day a Polish Count, who was one of our negotiators, took me out to dinner and asked me if I would like to take part in a little conspiracy. "You would be doing a great service to Poland," he said. I wanted to hear more before agreeing, and he explained that towards the end of the war the Germans had stolen the best horses from the Polish stud farms and that they were now in Southern Germany in the American Zone. The Americans were unaware of the true value of the horses, which were to be slaughtered to extract a certain serum for medical experiments.

"We want to kidnap the horses," he said, "and we happen to know that the order for the execution will be coming through your office in the course of the next few weeks. We would like you to hide the letter until we have returned the horses to Poland." I didn't hesitate for a moment and entered into the spirit of the adventure.

A few weeks later the Brigadier came into my office. He was a small, gentle man, rather vague, with a neat white moustache. "Sonia, have you seen a memo about some Polish horses? I'm told, from above, we ought to be taking some sort of action over them – something to do with our American friends." Looking totally blank, with the letter burning a hole in my in-tray, I said I had no knowledge of any such memo, but told him I would let him know as soon as it arrived. He turned on his heels and went back to his office and to the tapestry he was embroidering for his wife in England. Later that day, one of the Polish officers told me that the operation had been successful and that the horses had been kidnapped from the American zone, taken through Berlin and then by boat across to Poland. Years later the Count, by then living in London, wrote a book about the rebuilding of the Polish stud farms and about a young girl in the Control Commission who had helped to save the horses. I was not identified.

During this year, my determined suitor was writing long weekly letters and sending from England small luxuries impossible to find in Germany. Particularly welcome were the parcels of books – he sent *Great Expectations*, his favourite Dickens – and food to supplement our monotonous diet of Spam, beetroot, sausages and potatoes. He was living by himself, farming the estates, with only a small black cocker spaniel I'd given him. He was determined we should marry as soon as I returned home after my year of wanderlust. I was in a no-man's land of indecision. I knew in my heart of hearts I would never find anyone I loved and respected more; perhaps these feelings would grow into something deeper.

In the meantime I was madly infatuated with a much older married man. He had been a prisoner-of-war, had escaped and was in the Grenadiers, stationed nearby at Bad Oeynhausen. He gave me very little encouragement but knew how much I cared for him, and we gradually became inseparable. I told him about my life and indecision about the future. "You should marry him," he said. "I will never be able to leave my wife – she is in a mental home." Apparently she was a very beautiful woman and had already been unstable before their marriage. While he was in a POW camp, she had become completely insane.

Instead of going back to England for our leave, my girlfriend and I decided we would travel round Europe. We obtained two 'movement orders', and I stamped them with every official stamp I could lay my hands on so that they looked extremely important. Flourished in the faces of bemused German and Italian guards, they took us effortlessly on our train journeys through Germany and Italy. In Venice we stayed in a suite in the Danieli Hotel, which had been requisitioned by the Allies, for a nominal one pound a night. Afterwards we returned via Paris, where reality hit us and we had to conform with the accepted standards of civilised behaviour. But the code of morality practised by the occupying forces in Germany at that time was ambiguous. We had no feelings of guilt or of behaving dishonestly.

In my usual fashion, I was putting off any decision about the future until I returned to England. Once back, all the pressures were on me. In the year I had been abroad, the diffident young boy had become a determined and passionate young man, desperately keen to get married as soon as possible. My mother, worn out by her wartime jobs and unhappily reunited with my father, was more anxious than ever that her daughter should escape the limitations of family life and make a 'good match'. To be fair to her, she had become devoted to the intense, pale-faced young man who had used the flat whenever he came up to London rather than stay at his parents' unwelcoming apartment in Grosvenor Square. In the end I succumbed, convincing myself that I would never find a true soulmate in life, so I should marry this boy whom I loved and respected. His need I could fulfil.

In the frenetic preparations leading up to the wedding, I put into the recess of my mind my doubts and reservations. Good clothes were difficult and expensive to find in England at that time, and my aunt in Ireland sent over my wedding dress of white crepe, bordered by tiny pearls. Throughout the night before what is supposed to be the happiest day of one's life, I cried as if I were going to a funeral. In the morning, my mother's remedy was to give me a strong gin which only made matters worse. My friend's cousin had just started a florist business from her home and was meant to go to Covent Garden early in the morning of the wedding to create a spray of gardenias. It arrived with half the flowers turning brown from the fingers of the novice florist. Instead of telling me and letting me walk down the aisle with my ivory-backed prayerbook, my mother handed me the bouquet at the last minute, pretending it did not look like a wreath. As my father led me down the aisle, my eyes were glistening like the pearls on my dress.

Our wedding ceremony was taking place at St Paul's Church in Knightsbridge with the reception at the nearby Berkeley Hotel. Bunty and Julian's sister Karis were bridesmaids, while my mother and father and my grandmother were there to support me. The widowed Gwen, a sombre figure in black for mourning, came to the service. Julian asked Johnny Lowther, his Best Man, to keep an eye on her in case she did a bolt. He managed to persuade her to stand in the receiving line, but before the bridal toast proposed by Randolph Churchill, she was gone. What I did not know was that soon I would fall deeply in love with my husband.

Four

For our honeymoon, we spent a week at a small hotel at Lenno on Lake Como and then on to Paris to stay with King Peter and Queen Alexandra of Yugoslavia at their apartment in the Plaza Athenée Hotel. Alexandra's mother, Princess Aspasia of Greece, was a great friend of Julian's mother, and they had shared a house in Venice – The Garden of Eden. One night the royal pair took us to dine at the famous restaurant, La Tour d'Argent, where to my surprise Alexandra only ate a single apple, while we tucked into the many varieties of duck. She was always on a diet, she said. She was tall like me and gave me a beautiful red coat, which I wore for many years.

Back in London, we took a small gloomy rented flat in Earl's Court, which I disliked. So I persuaded Julian to buy a corner house in Wilton Mews, which I had fallen in love with. We could barely afford it as his parents, disapproving of our marriage, gave him no allowance. They had always hoped he would marry Princess Margaret, who was a great friend. But with a small inheritance from his grandmother Violet, we managed to scrape together the £5,000 for a long lease. Our immediate neighbour was Paul Richey, who wrote the famous book *Fighter Pilot* and became a good friend, as did his brother Mike who often sailed the Atlantic to America, single-handed in a small craft with a junk rig. Our other close friends were Sir 'Mike' and Christine West, who were great life-enhancers, unconventional and splendid hosts. Christine collected pictures by artists long before they became famous, such as Lowry and Bridget Riley.

Julian's priority was to look for work. Having been brought up in the country, he had an idea that farming should be more self-supporting. He had worked out a grass-drying scheme for cattle feeding, but to put it into practice he needed capital. As it happened, a close family friend, the painter Edward Seago introduced him to Lord Bearsted, chairman of the merchant bank of M Samuel & Company Limited, which decided to back the scheme. Consequently, British Field Products Limited was formed to establish a pilot plant, which could be the forerunner of some dozen others throughout Britain. After touring England to look for a suitable site, eventually Julian bought a fifteen-acre disused airfield in the centre of a large arable area of Norfolk near Fakenham. We made our first country home in the control tower, where rain seeped through the brick walls. It was a long way from Julian's home at Coleworth and the Melchett tradition of gracious living. But he had staked his future on the success of the enterprise.

Peter was born in our little mews house on 24 February 1948. It was a difficult birth and my doctor made me keep to my bed for three months prior to it. As he was a breach baby, I had apparently nearly died before giving birth. I do remember entering a dark tunnel with a bright light at the end, which I learned afterwards other people thought they had done – what is known as a 'near death experience'. But Peter was a splendid baby, and when I used to wheel him in his pram in Hyde Park, people used to turn and look at his golden curls and say, "What a beautiful girl."

But living in Norfolk in the control tower with a small child was no easy deal. Surrounded as we were by fields, with Julian at work and no friends or family to console me, I sometimes felt miserable and inadequate. In his highchair, Peter would refuse much of his food, and I was afraid he would waste away. But Julian's parents had mellowed towards him at the birth of a grandson, and his father sent him a cheque for £230 as a gesture of their new relationship. Sadly, in January 1949, Peter's grandfather Henry died in New York. He was only fifty. Julian flew there with his sister Karis and later attended a Memorial Service, held on the eve of Britain's recognition of the State of Israel. "It is sad," wrote Randolph Churchill in the *New York Times*, "that Lord Melchett, who did so much to promote a friendship between the English and the Jews, should not have lived to see this brought about."

At twenty-four, Julian inherited not only the title, but his father's public and political papers. Probably, Henry believed that his son was adequately provided for by his grandmother's settlement, but this had already been spent on buying our London home. To add to the difficulties of my husband, his venture into farming seemed doomed to failure. His hopes of expanding the grass-drying venture evaporated when a new government reversed the agricultural policy on animal feeding stuffs and withdrew the subsidy from British Field Products. As the representative of the

Samuel merchant bank, Julian remained a director when his company diversified into agricultural products. Later, the bank invited him to join them full-time, so he started as a clerk, setting out to learn the profession from the bottom.

Before that, we visited Israel and stayed at a bungalow at Tel Mond, a family house, where Julian had inherited a run-down citrus grove. His parents had sold the big house on the Lake of Galilee – the Villa Melchett. Although Julian was conscious of his Jewish roots, he was an agnostic and an anti-Zionist. He believed passionately in the existence of Israel, but with his single patriotism, he felt that the Jews should assimilate and donate to the country in which they lived. With his innate love of the land, he studied books on citrus farming and visited Palestine Plantations, as the place was called, and over the next few years, he had turned it into a profitable concern once more. He then sold it, and the proceeds gave us a modest income and a degree of financial security. We used to receive a crate of oranges every Christmas from the new owners.

Two years after his father's death, Julian made his maiden speech in the House of Lords, but he had no serious political ambitions. Although popular, he was not a particularly good speaker. By now Norfolk had become our second home in a series of rented dwellings. My first and favourite was a cottage at Burnham Overy Staithe. Its windows looked over the wide salt marshes and mud-flats with their narrow winding creeks to the foaming breakers of the North Sea. All around were low horizons where waves or land met sky. Then there was a house on the Holkham estate, and later a place in the shadow of Blakeney Church. A near neighbour was the artist, Edward Seago, who we had made Peter's godfather. Peter was a delicate baby, and I had a difficult time during the first years of our marriage, and slightly nomadic life. Although we had moved from the horrible control tower, I think I was a very inadequate mother. When Julian and I went abroad, I employed a nanny who had been recommended to me. On our return, I found her smoking and dripping ash onto his cot. She didn't last long.

My daughter Kerena was born in 1951 in our town mews house in London. She was a more robust child and much easier to care for. Luckily I found a reliable nanny to look after them both, before Julian and I went on a six-month trip to America, where he was to study banking in Wall Street. We stayed at a small hotel and, although we had been given a few introductions, we hardly saw anyone. Julian was usually too exhausted to go out, and he loved talking out all his ideas and ambitions to me. I was always his sounding board. Our only friends were John and Peter Loeb and their family, and we occasionally spent a country weekend at their Westchester house, playing tennis and swimming in their pool.

We spent some time in the mid-West so that Julian could inspect their grass-drying equipment. The only memory of that visit was of the insularity of the people and the enormous steaks they would give us to eat, sometimes overlapping our plates. But we had an exciting experience when we travelled to James Bay in Canada, north of Hudson Bay, to visit a Mond nickel plant. Flying a light aircraft over the beautiful Canadian lakes in the fall was a magical experience. Julian had decided to join a goose shoot and gave me lessons in how to use a gun. When we arrived, we were met by the horrified face of the owner. It was 'male only' he said, but he relented and a sheet was erected in the log cabin to separate me from the other twenty-four 'guns'. The next day at dawn, we set off to the hides in the marshes, accompanied by our native Indian keepers. They would put down decoys, and make the call of the wounded geese as the birds winged in over us. These were horribly easy prey and they soon fell at our feet. It was the first and last time I ever shot. But it achieved one good result – a published travel article and my first entry into journalism.

Soon after our return to England, Julian, having worked his way up the ranks, was made a director of M Samuel & Company Limited. He also became a director of the Guardian Assurance Company. We became great friends with Dick Bearsted, the Chairman of Samuel's, and his wife Heather. They had girls of the same age as Peter and Kerena, and we often stayed with them at their grand house Upton Park near Banbury, where we felt thoroughly spoilt by the lush way of life. Felicity, their eldest daughter, was later the mother of two sons, one of whom was to come second in the Grand National in 2011 – the youngest rider ever to do so.

In 1951, my sister Bunty married Anthony Kinsman. Once a Grenadier in the Brigade of Guards, he had been imprisoned during the war, but he had managed to escape to England before rejoining his regiment. His squad was one of the first into Hitler's bunker, and he took away several souvenirs, including a picture of Hitler, one of his prized possessions, also some headed notepaper for letters which would disconcert his friends on special occasions. He was extremely handsome, charming and with a wide-ranging wit. He worked as an underwriter at Lloyd's of London, entitling him after ten years to become an outside member on a small income.

Bunty had been a model at Worth, and at her wedding she borrowed one of their dresses and, unlike mine, her bouquet was a magnificent cascade of lilies. Peter was a page at the wedding and, shy as he was, almost stole the show by being surrounded by photographers and headlined in the papers as 'The new Bubbles', with his curly golden locks. For their honeymoon, the couple decided to sail to Paris, but not in a conventional style. They took a three-day crash course at Plymouth in sailing and navigation and bought a small sailing yacht.

Setting off in calm waters, they slowly learnt how to manage their craft, but halfway across the Channel, a storm blew up and the boat nearly overturned. In the galley, Bunty was conscious of a vast pot of cream flying towards her and hitting her on the face. Luckily she suffered nothing more than a black eye.

Making their way through the canals to end in Paris, their great difficulty was negotiating the numerous locks. At some they had to take down their mast in order to get through, slowing them up considerably. But once they reached the Seine they made their way to a place on the banks, where they could moor the boat. While they explored Paris, Bunty bought climbing plants which rapidly grew up the mast, much to the amusement of the Parisians. Eventually, they had to return to England and the job at Lloyd's at the end of their idyll.

They bought a small flat near Marble Arch at the top of a four-storey building. While on a short holiday in Spain, they lent it to my mother as a break from her Brighton life with my father. Unfortunately, while smoking in bed one night, Wendy set fire to the flat. When the Fire Brigade arrived, they saw this small figure sitting on the window-sill, shouting, "Help me! I'm just a human candle."

In 1953, Julian and I attended the Queen's Coronation at Westminster Abbey. Wearing Gwen's borrowed crown and robes, I remember the great occasion as an exhausting experience. We had to be in the Abbey two hours before Her Majesty, and the men and women were divided into separate groups. Most of the men had brought flasks of whisky hidden in their robes to sustain them. But the actual ceremony was enormously impressive with the Queen on the arm of the Duke of Edinburgh. She was looking magnificent as the glittering Crown of Saint Edward was placed on her head and her long train flowed behind her. Of the same age and the youngest peeress in the Abbey, I wondered how She would cope with the heavy responsibilities put upon her slight shoulders.

With two young children, our mews house was proving too small, and we searched London for a larger home. We particularly wanted to live in or near Chelsea, where we had many friends but, after endless searching, we were unable to find anything we liked that we could afford. We had passed several times a gloomy-looking house, covered in ivy and facing north, 16 Tite Street, which had remained on the estate agent's books for a year. In the end, I thought that, by making the most of the rooms facing south, removing the ivy and virtually brightening up the whole place, we should pay the asking price of £6,000 for a long lease – just within our budget. 16 Tite Street was Oscar Wilde's address, but the numbers had been changed since his day. However, it didn't stop endless devotees of the great man leaving green carnations on our doorstep. In the carpeted living room, we cut out a square to leave a parquet floor to use for dancing, and this room became the base for many parties.

I began working part-time at the Violet Melchett Health Centre in Flood Street nearby and for the NSPCC local branch. But the work I found most demanding was as a magistrate at Marylebone Crown Court. This was a weekly occurrence, and I sat with two other magistrates. Although some of the cases that came before us were interesting, most were petty crime such as shoplifting and drug abuse. But one day I saw, to my amazement, the transvestite April Ashley in the dock. She had apparently been arrested for hitting a policeman over the head with her handbag after creating a disturbance in a night club in Berkeley Square. Speaking in an exaggerated upper-class accent, she complained to us that she had been locked up in a male cell after her arrest. She had once been married briefly to the son of Lord Baden-Powell, who had started the Boy Scouts.

Although I was full of admiration for my colleagues who gave their services to the community in this way, I eventually resigned after eight years on the bench. The responsibility of passing sentences on young offenders was distressing, but my sympathies were often with the police in trying to bring about justifiable convictions. I felt my true role was as a mother, and as wife to Julian, who was very much in need of my moral support. Loving him as I did, and aware of his inner insecurities, I would listen to his endless outpourings on the inadequacies of some of his co-partners and of his frustrations at their inability to see into the future. Like most men with visions ahead of their time, he was sometimes open to criticism and suffered from the lack of foresight of his colleagues.

When not on holiday in Norfolk, we would sometimes go to Bembridge on the Isle of Wight in the summer to stay with General Mike and Christine West and their daughter Carinthia. Or we would go skiing in the winter to Kitzbühel, always with the children. I was an avid hostess and loved giving parties for a mixed bag of people. Occasionally we would have supper in the dining-room at the front of the house, darkened by an enormous camellia which we never had the heart to cut back. To my amazement, passing the house recently, I noticed that the new owners had allowed it to reach the top-floor bedroom. But most of our parties were buffet affairs in the large living-room on the first floor, which usually ended up with riotous dancing on our tiny parquet floor.

The most ambitious party we gave was in 1957 together with three other couples: Mike and Christine, my sister Bunty and her husband Anthony, and Sarah and Morys Bruce, later Lord and Lady Aberdare. We got permission to put up a large marquee in the square in Burton Court beside Chelsea Barracks and we sent notes to all the surrounding flats and houses apologising for the noise that might occur. Julian and Mike searched the musical clubs for a possible band. They came up with the idea of Mick Mulligan's

Magnolia Jazz Band and a trio led by Con Phillips and Humphrey Lyttleton's lot with George Melly (then relatively unknown). Invitations were sent, asking guests to bring a bottle of Bollinger non-vintage champagne. Bottle parties were common in those days, but a mixture could have been disastrous. Little did we know that an American hostess, Mrs Gilbert Miller, the wife of a wealthy impresario, was famous for giving an annual party at the Savoy. When she was told of our party which was on the same night, she was asked to change her date, but she was quoted as saying, "I can't do that as I am expecting the Duke and Duchess of Buccleuch, the Duke of Westminster, the Spanish Ambassador, and etcetera – I expect the only person I will lose will be Viscount Hambledon – he likes jazz." We didn't give much thought to Mrs Miller's ball and, in fact, it turned out that many of her guests slipped out and turned up at our bottle party, which went on until the early hours of the next morning.

One night at a dinner party, I sat next to Vane Ivanovic, a famous deep-sea diver (second only to Cousteau), and I asked him what was the most beautiful place he had ever visited. He said without hesitation Formentor in Majorca – he had built a house there. The following summer holidays, I persuaded Julian to rent a small villa, Casa Planas, just above the beach there, and this became our regular holiday spot. Two years later, we bought a piece of land just beyond and above the Formentor Hotel, where we eventually built our own villa – Casa Melchett. The land was off a dirt track overlooking a private bay with no other villa in sight.

In those days, it was the custom that when boys reached the age of eight, they would go to Prep School. I hated the idea of Peter leaving home, but I looked through all the schools I had been recommended to find one that would not be too harsh. In the end, we decided on Wellesley House in Broadstairs in Kent. The reason I chose this one was that it put the youngest boys in a separate building, where they were even allowed to bring their favourite toys. Going to Victoria Station to catch the 3.30 train where Peter would join the other boys made my heart sink. I had to watch his small disappearing figure in his cap and green uniform. Peter later told me that in all his time at school, these years were the most horrible. For the place was run by a severe teacher, who got pleasure from tormenting the more attractive boys. But he never told me when he was there.

Kerena was already at the Francis Holland School near Sloane Square. We spent the holidays in Norfolk, although Julian could only join us for the weekends. Many months passed in looking for a permanent country home. We found a house in Burnam Thorpe, the village home of Admiral Nelson, and we thought of buying it. We had the eminent zoologist and war scientist Solly Zuckerman staying with us in Blakeney at the time with his wife Joan, who was Julian's aunt. We took them over to see our prospective house. They were also looking for somewhere to live in Norfolk and they fell in love with the place. "Let's toss for it," said the Professor. Of course he won.

Our friends were very pessimistic about our ever finding anything suitable. In the end, however, simply going through an agent in Norwich, we found a farmhouse with 800 acres of land at Ringstead near Hunstanton called Courtyard Farm. We were told by experts that the land was too dry to be good for agriculture. Even so, Julian and Ralph Goldsmith, his old farming manager from Coleworth, were sure that it could be made profitable by planting lucerne. The house in the centre of the farm looked south to a muddy yard surrounded by large barns. It was a typical two-storied building, dating back to the eighteenth century. In one room on the ground floor, there was an open hearth and a large circular stone, on which the labourers used to sleep for warmth. The idea of living there filled me with gloom, but behind the house was a run-down garden surrounded by a high old flint wall. I felt that with a little imagination something could be done to make it liveable. In any case, with help from a friendly bank, it was what we could just afford.

In 1959 we bought two caravans and set them in a field close to the house, while we were rebuilding. This was my most productive year ever. I was pregnant with my second girl Pandora, and we were also making plans for constructing the house in Formentor. This was to be a small two-storied villa with a portico and a large terrace, and a steep path cut in the rocks to give access to a private bathing place. We all enjoyed caravan life, even when Peter and Kerena came home from school. Somehow, we also had my sister Bunty and her husband Anthony Kinsman to stay as guests.

In Norfolk, we turned the house back to front. We built a large bay window over the sitting room and cut a gap in the high wall of the garden and felled a few trees. We now had a clear view of fields, leading down to the marshland and miles of wind-blasted beaches. Because dyke experts from the Low Countries had drained the Fens and had made this land, I added Dutch gables to each end of the building. Eventually, the carstone and flint barns were restored, preserving their original character. Old tiles were found to repair gaps in the roofs and disused buildings were converted into modern stables. Julian was determined to create a model farm out of what a sceptical friend described as "a piece of stony land swept by the wind straight from the North Pole."

Five

Pandora was born in Tite Street on 11 September 1959, slightly premature. I had been too busy to buy a cot, so she spent her first few days cuddled up in a drawer in my bedroom. Peter confessed to me years later that he was quite jealous of this addition to the family, but in the future, when they had bedrooms next to each other in Norfolk, he would become her loving instructor, answering all her stream of childish questions in great detail. I had a splendid nanny, which was lucky as we had committed ourselves to a tour of the Far East.

Julian had become a director of the Bermuda-based Anglo-Norness Shipping Company, the brainchild of the Norwegian entrepreneur of modern shipping, Erling D Noess; he built tankers in Japan crewed by Italian officers, and he sailed his ships under the red ensign. I was asked to launch the Noess Sovereign, the third largest tanker in the world.

First we had promised to visit our friends Anne and Guy Millard, who were based at the Embassy in Tehran. They had been neighbours of ours in Chelsea, while Guy worked at the Foreign Office. Anne had become my greatest friend. She was one of the cleverest and most beautiful women I have ever met, with a sparkling sense of humour, and she gave brilliant dinner parties at their home in St Leonard's Terrace. She once confessed to me that she always had on her lap a list of interesting topics in case conversation flagged. Unfortunately, their marriage was going through a rocky spell (which later led to divorce), so our stay was slightly fraught. But we were taken to visit the Shah and his Queen in all their glory at the palace, and then we were lent a small aeroplane to visit the great sights of Persia. After a helter-skelter ride, we reached Persepolis early one morning – the most beautiful ancient sight I have ever had the good fortune to behold. We had seen Shiraz and Isfahan with their intricately patterned domed mosaic ceilings and other famous monuments, but standing where Alexander the Great had built his Summer Palace and looking south across the desert beyond was the ultimate enchantment.

People had told us that Angkor Wat was one of the strangest and most exotic of sites, and so our next stop was to be Cambodia. In those days, there was only one run-down hotel near the ancient seven-mile site with trees growing out of the old monuments. With a guide, we trekked down the long entrance, lined with carved figures of gods. It was certainly strange, but I found it creepy and full of foreboding, as if a prophecy of the dreadful times of the Khmer Rouge to come.

We flew on to Hong Kong, where Julian had business meetings for the M Samuel bank, and we were taken by boat to Macao, more famous for its casinos than its natural beauty. But our next destination was Tokyo. We met our friends, Heini and Fiona Thyssen. The steel Baron had interests in shipping and was one of the guests, as were John D Rockefeller and his wife. We were all taken to visit Mount Fuji and the tea gardens of Kyoto, with its intricate stonework amongst the plants. But our objective was the devastated city of Nagasaki, already recovering from its atomic bombing. Thousands of Mitsubishi workers congregated for this milestone in the shipping industry. I had decided to make my speech in Japanese, and I had it carefully translated. At the dinner before the launch, which was to take place the next morning at 8 AM, the Chairman of Mitsubishi said how glad he was that I was to speak in Japanese and asked me to tell him what I was going to say. When I had finished, he rocked with laughter and asked me who had translated for me. When I told him his name, he said, "Oh dear, you should have gone to a woman – we have slightly different ways of expressing ourselves." To my horror, I had to relearn my speech late into the night with a female interpreter, who got rid of the male overtones.

But after my garbled speech at the actual launching, I was handed a little silver axe to cut the bowline of the £4,500,000 vessel. A balloon soared high into the air, and a flock of doves was released from it. The third largest cargo ship in the world slid into the sea to sail under the red ensign. Against a backcloth of mountains, Julian spoke with fervour about the aims of the international organisation "to build, own and manage these great vessels of the future and to transport the raw materials of the world across the oceans at the lowest possible cost." After thanking him, our host turned to me and said in English, "Now we have cocktail party as is custom in your country." It was only nine in the morning. But what the hell. A Martini for breakfast.

Instead of continuing our trip, we had to return to London. There had been an urgent telephone call to say that a fire had broken out in our London house. Apparently it had started in the linen room on the top floor. When our nanny saw the blazing fire, she ran downstairs carrying Pandora and followed by Kerena in tears. The fire brigade was called and prevented the flames from spreading throughout the house. Until it was safe to return, the nanny and the children stayed with our neighbour, Bob Boscowen, a war hero and pilot who was to serve in Parliament.

In the sixties we lived our life between Norfolk and London. During the children's holidays, I would be with them at Courtyard Farm, and Julian would join us for the weekends. Much of the time was spent riding round the fields or down along the seashore. Sometimes there would be the dreaded gymkhanas, which the children loved. It meant me rising at dawn to drive far and wide across the county, pulling the horsebox behind my car. Peter and Kerena were not usually as expert as most of the other riders, and often I would hear the loudspeaker blast out at the end of the contest, "Would all those who have not yet won a rosette please wait for the last round." It would often be nearly dark by the time we reached home.

Peter went to Eton, aged twelve, and Kerena followed him two years later at a nearby boarding school called Heathfield. We chose it because of its reputation for having a high standard in music and that was my daughter's great gift – playing the guitar and the piano. She also had a good voice, but she hated singing in public. Otherwise, I was still working regularly at the Violet Melchett Infant Welfare Centre in Chelsea and entertaining regularly. I loved creating a mixture of guests, old and young, famous or obscure, with a few 'cads' thrown in for good measure. People on the way up met people on the way down.

In the meantime, Julian's capabilities were being recognised in the sphere of politics. In 1961 in the uniform of a RNVR lieutenant, he replied to the Queen's Speech in the House of Lords after the Opening of Parliament. He condemned the recent Russian nuclear explosions, which he said had shattered the hopes of reaching a better understanding and had shocked the world. Lord Hailsham recalled hearing Sir Alfred Mond speak when he himself was an undergraduate: "I would never have dreamed that old character with a strong German accent I had heard in Oxford would have such a typical English grandson as Julian."

Quinton and Mary Hailsham were great friends. He would always arrive at our house on his bicycle, which he tied to the railings. Other close friends were Ian and Caroline Gilmour and Richard and Susan Crosland. In his diary, Richard wrote, "I found I was there with Eddie Shackleton (son of Sir Ernest Shackleton, the polar explorer), Frank Giles (Chief Correspondent of the *Sunday Times*), his wife Kitty and Beatrice Miller, editor of the *Queen* magazine (later editor of *Vogue* for many years). The Melchett house is vigorous, rather like Pam Berry's house, and I saw George Weidenfeld and Eddie in deep conversation."

I tried to mix the worlds of politics, the arts, business, the press and television. I felt that there should be no barriers of age, profession, class or money. Although I was considered by the papers to be a leading hostess, our private lives sometimes went through difficult patches, as I imagine do most marriages. We had married young and had no premarital sexual experiences. We were both attractive to other people and had flirtations and flings at the time which proved hurtful, but in the end seemed to bring us closer together.

Infidelities in marriage at that time were not all that uncommon. When we went to stay for a weekend with our friends Catherine and Harry Walston in their house outside Cambridge, it was well known that Catherine and Graham Greene were having a passionate affair. In fact, he was often in the same house party, along with several Catholic priests. I knew that Graham had a villa in Anacapri, and when I told Catherine it was a place I had always dreamed of visiting, she arranged it immediately. Several months later, my sister Bunty and I with two male friends spent a glorious two weeks in the small whitewashed villa high up on the crags of the island. The rooms were sparsely furnished except for shelves of books, and we used to climb down the steep rocks to dive into the sea below. Before we left, I was deep into Graham's copy of the *Oxford Book of English Verse* and had it with me on our return journey. I have to admit this was the only thing I have ever stolen – and how I regretted it. On his next visit to his villa, Graham realised its absence and asked for its return. Luckily, my shame didn't spoil our friendship and he forgave my sin.

Catherine, a beautiful American, was passionately in love with Graham, and they shared a small flat in Dublin. Sadly in later years, she had a bad fall there, was put on strong painkilling drugs, and became addicted. The last time I saw her was in the Walston flat in Albany when Harry, her husband, was looking after her like a nurse.

Whenever I had the time in London, I visited all the main art galleries. I had begun to collect the paintings and lithographs of some of my favourite artists. As soon as they became affordable, I bought the works of some up-and-coming painters including Stanley Spencer, Matthew Smith, John Piper and Graham Sutherland. Edward Seago had painted portraits of Julian and myself, and I bought a small painting by him of Lake Como as a reminder of our honeymoon. When I went to the sculptor David Wynn's first exhibition at the Marlborough Gallery, I fell in love with a study of egrets which I later took to Majorca and had made into a fountain in pride of place on the terrace.

The children's summer holidays were always spent in Formentor. The Vane Ivanovics were near neighbours, as were Daphne and Whitney Straight, and we usually had friends to stay. One year George Weidenfeld brought his daughter Laura, when he was between marriages, and although I don't think he went anywhere near the sea, he was always full of fascinating stories and inside information. He even taught Laura how to play chess. We had a small sailing dinghy which Julian loved. When Jean and George Galitzine came to stay, she proved to be terrified of sailing, but said she always felt that with Julian in control, nothing could go wrong. The ballerina Moira Shearer and her husband Ludovic Kennedy agreed. Ludo said of Julian later: "He had a mastery of everything he did, it gave you complete confidence, and he was totally independent about politics. When he'd finished talking, you couldn't say whether he was Liberal, Conservative or Labour." Lord Hailsham had no doubt: "He was a very independent peer whose speeches were not always in accordance with Party lines."

We also had a speedboat behind which we all loved waterskiing. One day Julian had the idea that we should all four ski together on single skis, with Pandora, at the age of two, carried on his shoulders. Geoffrey Keating, a brilliant photographer, perched himself on a high rock above the bay and, after several false starts, he took the perfect picture. That night, as it was a full moon, I decided I would water-ski in the nude. It was exciting skiing down a moonbeam and, with Julian steering the boat, I felt extremely safe. Apparently bets were taken by some of our neighbours as to whether I was naked or wearing a bikini. We never gave the game away.

Sometimes I went to Formentor in my open white Alvis coupé. One summer, Peter and I drove back to London. As we sped north along the Route du Sol, I was in a particularly light-hearted mood, and we were singing at the tops of our voices. As it was getting dark, I realised I hadn't booked a room for the night. I wasn't particularly worried, but after being turned away from at least a dozen hotels, we eventually found a rather seedy-looking establishment which offered us a room. I thought the large bejewelled lady behind the desk looked rather dubiously at us, but it wasn't until the next morning we found out we had spent the night in a brothel – a fact Peter was able to boast about back at Eton.

One summer, Caroline and Ian Gilmour came to stay with their children, Caroline fell so in love with the place that they decided to buy a plot of land just above us and build their own house. I was not totally pleased, especially when the voices of their guests, usually the braying of leading politicians, were carried by the wind across to our terrace.

In London I loved giving parties and, as our circle of friends widened, I became known as a 'political hostess' by certain elements of the press. The qualities of the great political hostesses of the past were so varied that any modern aspirants would quickly discover there are no easy rules to the game. I suppose the most frequent and general motives for entertaining are to give pleasure, to act as a catalyst, create new friendships and amours. For this you need a constant curiosity about people, an ability to keep abreast with new ideas, a gift for organisation and a certain degree of creativity. Sibyl Colefax had all these qualities, although the greatest lion hunter of them all, Osbert Sitwell, rather unkindly called her salon Lyon's Corner House. Her desire to please outweighed her desire to impress. Unlike Mrs Ronnie Greville, who was clever and bitchy, Sibyl detested malice and intrigue. I believe only the extremely dedicated should persevere in such social activity. The pitfalls often deny the benefits, especially the jealousy incurred by the uninvited. Although you may never have been entertained by them, they still think you are having parties and ignoring them.

The term 'political hostess' is hardly relevant now, when politicians are no longer the stars they once were. The lions of today are film and television stars, pop idols, media personalities and well-known writers and artists, who are surrounded by enough unsophisticated and young guests, easily impressed and deferential, thus making everyone happy. As Sibyl Colefax illustrated, money should not be an obstacle or an excuse for not entertaining. The only reason is meanness. No one has ever minded being asked to bring a bottle, and who has complained of sausage and mash?

Drue Heinz, one of the most imaginative and successful hostesses, once gave a party at which the food was a mixture of the fifty-seven varieties of her famous firm's products. She also gave a brilliant party in a field outside her house near Ascot and turned it into a fairground with a roller-coaster and a coconut shy. People sat on bales of straw and her guests consisted of many members of the Royal Family as well as friends from all walks of life.

I always had a fairly large proportion of men to women at my parties. Even the most ardent feminists don't appear to enjoy talking to each other the whole evening, while men will prop up the bar and talk politics forever. A number of attractive girls is a 'must' and, if you get a sprinkling of clever men and women together, some sparks are bound to fly – sometimes liquid too.

One of my parties became quite famous. Because of her sacking from *TV AM*, with a shaking hand, the newsreader Anna Ford threw a glass of red wine across my crowded room at the dashing Jonathan Aitken. It missed and dowsed an innocent bystander. Another disaster was when a hired butler got very drunk beforehand and announced Princes Margaret in a very loud voice as Her Royal Highness Princess Elizabeth. With her usual aplomb, she turned to her husband and said, "Well, Tony, it seems we've gone up in the world."

A rule of mine was never to relax until towards the end of the party. Otherwise you are the only one who will think it has been a roaring success. The start should be orchestrated, trying to introduce people to sympathetic strangers, to keep them on the move unless happily engrossed elsewhere, and to see their glasses are constantly full of their chosen drink.

In spite of the perils, there can be a great reward for the host or hostess – the possibility of aiding young friends by introductions to influential people and even starting a romance. Bernard Levin told me that his attachment and later marriage to Liz Anderson started on the doorstep of my house when he offered her a lift home. Who will disagree that a card in your post, among the brown envelopes, asking you to participate in some future festivity always lifts the spirits?

I was still working at the Violet Melchett Centre when, in 1964, I was put on the main Board of the NSPCC under the chairmanship of Lady Holland-Martin. It was heartrending to be presented with the details of the amount of cruelty perpetrated on some of the tiniest children. Part of my work was to act as a fundraiser, and I chaired several charitable occasions, such as a film or a theatre *première* for the cause. It always helped to have a member of the Royal Family as the guest of honour, and Princess Margaret and Princess Alexandra were great favourites. It meant a lot of hard work, setting up a committee of friends, filling the theatre or cinema and arranging a party afterwards in a grand house or friendly restaurant. For myself without a secretary, this work ate up my time, but fulfilled me.

Ever since Julian had inherited the title, we were asked to the Opening of Parliament each year. On one occasion, I had a minor disaster. I had forgotten to put my diamond necklace into its tiara frame, and tiaras were obligatory then. So I had to telephone the man from Cartier's and ask him to dash round and fix it. While he was fiddling with it, he snapped it clean in two and then calmly told me it would take two weeks to repair. As this was impossible, I managed to sew it together myself with strong white cotton. We arrived so late that the procession down the Royal Gallery was about to start, and we were only just allowed into the chamber. Everyone else had been there for about an hour. I always enjoyed the occasion and I believe that pageantry is something we really excel at in this country.

Six

One weekend, June and Randolph Churchill asked us to stay with them at their house in the country, which was near Chartwell, Winston's country home. When we arrived, June asked us whether we would like to share a bedroom or have separate rooms. Looking rather amazed when we said we only needed one room, she said, "How odd, most of our friends always opt for two." I was very fond of June, and her daughter Arabella was a great friend of my Kerena. Randolph could be amusing when sober, but he became belligerent when drunk, which was all too often. Once he was said to have become so impossible that some fellow members of White's Club, where he was lunching, pushed him down the stairs to sprawl on the pavement of St James's Street. He was in very good form when we arrived, but when we sat down to dinner that night, everything changed. He asked the butler to pour the bottles of wine, and when Randolph was told that they had run out, he turned red in the face and ordered the poor man to cycle to the local pub where he had an account. When the butler returned empty-handed, he said that the pub-owner had told him that his master's credit had run out. He was then sent to a pub at the next village to open a new account and eventually we had a late dinner, accompanied by delicious claret.

The next day we were to lunch at Chartwell with Sir Winston and Lady Churchill. We were the only guests, and I was terrified to be sitting next to the great man, whom I admired enormously. On my other side was Randolph and before long they were having a furious political argument across me. I remember having read that Winston was a great admirer of the evangelist Billy Graham and, to break up what was becoming a more and more heated exchange between father and son, I turned to Winston and asked his opinion of the evangelist. His eyes lit up and he spoke of his enthusiasm and admiration at great length. His wife Clemmie, across the table, looked very relieved and lunch passed off peacefully. Afterwards, Winston took me into the garden and proudly showed me his goldfish, while he fed them some crumbs.

Sadly it was soon after this that Winston died, and Julian and I went to the ceremony at St Paul's Cathedral, deeply moving and miraculously organised. The pall-bearers included two Prime Ministers, Clement Attlee and Harold Macmillan; two Field Marshals, The Earl Alexander of Tunis and Sir Gerald Templer; and an Admiral of the Fleet, The Earl Mountbatten of Burma. Of course, members of the Royal Family attended. After the service, the launch Havengore took the bier to the Festival Hall pier to be carried ashore and there conveyed by motor hearse to Waterloo Station and then by train to Blenheim Palace, where Sir Winston was buried at a private ceremony.

His daughter Mary and her husband Christopher Soames the MP were good friends of ours, and when Christopher became Ambassador in Paris, Pandora and I stayed with them in the Embassy. Mary was a brilliant and effortless hostess and gave unconventional and entertaining dinner parties. Emma, their pretty teenage daughter, was going through a rather wild stage, and I remember her once rushing through the dining-room during a formal lunch party, wearing the skimpiest of shorts, but Mary remained unperturbed. Several years later, Mary would become my Chairman when I sat on the Board of the Royal National Theatre.

Peter was now at Eton where he made many friends. In the Lent and Michaelmas halves, he played the Field Game and the Wall Game which the Duke of Wellington had in mind when he declared that his battles were won on the playing fields of Eton. In summer, Peter decided against playing cricket to become a 'wet-bob', a term used for those who sculled as well as rowing in eights. On the Fourth of June, a holiday to commemorate the birthday of King George the Third, parents would descend to picnic on the grass and watch their sons play their chosen sports. We would stand by the side of the Thames as the boats paraded, the crews with flowers decorating their boaters and wearing monkey jackets and smart white trousers. Afterwards, there would be a display of fireworks. In his last year when he was head of his house, Peter's eight were slightly intoxicated, and when they stood up with raised oars the boat capsized and they all landed in the water. The audience was delighted.

During the winter holidays, he would join me in Norfolk and help with our regular shooting weekends. We chose some of our guests rather for their good cheer than their good shooting. Julian preferred shooting wild birds, but did breed a few pheasants to augment the game, and our two Labradors were kept in kennels in the yard. They loved following our horses out riding, especially along the sands. They were also trained to retrieve the birds during the shoot. Afterwards I would give everyone my favourite recipe of curry and rice with all the trimmings, which we ate in the living room overlooking the garden. Our regular guns would be Harry Walston, George Jellicoe, Eddy Shackleton, Hugh Fraser, Ian Gilmour, Duncan Sandys and Aidan Crawley. They would bring their wives, who would sit on shooting sticks beside them where they stood to wait for the birds to be driven towards them over the trees by beaters. Peter's responsibility after the shoot was to enter every detail in the Game Book. I remember one year Antonia Fraser decided to blast away, impressively dressed in brown leather with a peaked cap.

The farm was more than a weekend pursuit for Julian – a major commitment and a working proposition. He was determined that Peter should learn step by step how to take it over, when the time came. He became instructed in forestry and planted many small woods and copses. Riding across the field with the family, he always carried a notebook and often dropped his reins to write down where a crop of wheat might be blighted, or he would mark the spot in a hedgerow where a newly-planted oak was being attacked by rabbits, so the foreman could be told. The farm was both his refuge and his challenge. On the day he was invited to give the opening address at the Oxford Farming Conference, his passionate involvement in agriculture was fully vindicated.

To enable Julian to spend more time at Courtyard, the Samuel bank had provided him with a small Cessna aircraft, which he kept at Elstree. The flight only took forty minutes. He had a pair of runways constructed so that he could land and take off at the farm, irrespective of the direction of the wind. The foreman was warned by telephone of his expected time of arrival, and he would switch on the landing lights, flashing red ones on top of the barn, while green and white ones indicated the approach to the runways. At the sound of the plane, he would also stand by with a fire extinguisher in one hand and a crowbar in the other.

I was always rather nervous in the Cessna, especially when we flew to the weekend parties of friends, usually landing in a bumpy field. After one dance, Julian had such a hangover that I was determined to learn to fly myself, as a safeguard. I took lessons at Elstree and learnt to take off and land, but before I achieved my flying licence, I was made to see how to straighten the plane when it was in a deep spin. This made me feel sick, and I had to give up the challenge. But at least I knew that in dire circumstances, I had a fundamental knowledge of flying. Once when we went to stay for a weekend with the St Oswalds at their beautiful Robert Adams house Nostell Priory, where Chippendale had made most of the furniture, we had a frightening experience. Our host had told us he had the perfect field for landing in front of the house, but as we approached, we saw several sheep in our way, which he had forgotten to have removed. The rest of the guests were all gathered at the top of the high flight of stone steps, watching as Julian luckily managed to swerve in between the stray flock.

We would always try to spend the Easter and Christmas holidays at Courtyard, often with some of our London friends. We treated the children in a grown-up way, often allowing them to stay up after dinner and get involved in lively discussions on any conceivable subject, which sometimes continued late into the night. Our informal country lifestyle was in marked contrast to our high-powered London life. One Christmas morning, Julian and I led a reluctant holly-decked and bemused Shetland pony into Pandora's bedroom. Our gift was greeted with shrieks of delight and immediate demands for a ride in the snow in pyjamas and gumboots.

In London, Pandora attended the Garden House School off Sloane Square, where a famous picture would appear of Princess Diana in a see-through chiffon skirt. Later, Pandora was educated at Lady Eden Nursery School in Fulham. Drusilla Shulman and I were great friends, and as her daughters Alexandra (later the editor of Vogue) and Nicky (the writer and the Marchioness of Normanby) went to the same school, we used to take it in turns to drive them to their first classes. Not being an early riser, I would usually just put a coat over my nightdress and run them there in my car. Nicky was a vague and disorganised child with her school socks always in concertinas round her ankles. Little did one realise she would grow into a great intellect and beauty and marry first Edward St Aubyn and then the writer and landowner Constantine Phipps.

On the face of it, we were leading an ideal life, but disenchantment lay ahead. A merger was proposed between the Samuel bank and Kenneth Keith's merchant bank, Philip

Hill, Higginson, Erlanger. Kenneth Keith had masterminded several takeovers during his meteoric rise in the City and was feared for his ruthlessness. The Samuel family were slightly dubious, but Julian persuaded them that the danger was outweighed by the advantages. By April 1965, plans were announced to merge the two banks and their assets of more than £200,000,000. Hill Samuel was born. On the eve of the announcement, the main instigators, Julian and Kenneth Keith, dined at the home of Woodrow Wyatt, who applauded the venture.

Before the end of the year, however, the honeymoon was over. Disillusion set in. The merger had been described in banking circles as 'an alliance between the Gentlemen and the Players', and Keith acknowledged the difference: "Being a (Samuel) family affair, they felt they should be treated as in the old days and be consulted about everything and when they weren't they got rattled. We were used to acting without board meetings and they weren't. I suppose we were unduly brusque and arrogant. We thought we were better than they were." Within months Julian wanted to reverse the merger and the personality clash between him and Keith became insurmountable. The Samuel family weren't behind him and, after a prolonged battle of wills, Julian never again attended a lunch or a meeting if he knew Keith would be there.

Of course Julian would describe to me step by step what was happening, and I was deeply concerned how much was taken out of him. But at the age of forty-one, he still held more than a dozen directorships, including one with Guardian Assurance. He persuaded them to become major shareholders in British Field Products, a rapidly expanding enterprise. Its activities extended to selling seed and corn, the drying of grass and the renting of land to grow lucerne. In 1964, the company had acquired Weasenham Farms Limited with more than 14,000 Norfolk acres, with Julian as its chairman. Its success helped to block out the memory of the failure of the Hill Samuel merger.

In the meantime, in 1964, I was writing a novel, *Tell Me, Honestly*, which was in the form of a series of revealing telephone conversations between London society hostesses, journalists and politicians. Written under my maiden name of Sonia Graham and based roughly on the idea of *Les Liaisons Dangéreuses*, it was born out of my disenchantment with the insincerity and futility of much of the London social scene. Published after the Profumo Affair, many people were busy speculating who were the characters in the book. George Weidenfeld took me to the Schloss Hellbrunn outside Salzburg in Austria to attend the Prix Formentor. I met Mary McCarthy, Jonathan Miller and Jorge Semprun, the previous winner of the £3,500 prize, also the present winner, a beautiful twenty-seven-year-old German woman, Gisela Elsner, for her novel *The Dwarf Giant*.

Soon after returning to London, I went to Africa to write an article for Vogue on game parks. I called it 'From the Tops of the Trees to the Mountains of the Moon'. I travelled with my friend, Anne Millard, and John Bennett, the High Commissioner in Rwanda, helped with all the arrangements. In tiny chartered planes, we visited many famous reserves. John drove us in his jeep to the foothills of the snow-capped mountain ranges of Kenya and Kilimanjaro. In Rwanda at sunset we watched the giant Watutsi perform their colourful tribal dances. But the highlight of our visit was staying overnight at Tree Tops outside Nairobi. That hotel had become famous, because there Princess Elizabeth heard of her father's death, and that she would be Queen.

Built high in the trees, the rooms overlooked a water hole in the Aberdare forest about a hundred miles from the airport. We were met by our white hunter, Colonel Hayes-Newington, ex-Indian Army, toting guns to protect us from wild animals. As the moon came out, people talked in whispers, looking expectantly into the forest for the animals to make their entrances. Slowly, hesitantly came the rhinos, warthogs, wildebeeste and buffalo. The circus parade continued all night with the animals drinking, snorting, puffing, blowing and listening for the more dangerous beasts lurking in the darkness beyond.

One experience I never forgot. We were to fly over Mount Kilimanjaro in Tanzania, Africa's highest mountain. We set off in a Cessna Skyknight with a Turkish pilot. There were two oxygen cylinders in the plane – essential as we would fly to more than 19,000 feet. As we neared the mountain, the pilot tried his oxygen tank – it didn't work. We gave him ours, which he accepted with alacrity. Deprived of oxygen, with the heady feeling of champagne in our blood, we flew round Kilimanjaro, thankful that our pilot was not feeling so intoxicated, and he managed a safe but bumpy landing. Uganda was our final destination, and we flew northwards, crossing the westward tip of a stormy Lake Victoria, taking on the colour of the bleak sky. Here, some argue, is the true source of the Nile or at Ripon Falls, where it flows north to Murchison Falls and Lake Albert.

Another tiny charter plane with a Greek pilot this time, took us to the Paraa Safari Lodge overlooking the Nile in the centre of the Murchison National Park. The highlight of our stay was a trip by river steamer to the Falls, a fantastic spectacle of the Nile thundering through a twenty-foot gap in a series of cascades to detonate in the tranquil water below. Hippos appeared a few feet from the boat; crocodiles sprawled on the banks, their scales glinting in the sun and their tiny, malignant green eyes ignoring us passing by. Most delightful though, was the time at the Queen Elizabeth Park, nearly eight hundred square miles in the extreme west of Uganda, bordering on the Congo. To the north lay the jagged Ruwenzori Range, the dream Mountains of the Moon. Looking from the Mweya Safari Lodge at the momentous peaks and ridges, I couldn't help being aware of the underlying mystery, the vastness and beauty that is Africa. One day I hope to return.

We flew to London to my routine life of work and social events. Some took place in Millionaire's Row, where nearly all the Embassies had their Residences. The most impressive was the French Embassy, backed by a beautiful garden and always full of a cosmopolitan mixture of people. But a favourite was the Dutch Embassy, where Gabby Bentinck held amusing and informal parties and became a great friend. Another was the Philippine Embassy where we met the infamous Madame Marcos, the lady with more than one thousand pairs of shoes. The Ambassador was a charmer and became Pandora's Godfather. For her Christening present, he gave her an inlaid wooden box with endless tiny drawers each containing a jewel or a poem. But in spite of all the parties and our happy home life at Courtyard and Chelsea, our future was about to be transformed.

In April 1966, the Prime Minister Harold Wilson appointed Richard Marsh as Minister of Power with a directive to nationalise the steel industry. His choice for the demanding post of Chairman was Julian. We were in Majorca at the time and we were amazed when a man in a smart white uniform arrived at the villa and said he was the British Consul in Palma and had an urgent message from the Government. Changing quickly from his swimming trunks, Julian read the grand sealed document handed to him. After the Consul had left, Julian and I discussed this surprise proposal. We felt we had to give it a great deal of thought. In my heart of hearts I was against it, as I feared the strain put on the shoulders of my husband might be insupportable. But equally, I felt it had to be his decision alone.

When we returned to London, Julian and Richard Marsh had several talks and, as Richard became more keen, Julian grew more apprehensive. He knew that the Labour Cabinet was hardly enthusiastic. A Tory peer with an Etonian background was not exactly what they wanted. But in Richard Marsh's words, "they were won over by his extraordinary charisma, which was a mixture of a stubborn streak and an enormous strength of character and charm. I think he was the most impressive man I ever met." Sir Henry Benson added that he had suggested Julian because of his self-confidence, high intelligence and sense of humour. Before accepting Marsh's invitation to mastermind the biggest amalgamation ever attempted in British industry,

Julian consulted individually the heads of the fourteen major iron and steel companies, together employing 270,000 workers. His task would be to weld them into one financially viable corporation, something that he knew could not be accomplished without the consent of their chiefs. Only one resigned, the rest backed Julian's plans. He stood to add yet another dimension to his Mond father's and grandfather's definitions of the word 'rationalisation'.

Before accepting the chairmanship, he consulted his close friend, the brilliant barrister Mark Littman, who encouraged him to accept. Mark became Julian's chief legal adviser and, ultimately, a Deputy Chairman. Julian's vision was to see the steel corporation as a manufacturing business, international in operation, marketing and acquiring raw materials. The Glaswegian scientist, Dr Monty Finniston, was Julian's technical and political counterweight. Eventually he would become Deputy Chairman and, finally, Chief Executive. Julian was criticised for choosing two Jews as deputies, a factor he had never considered. He chose people for their character and ability without regard to their family or background. Nor was he perturbed by the outcry at his own appointment. Some members of the Labour Government were antagonistic, while the Tories called him a traitor for furthering nationalisation. He responded that his primary interest was business, not politics, and the need to run a major industry effectively was more important than theoretical arguments about public and private enterprises.

As a deeply sensitive person, his unfailing air of affability masked the fact that he really cared about hurting people. The hardest part of the job was the wide-scale closure of plants and the sacking of 50,000 men during the first years, some of whom had spent their entire lives in the steel industry. He admitted that he found the social problems emotionally exhausting. He told the journalist Susan Barnes, "One of the first things I established was that we gave two years' notice to any major plant closure so that the workers could be retrained for something else."

He told me that he felt it was his personal duty to tell key men in the industry, often nearly old enough to be his father, that they had come to the end of the road. This one task he never delegated. Before these meetings, when he had to travel to the various plants, I knew how much he was hating the gruelling job ahead, which took more out of him than anything else. I would wait anxiously for his return and, although he hated talking about these confrontations, I could tell by his face how demoralised he was. He was never the ruthless businessman.

In the meantime, I tried to keep our lifestyle as normal as possible. In August we went to Majorca as usual, although Julian could spend less time with the family. That summer, I took my mother with me and the children. She was living in a flat in Worthing with my father, and she was happy to get away, as their marriage was not getting any better. Julian was to follow a week later. Two nights before he was due to arrive, my mother got extremely drunk, but when I put her to bed, I thought she would sleep it off. Suddenly in the middle of the night, I smelt a terrible smell of burning. It was coming from my mother's room below me. Rushing down the steps, I saw the room was on fire and my mother had set the bedclothes alight with a cigarette. Pandora's room was next door, and the first thing I did was to make a dash and carry her to safety. My mother had somehow got into the bath, and eventually Peter and I found a fire extinguisher and managed to stop the flames. But the aftermath was dreadful – that foul smell only a blaze can produce. The walls of my mother's room were black, and I had the awful thought of what Julian would find when he arrived. I sped into action and got some painters round to repair the damage, and in the meantime Peter and Kerena, Pandora, my mother and I spent the day in our boatman Cosmé's fishing vessel. When Julian arrived, I spared him the details of our night of horror.

Seven

On returning to London, Julian threw himself wholeheartedly into the job of proving that he could be a major industrialist. While reorganising the industry, he also set himself the task of absorbing its technology and learning enough to try to assess its future in a changing international scene. Pressures mounted and in April 1967, the British Steel Corporation was formed with the industry divided into geographical areas. We made a trip to America to study the steel industry in Pittsburg, Chicago and Ohio. I remember one American steel magnate greeting Julian by saying, "I've been in steel for more than thirty-five years. How long have you been in it?" Julian's reply was, "Barely thirty-five minutes. That's why I've come to see you."

The intensity of the work was beginning to take its toll, and after Christmas he was taken into the intensive care unit of Westminster Hospital with a minor heart attack. He would be away from work for six months. There was no talk of retirement, and in the summer of 1968, he was back at his desk to fight a series of financial battles with the Treasury for the Steel Corporation's right to act as a public company, not a public corporation and to reorganise itself into product divisions like ICI and other major corporations, rather than in regional groups. He also renewed his own contract for six years at £16,000 a year.

We now had the use of the Steel Corporation's twin-engined aeroplane. Although the smart uniformed pilot who met us at Elstree would offer to fly us, Julian always chose to take over the controls. I must say I preferred our small Cessna, which had now been returned to Hill Samuel. I found the Corporation's plane rather pretentious. The other thing I found difficult was all the criticism over what was considered to be Julian's vast salary. Originally, he had demanded for himself and his Board more money than was being paid by any other nationalised industry. His argument was that he needed the money to enable him to hire the best people in England and abroad. There were snide cartoons in newspapers and headlines on placards on the pavements as we drove past. All very hurtful and unpleasant.

My friend Anne Millard suggested I should escape from all of Julian's worries and go for a week's holiday on a cruise round the Caribbean. We would explore some of the smaller islands. My idea of a cruise had always been old ladies and men sitting on a chilly deck wrapped in rugs, their only recreation being a gentle game of quoits or a morning constitutional round the deck. But my apprehension proved wrong. The cruise lasted a week and took in eight islands on a Greek ship called the *Stella Solaris* and carried about one hundred and fifty passengers. We boarded her at San Juan, Puerto Rico – the nightmarish Las Vegas of the Caribbean, full of one-armed bandits, Hamburger Heavens and casinos. Thirty pairs of curious eyes of the Greek crew stared at us as we walked up the gangway. To what? To where?

There were deckchairs arranged like soldiers on the sun deck. I'd been right all along. In our cabins we found horror upon horror – a programme of our cruise. Day one included an 'excursion around St Croix', a 'get together dance in the Olympia Lounge', 'bingo in the Aegean Lounge', 'crapshooting on the aft-deck'. Later in the week there was a 'masquerade parade', a 'Caribbean hat party', 'Ekleipsis à la Grecque', and 'musical tea and horse racing'.

Escape was impossible and, as it turned out, we were lucky. Very few passengers on our boat had anything to do with the organised programme. They just went their separate ways, to lie on golden beaches, taste the freshly caught lobsters at one of the small island hotels, explore the local rum or spice factory, or even stay on board and do nothing.

On this Greek ship, there was no nonsense about being asked to join the captain's table. The Captain – a very Socratesian figure with pale grey eyes and beard – sat with his officers, all in immaculate white. He gazed at the world from his Olympian heights. As far as I know, he never left the ship. From the first day, when we had to line up in front of him on deck dressed in lumpy orange life-jackets, to the last, he inspired complete confidence. We ate delicious taramasalata and moussaka, washed down with ouzo and retsina, while the crew entertained us with songs and Spiro, a serious Anthony Quinn-like Zorba, danced a serpentine jiggle with masterly control, as the ship appeared to be at an angle of twenty-two degrees.

We sailed every night and stopped at a different island each day. A favourite with many people was Martinique, the birthplace of the Empress Joséphine. I found the beaches bleak and uninviting – black lava sand washed by relentless breakers. I loved St Lucia and St Barts, but my favourite was Grenada with its Grande Anse beach. Sometimes local dancers would entertain us on board before we weighed anchor and sailed away. Perhaps perpetual motion is the answer to dull care, as on an eight-day cruise, I learned the delights and the pitfalls of this short odyssey.

In the meantime, Peter had moved from Eton to Pembroke College, Cambridge, where he was studying law. He lived in digs outside the college with an old Etonian friend so that he could keep Henry, a small black mongrel. He was devoted to the dog. Once on holiday in Norfolk, Henry jumped into an icy river to retrieve a pheasant shot by Peter. The current swept Henry away. Without hesitating, risking his own life, Peter dived in and eventually rescued his beloved pet.

Julian and I were visiting Australia for meetings connected with steel when we learned that Peter, in his final year at Pembroke College, had been taken very ill with severe colon pains. At first the specialist said there was nothing they could do for him except to recommend rest. But while recuperating in Norfolk, he was struck down again and we drove him immediately to the Westminster Hospital. There, a brilliant young specialist agreed to do a series of then still unusual and rare operations to bypass a diseased colon.

Months of convalescence followed each operation, but it was only after two failures that the third operation was successful. For the sake of Kerena and Pandora, who were unaware of the serious illness of their brother, Julian and I tried to carry on living with some semblance of normality. In August 1968, Julian took the two girls to Formentor with a group of their friends. Staying on at Tite Street, I would walk to the Westminster Hospital every day. Peter's room was beginning to look like a Heath Robinson drawing with so many odds and bobs of hospital equipment cluttering up the space. He was always cheerful and full of jokes for the nurses, but after each operation, he told me later, he could always tell by the expression on my face whether the process had been successful or not.

In between major surgery, we would go to Norfolk and take walks along the windswept beach between Hunstanton and Holkham. When Peter eventually began to recover, we rented a small flat in Eccleston Square, where he could feel some degree of independence. In 1970, he went to Keele University, to take an MA in criminology. He lived in half a farm worker's cottage near to Quentin and Sue Crewe's house. They were enormously hospitable and always remained good friends. Later he would do research work in criminology at the Institute of Psychiatry and the London School of Economics.

Julian was also having a battle for survival on the political front. Time and time again, he found himself blocked by the new Conservative Government over a long-term development plan. Yet when Peter Walker, an old friend, became Secretary for Trade and Industry, he defended Julian's scheme and suggested that the Cabinet should discuss it with him. That unique historical meeting was the most crucial of Julian's career. Afterwards, the Government agreed to the biggest modernisation and expansion programme in the steel industry's history, involving an investment of three billion pounds over the next ten years.

Julian was also involved at an international level. As President-elect of the International Iron and Steel Institute, we were asked in 1972 to host a dinner and reception in London's historic Guildhall. It was a glittering occasion and leading industrialists came from all over the world. I pushed the boat out and bought a glamorous pale-blue jewel-encrusted chiffon ball dress from Dior. I danced in the ancient crypt with the Prime Minister Edward Heath, who later became a great friend.

Julian still had many critics within the nationalised steel industry, but in the fifth year of its creation it was said to be in better shape than at any time since the war. "He was right to devote so much effort to the political battle," wrote Keith Richardson, the Industrial Editor of *The Sunday Times*. "By doing so he convinced most of his critics on both Left and Right that the British Steel Corporation should be left alone to get on with the job. For the first time since the war steel is out of the main political arena and has a chance to build for the future. That has been Melchett's immense achievement."

I was seeing less of my sister Bunty, as she and her husband Anthony had tired of the bright lights of London and had escaped with their four young children to the Lake District. There they had settled in a National Trust castle at a peppercorn rent. Dacre Castle was a derelict medieval fortress by Ullswater. There, in the great King's Room, a stone-walled hall associated with King Athelstan, Bunty covered the arched windows with velvet curtains, which she made herself. They both loved hunting and hired two horses and also acquired two whippets, two peacocks, two falcons, a donkey and a large floating population of pigeons, ducks, homing budgerigars and a villainous raven.

Bunty studied falconry, which often meant staying up all night with the bird tied to her gauntleted wrist by a leather leash. When I travelled to Cumbria to be with her, I slept in a small bedroom, which had formerly been a chapel. She and Anthony seemed extremely happy leading an unconventional life with various animals wandering at will throughout the castle. The peacocks, however, were kept outside by putting a large mirror on the lawn, so that they could admire themselves. Bunty wrote a book about their experiences called *Pawn Takes Castle*, which described both the pleasures and horrors of living such an extraordinary life.

The summer following Peter's illness, we spent a wonderful August at Casa Melchett. Julian had ordered a diesel motor boat, *Sondora*, to be built in England, and he had her fitted with every conceivable aid to navigation. He also had our Majorcan boatman Cosmé flown over to be trained in her maintenance. He intended to use her to explore the Balearic Islands and he meant to leave nothing to chance. He, Peter and Cosmé motored her to Majorca, and there were screams of delight when they arrived at the steps of our villa.

Soon afterwards, we decided to go round Minorca in her, taking with us Pandora's friend Jane Gilmour, the daughter of Caroline and Ian, our neighbours. When we set off, the sea was calm, but just as we were nearing the top of the island, a storm got up and we had to consider turning back. I was all for it, particularly as I felt responsible for my friend's child as well as Pandora. But Julian and Cosmé thought we could make it, and with the waves pounding the windscreen, we survived an extremely rough passage round the island and eventually back to Formentor. I don't think I have ever been so frightened in my life.

On our return to London, normal life continued with its mixture of work and social gatherings. Every weekend Julian and I flew to Norfolk where I was joined by the children during their school breaks. Pandora was enjoying boarding school, Cobham Hall, and won a prize for her piece, 'Bob-bob-bobbing, I came bouncing over the waves':

Now I must describe myself. I am a Schweppes Tonic bottle, with a gold screw top of which I am very proud. I've a secret message inside me which was put in by someone who was stranded on a desert island. He hoped that I would reach the shore but I never did, so here I am bobbing on the waves. Today I was nearing a huge port with ships in all directions. I was very frightened and all the tonic that was left inside me had all fizzed up, because I had been bumping up and down all the wastes of the boats around me. Help! The Queen Elizabeth was heading straight for me. Help.

"I'm going to be run over!"

I could hear her huge engines pounding in my ears, the noise becoming louder and louder! For a moment I thought I was going to be squashed into glass fragments, but by pure luck I was just saved.

Soon I was in the open sea again and it was full of rubbish. "Ugh!" I have just floated into the most revolting piece of orange peel! How can people be so disgusting, dropping their rubbish into the sea?

"Hello, what's that? It looks like another bottle."

And, sure enough, up floated a handsome brown Ginger Beer bottle.

"Hello. Who are you?" I asked.

"I have been dropped into the sea by my unkind master."
The poor thing looked so upset I felt very sorry for him.
"Stop sniffing," I said, thinking that I might start myself."
"I say, why don't you come with me on my adventure?"
"Gosh, thanks! I'd love to," said the now much cheered-up Ginger Beer bottle.

So off we went together, bob-bob-bobbing over the waves. After that I became great friends with the Ginger Beer bottle, and he calls me 'Tonic' for short, and I call him 'Ginger'. So Ginger and Tonic lived happily ever after, bob-bob-bobbing over the waves.

On 10 June 1971, Julian and I were invited (or rather, commanded) to a dance at Buckingham Palace for the Duke of Edinburgh's birthday. A formal sit-down dinner was followed by the dancing, and then a breakfast of scrambled eggs, grilled bacon, chipolatas and mushrooms. I was lucky enough to dance with Prince Philip, who is very good on the dance floor, and although I had thought the evening might be rather frightening, it was very relaxed. I wore the same Dior dress I had worn for the dinner at the Guildhall. The Queen was thoroughly enjoying herself and I had never seen her look so happy.

Our next Royal occasion was the Opening of Parliament by Her Majesty. I had always found this an extremely exhausting occasion as we had to be seated for over an hour before the Queen made her entrance accompanied by the Duke of Edinburgh. Then, of course, in all her regalia, she had to read out a rather boring speech composed by the Prime Minister. I am sure it had little to do with her own opinions. But Queens must never now speak out, as they once did.

In October, we went to a luncheon at Hampton Court Palace in honour of Their Majesties the Emperor and Empress of Japan. In his address, the Emperor said it reminded him "of his first visit as a young man, under the reign of His Majesty King George the Fifth." He went on to say how impressed he was by the courage, strength and endurance the British people had exhibited in the face of national troubles. Most important was that our two countries should remain interrelated and interdependent, which is what we had tried to do in recent years. "It is reassuring to know that the two countries, at either extremity of the eastern hemisphere, are proceeding toward the same goal with or without a written alliance."

I found this a moving occasion. This time I refrained from speaking to my neighbour in Japanese, as I had done at the shipyard at the launching of the oil tanker in Nagasaki. Blunders do make one wary.

The following year of 1972 was almost too busy. Julian needed all the help that could be given him, and we travelled intensively, visiting steel plants all over the country. I have a photograph of myself in a hard helmet standing by a blast furnace in Teeside, and showing the Queen and Prince Philip round a new plant at Port Talbot. But it wasn't all work. One weekend Julian and I stayed at Cliveden with Bronwen and Bill Astor. Stephen Ward had a cottage on the estate and would join us to swim in the pool and for meals with the other guests. But I never saw any sign of Christine Keeler or Mandy Rice-Davies. Drinking champagne and relaxing on the terrace overlooking the Thames, no one could have predicted the scandal that was to follow with such far-reaching tragedies. Stephen Ward, a well-known osteopath, was assumed to be having an affair with Christine Keeler, who was also meant to be living with a Russian spy. This was never proved, although John Profumo had to resign from the Macmillan cabinet. Ward was blamed, and after a court case, he committed suicide. Bill Astor was never a very strong character, unlike his formidable mother Nancy Lady Astor, and so he was deeply scarred by the whole episode. I met Bronwen years later, when she was living in a house near the health farm Grayshott Hall, and she told me that the scandal had precipitated his early death. She had become deeply religious and lived an extremely puritanical life with priests amongst her guests.

When Pandora was eleven years old, we sent her to board at Cobham Hall in Kent. I had heard very good reports of the school, both scholastically and artistically. Painting was my daughter's passion and still remains so, professionally. The girls were allowed to keep pets and Pandora had several guinea pigs, which she bred and sold to school chums. Her best friend was Sarah Cameron, now the literary agent Sarah Lutyens. Thirty years on, they are still very close.

A year after she had been at Cobham, Julian and I were in London, about to attend the first night of a film premiere. We had a wonderful chauffeur called Ron, who had virtually become part of the family. He had been a Pearly King in the East End before becoming a chauffeur, and Pandora loved to see him in his full garb covered in lustrous buttons. This particular night, he took a call on the car telephone and handed it to Julian. The school were ringing to say that Pandora had had a serious accident and was being taken to hospital. We immediately reversed and sped to Kent. The doctor told us that she had a hip fracture and needed an operation as soon as possible. In the ambulance travelling to the Queen Elizabeth Hospital, Pandora was deeply sedated and was out of pain. The surgeon in London told us that this was a seriously complicated fracture and would need a four-hour operation. Still in our party clothes, Julian and I sat in the waiting room, frantically worried for our youngest child.

Later Pandora was to tell us that the accident had occurred while they were playing 'newly-weds' on the school lawn. While being carried, she was dropped when her 'husband' slipped. Although she was in excruciating pain, the games mistress made her climb the steep winding staircase to brush her hair in the dormitory before she was taken to the local hospital. Luckily, the operation was totally successful, and within a few months she was walking freely, and able to return to school.

Julian was working harder than ever, and he persuaded the Government to align the steel industry to meet the competitive challenge of entry into the Common Market. The Corporation's borrowing powers were raised by £750 million to one and a quarter billion pounds between 1971 and 1974, in order to reduce the industry's capital by up to £350 million, so enabling it to write off losses expected to total £240 million and to create a reserve fund to meet the closure of obsolescent plants. Sir John Eden, then the Trade and Industry Minister, said: "We are clearing the slate." Julian welcomed the Bill, as "a really important step forward."

During this period I was asked to launch the Wear's biggest tanker, the *Orienda Bridge*, at the North Sands shipyard. This time my technique was the conventional cracking of a magnum of champagne onto the bow of the ship and naming her. Luckily I did not miss. Later that week our friend Sam Spiegel gave a lavish promotional dinner for his film *Nicholas and Alexandra*. At a promotional dinner, my neighbour was talking about taking his daughter to visit Father Christmas at Harrods the next day. On my other side was an extremely attractive man I knew quite well. "I'll make you a bet. Let's have lunch tomorrow and you become Santa Claus for an hour." Why, I shall never know, but I agreed – possibly after too many glasses of champagne.

After lunch the next day, I approached the real Father Christmas in Harrods and told him my plight and threw myself at his mercy. To my surprise, he agreed, took me into a small side room and gave me his clothes and long white beard. I got away with it for about an hour and happily none of the children suspected, especially as I put on a deep husky voice. But in the end, my light-hearted joke was discovered and one of the managers of the department said very sternly, "We take Father Christmas very seriously here. One has to be careful where children are involved." What made it worse was that my cover was blown a week later in the Private Ear of the *Sunday Times*.

Sam was very amused, and later in the following year, he and his American wife Sandra took us in his beautiful yacht, the *M.Y. Malahne*, on a cruise round Corsica. We stopped at several beautiful ports such as Saint Florent and Calvi, but Sam was in a restless mood and for some reason wanted to reach Brigitte Bardot urgently, as so many other people did. At a small port, we stopped at the only shop nearby, which happened to be a butcher's, and Sam spent ages trying unsuccessfully to reach the famous star on a very ancient telephone. There were endless lines of various salami hanging from the rail of the shop, and Sam was tucking into his favourite food. After some time, he gave up and radioed for his yacht to send a dinghy to take us on board. Later that night he became extremely ill and had to be flown straight back to England and hospital. Luckily he made a speedy recovery from that close call.

My musical daughter Kerena was going through a hippy stage and living in the basement flat of my friend Nuala Allason in her historic house in Cheyne Walk. There she could pluck her guitar to her spaced-out comrades without disturbing anyone. When she joined the family at Casa Melchett, she would play and sing for us on the terrace, either one of her own or her favourite Joan Baez numbers. With her lovely blonde hair cascading down her back, we would sit enthralled in the evening sunset. But whenever I asked her to perform in front of friends or guests, she adamantly refused.

Back in London, Margaret, Duchess of Argyll, gave a party at the Dorchester Hotel to celebrate the eightieth birthday of Paul Getty. We had stayed with Paul at his mansion, Sutton House, and it wasn't an altogether agreeable experience. We were met by his ten black hounds barking their heads off, but luckily kept at bay by their keeper. Although he must have been one of the richest men in England, he was known for his meanness. He kept a telephone box in his hall where guests had to pay before making their calls. But the party in London was a great success with friends including George

Weidenfeld, Pat 'Bubbles' Harmsworth, Eddy Shackleton and Fiona and Heine Thyssen. An ex-screen siren, Pat was herself a great hostess. At one of her dinners, I sat next to David Niven, who was just as entertaining as his book, *The Moon's a Balloon*. Across the room, she had gathered an eclectic mixture of guests from royalty to Andy Warhol. She was famous for always being late, even at her own parties. Years later, when I was Chair of a gala in aid of the National Theatre and Princess Margaret was the guest of honour, Pat's husband arrived alone and stood in line with the rest of the committee. I asked where she was. "In the bath when I left," he replied, "but I expect she'll make it." Indeed, she stepped out of her chauffeur-driven car and slipped into line a moment before the royal entrance.

Pat was also extremely generous and once offered her flat in Madison Avenue to me when I was visiting New York. The Irish writer Edna O'Brien came along as she had to see her literary agent. It was a sumptuous apartment and we settled in, with me choosing the second largest bedroom and Edna opting to sleep in the linen cupboard, as she found the other rooms were too noisy. After we had been there a few days, we were greatly surprised when Bubbles suddenly, without warning, made an unexpected appearance. Immediately, the flat became a madhouse with trunks full of ball dresses lying all over the floor. The telephone never stopped ringing and invitations flooded in for dinner parties. Edna's and my tranquil life came to a crashing halt. Bubbles always carried with her a canvas bag with a bottle or two or champagne, in case there was none on offer. They provided her nickname and accompanied her over-the-top flouncy dresses. She was certainly a life-enhancer, always in ebullient form, also a wonderful and devoted mother. Being Godmother to her only son, Jonathan, I got to know a different side to her public persona.

At a party, given by Vere Rothermere for the *Daily Mail* to honour Hungary, where his father had once been invited to become Regent, we saw Mrs Thatcher seize the microphone to trumpet about her last visit to Budapest.

"I went and bought a handbag," she said, while we all ducked, fearing a swipe from the swinging leather. "I bargained. They listened to me, and that's why it's good there now. Free market."

Early in the new year, Julian and I were invited by the Prime Minister, Edward Heath, to a supper at Lancaster House following a gala performance at the Royal Opera House to celebrate the entry of the United Kingdom into the European Common Market, in the presence of the Queen and the Duke of Edinburgh. But all too soon this grand social life was to come to an abrupt end. Under the terms of Julian's appointment as Chairman of the Steel Industry, he was allowed one directorship with a bank. His reputation as an unpompous tycoon with a dynamic personality, was spreading. In the summer of 1972, he was appointed a non-executive director of the Orion Bank. This was another gateway to international activity, if he chose, as many suspected he might, not to renew his steel contract in two years' time. Soon afterwards we flew to Venice for the weekend for the annual board meeting of the Orion Bank. We stayed at our favourite hotel, the Cipriani, and we were happier than we had been for a long time. He took me to see places he recalled from boyhood holidays – Princess Aspasia's villa, The Garden of Eden and the Casa Leone facing it on the Giudecca, where his parents had entertained so lavishly. Now all the buildings were looking a little derelict.

Across the lagoon, the island of Torcello appeared just as beautiful as he remembered it, and he decided to hire a motor boat to drive me there for dinner. Afterwards the moon came up and, arm in arm, we walked round the tiny island. The houses were bathed in a soft haze and I felt a hint of the eternal as we stood in the cathedral. For the first time, I was aware of the inevitable, transitory nature of life and a sudden certainty that Julian and I would be together forever. A strange sensation. That night, we made passionate love.

The next day, Sunday, 10th June, we sunbathed by the swimming pool, and we were joined by William de Gelsey, who was to become the Orion Bank's joint managing director. His friendship with Julian dated from the day when, as a Hungarian refugee, he came down from Cambridge with a chemistry degree and an introduction to Henry Melchett, which led to an ICI position. Suddenly, someone produced a Sunday paper with a long article about a proposed merger between Hill Samuel and Slater Walker. Julian went white when he read it. It must have made him relive the horror of the M. Samuel merger with Philip Hill, and his resignation.

Later that afternoon, we went sightseeing in St Mark's Cathedral, and we visited the Doge's Palace. I felt strange, as if in the Hieronymus Bosch painting of the little people on the edge of the world. Julian wanted to leave. He suddenly

Julian and I, before attending the Coronation of Her Majesty the Queen

With Princess Margaret at a charity gala

With Prince Philip and H.M. The Queen at th
opening of a steel works

All dressed up with Peter and Kerena

Young Bunty and I go riding

(Right) Nicholas Coleridge, Craig Brown, Guy Lubbock, Edna O'Brien and my family at a rented house in Tuscany.

The family water-skiing at Formentor

With Andrew, just after our wedding

(Right) Mike Richey, enjoying a drink and cigar

With my three children, Peter, Pandora and Kerena in Norfolk

felt tired. After dinner, we sat at a small table in St Mark's Square and bought two yo-yos from a small boy. Yet back in our hotel, I felt drowsy and happy, at peace with all the world.

Eight

In England, three days later, I made Julian have a medical check-up and the heart surgeon pronounced him completely fit. Later, he was to meet Monty Finniston to sort out a batch of new problems. Monty suggested that he, his wife Miriam and I go to Majorca for the weekend to work in a relaxed atmosphere. So then we flew away in a company aircraft together with Julian's secretary, Phyllis Rumbold. It was a glorious day and everyone was in great spirits.

The Finnistons had gone into Palma and were to join us later. We were met by a car driven by our gardener. Julian sat in the front and I directly behind him next to his secretary. His left arm was resting across the back of the seat as he turned round to talk to us. The sleeve of his blue shirt was rolled up and the blond hairs showed on his brown arm. He was happy and excited to be revisiting our villa, cutting down the size of the bedrooms as we worked out the price in pesetas per square metre. I remembered how little money we had in those days, but we had always been a bit reckless. As Julian turned to talk to me, our eyes met and something told me we would make love that day. I quickly turned to Phyllis, knowing she must feel excluded from our happiness.

We drove for an hour. The last stretch of the road was precipitous, winding round the side of a mountain. At the top, cars were parked overlooking the view. I had never liked that scene, finding it too spectacular, like a picture postcard. We passed the Hotel Formentor with its formal flowerbeds and uniformed porters, and we reached the steep road up to the villa, still littered with craters and boulders. We preferred to keep it that way to deter encroaching tourists.

As we pulled up at the small iron gate of our villa, it was immediately opened by our smiling cook, Madalena. Greetings and news of the children were exchanged in Spanish and we moved through the stone archway to the large cool terrace where lunch was already laid out on the wooden table. The sunlight made beautiful patterns through the slatted green canopy. I had thought we'd eat straight away, but Julian was already halfway down the steep uneven steps which led through the oleander, bougainvillea and plumbago blooms. Phyllis said she'd rather wait, but I grabbed a bikini from my luggage and Julian's swimming trunks and I followed on down. Sitting on the flat jetty, I dangled my feet in the water. "Icy," I said, but Julian had already dived in and started swimming towards the tiny island about a quarter of a mile away. We usually swam there and back in one go.

At a half-way point, a rock stuck out of the water. Julian was sitting on it, and as I was about to pass by, he called out, "Don't be in such a rush. Stop and give me a kiss." I sat on the rock for a moment and felt a deep contentment. This villa, our creation, had been the scene of many a family drama, witness to the different phases of our marriage, the disappointments in Julian's careers, our occasional infidelities and following jealousies. But today, the calm, clear water reflected my mood of transparent happiness. I swam on to the island, rested a moment and then swam back to the jetty. Julian had put on his trunks and was lying face downwards to soak in the sun. Lying beside him for a moment I realized by a gentle snore that he had gone to sleep.

"Darling, wake up. Let's have lunch."

Silence. I prodded him. No movement. A wild panic possessed me as I looked at his immobile body. I used all my strength to turn him over. I put my ear to his heart. He seemed to be breathing. I tore up the steps, calling for Phyllis to telephone for a doctor, who I knew would take ages to come. My bikini top was dangling round my neck. How stupid I must look! How ridiculous to think of something like that now.

I grabbed the heart pills which the specialist had prescribed in case of an emergency. Then I found some water and rushed back down the steps, followed by the gardener and Madalena. As I tried to get him to swallow the pills, I felt helpless and futile. I tried the kiss of life, which I'd never been taught. I tried massaging his heart and felt he was just breathing. All the time, the sun was beating mercilessly on the rocks. The time it took the doctor to arrive from the village was the worst time in my life but, after what seemed like an eternity, he was there.

"I think he's still alive," the doctor said. "Look for a large, flat stone while I massage his heart."

"A large flat stone? What on earth for?"

"To put under his head."

The only stones I could see were small and round. When I found a flat one, I took it to the doctor.

Madalena was weeping.

"I'm afraid he's dead," said the doctor.

"No," I said. "We must get him to a hospital. There must be something to be done."

He took my arm, leading me up the steps.

"There's nothing anyone can do. It was a massive coronary. I will make all the arrangements."

I stood on the terrace and, as if in a trance, watched as the inert body of my husband was carried up the steep steps in a canvas chair and put to lie on our bed. Suddenly, a woman from a neighbouring villa was holding my hand and saying words of comfort. We hardly knew each other and certainly we had never been friends. Why was this stranger here now? All I wanted was to be left alone with my husband. My grief was immeasurable – I wanted to be dead too … but there were the children.

As the twin-engined executive jet flew through the night sky the following day, I sat on the front seat on the right. Opposite me was Julian's secretary, notebook on her lap, taking shorthand from Monty, now acting Chairman of the Corporation. His wife Miriam was sitting next to him. I looked at the stars which seemed more beautiful than I had ever seen them before. The pain accumulated. Twenty-four hours ago in sunlight, Julian had been where the secretary was now sitting. I had looked across at him at one moment when he was sharing a joke with Monty. I had thought how well he looked – still brown from the previous weekend in

Venice. Tears were now running uncontrollably down my face, and I made no attempt to wipe them away.

Miriam said to Monty, "Must you go into all that now? You're upsetting her." But I hardly heard her and allowed tears to fall relentlessly down my face, until I realised the plane was beginning to reach the runway and make a landing. I had to be strong for the children – they were all being brought by the chauffeur, Ron, to the small private airfield to avoid the press and publicity.

As I stepped onto the runway, Peter and Kerena and Pandora ran towards me, and I enveloped them in the cloak I was wearing. We stood clinging to each other without speaking for several minutes.

"Let's go home," I said.

Peter sat in the front with Ron and, turning round, said, "I tried to telephone Gwen to tell her the news but unfortunately the press had reached her first."

Obviously she would have been deeply upset at the death of her second son. Half of me was trying to comfort my daughters, but the other half was a jagged void, still not accepting, refusing to accept – it must be a nightmare from which I would wake. But the nightmare went on. There would be no waking.

Back at the house our 'daily' opened the door. For once she was speechless – the tiny, gallant woman who had worked for me, shared my disappointments and triumphs, who revelled in minor disasters and turned them into jokes. She was subdued and almost distant.

"Here's a letter from the Palace," she said.

Opening it in disbelief and reading the brief words of

condolence, I thought – how efficient to be so quick – and then – how thoughtful.

"I'll get you a nice cup of tea, dear," the daily said.

But we had things to be talked over and arrangements had to be made. I had to get Julian's body back to England and I made Peter promise to fly out to Majorca to accompany the coffin. He thought that it was unnecessary and that I was being unreasonable. I became hysterical.

"You can't let him come back all alone. If you won't do it, I'll go myself."

But he knew, and I knew, that I wouldn't be able to face it.

"Of course I'll go," he said.

He would have to shoulder many responsibilities in the coming months and years – this, his first duty.

The next few days and nights were blurred. I took pills to steal a few hours of oblivion. I refused food, but people said, "You must make yourself eat. You must think of the children."

Cups of tea and hot milk drinks were given after road accidents to ease the ends of the nerves. In my dazed state, I felt mutilated, as if only a part of me was left. A philosopher had once said the world only existed in the eyes of God and that matter had no real existence. I had existed because one man had believed in me. Now I had no existence. Friends wrote and telephoned and sent me books – books by doctors and philosophers … come to terms with your grief … give in to it … Americans had invented the best expression, 'Let it all hang out'. But this I found impossible – perhaps it was my upbringing. When Bunty and I had had minor illnesses in our youth, we were told to suffer in silence and not complain. But our *ayah* had listened to our moans and groans and given us betel-nutty kisses.

My great friend, Anne Millard, now a divorcee, had suffered a nervous breakdown, but she was a friend who would understand. She had known us both well and had even had a brief affair with Julian. Yet to me, this wasn't an act of betrayal.

"I feel I'm acting a part," I told Anne. "I was never made for tragedy. I don't know how to behave. I even resent Julian for being dead. I can't forgive him for deserting me, for turning me into an object of pity, a widow." How I already hated this word which always seemed to conjure up sad, silver-haired old ladies. "I feel I'm playing a role for which I'm totally unrehearsed." My previous roles had all been positive, full of optimism, excitement and challenge. Disappointment and minor tragedies, yes, but always to be shared.

"I do understand," Anne said, "but you're stronger than you realise. Somehow you will slowly learn to weave him into the fabric of your life. But now I know how you must feel. Unhappiness is like being in love, it isolates. Grief never contaminates, though you may feel like a leper."

Anne's words of wisdom helped, but sadly she herself was to die a year later. She never really recovered from her breakdown and sank lower and lower into a pit of depression. In the end she committed suicide by pills and drink. She was found on the floor with a mass of photographs of herself, as a great beauty, all torn or cut into fragments. What a loss of such an intelligent and special woman. I would miss her dreadfully.

In the meantime, Peter helped me with all the practical details surrounding Julian's death. The funeral was in a private mausoleum in East Finchley. Since he had served in the Fleet Air Arm, the coffin was covered with a Royal Navy ensign. It was surrounded by a handful of relations, most of whom had never been particularly fond of either of us. After a short service, we left the dark, damp mausoleum and stepped outside into brilliant sunshine. Through my tears, I looked at the late daffodils all around us and felt, with the heightened sensibility and awareness that grieving brings, that the world had never shone with such brilliance or hurt more intensely.

William de Gelsey suggested I borrow his house in the South of France for a fortnight. This practical gesture of help was a lifeline, and my friend Nuala Allason said she would go with me. But before we left, there were a million things to do. The first was to give away Julian's clothes. I couldn't bear to see them hanging neatly in our bedroom. I gave everything away, his watch, his cufflinks, his hairbrushes. I was amazed how little there was. He had always been ruthless at keeping his personal possessions to a minimum.

"Don't you want to keep anything?" people asked in shocked voices.

On the table by my bed, I kept the red leather marker showing the page of the book he had been reading before we left London. I kept all his photographs and letters, and the albums. I had spent many a contented hour pasting in happy holiday reminders of children and friends, also some press-cuttings – a potted history of our life together. The last album was only just begun and the final pages would remain blank forever.

There was the Will and the bequests to be dealt with. Everything was in immaculate order. He had left me well provided for, with a short impersonal letter to me in his own hand, warning me to keep away from expensive solicitors. Once in Norfolk, walking round the farm, he had tried to explain about his Will. I had refused to discuss it, thinking it morbid. Now I was relieved that everything was so clear and straightforward.

I had to go to the Norfolk farm to see the people who had worked for him and give them their gifts. Give, give – it was easy – what need had I for possessions when my whole reason for living had suddenly gone? All the things we had given each other to demonstrate our love now seemed superfluous. We possess through our possessions. In divorce, where there is bitterness, possessions are used as weapons to hurt and dispossess. The giving was easy. More difficult was having to stay in the house we had converted fifteen years ago.

That evening, as it was beginning to grow dark, I walked in the garden through the gap in the wall and down towards the sea. If only I could just go on walking for ever and ever. I lay on the damp grass and remembered another evening. I had been at the farm with the children during their school holidays. Julian had flown in late one Friday, looking exhausted after a week of some unsuccessful business negotiations. I had led him into the garden to show him something of which I was proud. It was a climbing 'Rose Philippe', a tiny white rose I'd planted to grow up an old apple tree. I'd got the idea after a visit to the white and blue gardens of Sissinghurst.

"Look, it's worked," I said. The tiny clusters of roses were showering over the top of the old tree like an enormous umbrella.

"And you said you'd never make a gardener," he replied. "It's beautiful."

I knew he was really looking at the crops beyond the garden, through the gap in the wall to the edge of a barley field. Suddenly the clouds cleared and a full moon bathed the farm in light and the dew glistened on the damp grass. We didn't speak, but the magic seemed all around us. For years we had worked building our lives ... children, professions, friendships, houses. That night, perhaps because of the magic, we both felt a sense of fulfilment and awe.

I suddenly realised I'd been lying on the damp grass for ages. My dress was soaked through. I walked slowly back to the house and the small guest bedroom where I'd chosen to sleep. I passed our two portraits painted by Edward Seago. We had been very young, and our eyes looking out from the canvas were cold and impersonal.

'Who are these people? Nothing to do with me.'

Then a fierce feeling of hatred invaded me, hatred for the house, for that garden, for a God whose cruelty could be so random, but most of all, hatred for myself. The bitterness mounted. Suddenly I saw clearly what I must do. Of course, it was logical. I went to the kitchen and took the sharpest knife I could find. I carefully took the portraits down from the wall. First I slashed my face, the cold eyes, the young, smiling mouth. Cut – cut – cut – the canvas was difficult to destroy, but I was feeling strong. Then I turned to the portrait of Julian. Yes, he must go, too. One could not live without the other. Something stopped me cutting his face, but I slashed all around it, until the portrait was unrecognisable.

Back in bed, I felt almost peaceful. 'They will say – "She went mad. She did it in a moment of madness." But it wasn't madness. It was just something I had to do.'

In London, the outside world continued as before. Stepping off the train at Liverpool Street Station, I could see that life was going on as usual, but I could no longer see it in the same way. Everything seemed to have changed and taken on a new significance. Travelling through the City, I was transfixed by the beauty of St Paul's, Wren's great dome in its crowded isolation. Driving along the Embankment, the opal river glistened under the clouds. The world had never seem so defined and yet so distant. I appeared to have stepped outside life and didn't know how to step back. My being seemed to be on the wrong side of the looking-glass.

The letters continued to pour in. Most were spontaneous, generous and emotional. They said he had been much too young to die. All his virtues were listed: his courage, his vision, his sense of humour. The letters all helped, but the ones which helped me most also spoke of how much I had supported him, of my virtues and of the future, and how I must have the courage to continue. The obituaries in the national newspapers were fulsome in their praise. I put them all carefully away in the top of my cupboard.

I had sent Pandora back to boarding school. It seemed harsh, but the best solution. Later she would go to St Paul's Day School, so that at least we could be of some comfort to each other. Kerena was planning a trip round Southeast Asia with Richard, her boyfriend. Peter was staying at his flat in Eccleston Square and would 'hold the fort' while I was away.

There was to be a memorial service in Westminster Abbey, and a lot of planning was involved. We all went to the Chapter Office to meet the Dean and the Chaplain, also to discuss the protocol and the details of the service. We sat round a large refectory table with pads of paper and pencils, as neatly arranged as for a board meeting. The clergymen were solicitous throughout. 'This must be commonplace to them,' I thought, 'just a routine.' There were to be Government representatives and many important business associates from overseas. Seats had to be allocated. I felt I wouldn't be able to face it, but I owed it to Julian to observe the conventions of my faith and to fulfil this final obligation.

"And the music and hymns? Have you any preference or will you leave it to us?"

I realised I was being asked a question.

"We'll let you know," Peter said, "when we've given it some thought."

Going home in a taxi, we suggested hymns to each other and snatches of our favourite music. Kerena sang in her beautiful voice the opening bars of the hymn of Blake's poem, "And did those feet in ancient time ..."

The taxi driver turned his head. "That's one of my favourites," he said. "Been to a wedding, have you?"

Before the service took place, my friend Nuala and I hired a car and drove from Nice airport along the coast to the outskirts of Villefranche. I took all the letters of condolence with me, and every morning was spent in replying to them. Sometimes I was overcome by the raw shock, as if I'd undergone a mammoth amputation. At such moments, I thought of suicide. It would be so easy. But I knew that to give up on life would be total cowardice, inflicting a further terrible wound on the children and my own elderly mother.

It didn't seem possible that the days could move on so relentlessly. In the afternoons we would walk down to the little public beach below the villa. One hot day, with the sun blazing on the pebbles, I took my first faltering steps into the sea. I wanted to swim far out, but there were white buoys, bobbing on the water and protecting swimmers from speedboats. Back on the beach, I lay on my towel, hardly aware of the pebbles pressing into my skin. A French couple were helping their children build a sandcastle by the water's edge.

This was a beach scene I had taken part in and witnessed a hundred times, but now I saw it with exaggerated clarity, as if for the first time. The serious expression on the boy's face as he patted the sand into the bucket and tipped it carefully onto the castle. The little girl, emptying buckets of water into the moat. The father was enjoying himself, but the young mother was bored and went back to her magazine. The scene was of such ordinary contentment that I wanted to scream out, "Don't take it all for granted. Don't you realise you're a complete family? It may never be like this again."

Sometimes in the evenings we drove up to the attractive hill towns to dine in bistros under pergolas, covered with wisteria. Everywhere I looked, I was aware of couples, flirting young couples more engrossed in each other than their food; elderly married couples, comfortably silent, eating and drinking with total concentration; gay men and women in earnest fond conversation. "They probably think we're together," Nuala said.

We talked of the future. I would have to find work, but I had so few qualifications. I remembered once writing in my diary, "Since everything man needs has to be discovered by his own mind and produced by his own efforts, the two essentials of the method of survival proper for a rational being are thinking and productive work."

Yes, I'd have to try and get a job, but for now, I could only just limp through each day with its anxieties bordering on panic. The nights were the worst. The doctor had prescribed pills but, after two or three hours of drugged sleep, the nightmares started. I never dreamt of Julian, yet the themes were recurrent ones of physical struggle against impossible odds, and sometimes I would wake sweating with fear. The day always began as if there was a thick wall of fog which I somehow had to break through.

Drink numbed the pain, when it became unbearable. This I knew was considered cowardly and was merely postponing the day when life had to be faced in all its rawness. But why was it so terrible? You put sticking plaster over a wound to stop it bleeding, a temporary dressing until the skin heals itself. Was it so wrong to use any available means to swab the internal bleeding of a creature in torment?

Back in London there were the final arrangements to be made before the memorial service. A bus to bring people from Norfolk. Seats to be allocated to VIPs in correct pecking order. Pandora to be brought up from school. And when the day arrived, I realised I had nothing in black suitable to wear.

I found a dark brown suit, once a perfect fit, which now hung loosely over my thin body, and I wound a scarf round my head. What did it matter? What did anything matter except getting through the ceremony with some dignity? The conventions of life seemed without any significance.

My mother and Gwen joined me as we took our seats in the front row of the West Transept of the Abbey. The organist was playing music by Bach and Handel. I was aware of a host of familiar and unfamiliar faces, their blank expressions controlling any emotions in the true British tradition.

As the choir broke into 'I will lift up my eyes unto the hill from whence cometh my help', Kerena started to cry.

"Not here, you mustn't," whispered Pandora. "Later you can."

The Dean ended the service with:

No man is an island, entire of itself
Every man is a piece of the continent, a part of the main …
The death of one diminishes all,
For all are bound together in the bundle of life.

Peter took my arm and gently steered me through the Abbey. I was clear-eyed and held my head high. Outside, people surrounded me, took my hands and kissed me. Many had tears in their eyes. He had been much loved.

Nine

Although it seemed the best idea to send Pandora back to Cobham, she told me years later that she had been miserable and would much have preferred for us to have stayed together. But the following term, she was accepted as a pupil at St Paul's Girls' School, which had a high academic reputation.

As the months passed, we tried to settle into our new roles. My daughter had usually been so extrovert and ebullient, but now she had become withdrawn and difficult, retreating into her own shell of grief. She would take the bus to her new school every morning and I would collect her by car in the afternoon. Waiting for the school gates to open, the other parents would be standing around chatting happily to each other. Some I knew slightly, but, not feeling like facing anyone, I remained in the car pretending to read a book. I couldn't bear the flicker of embarrassed awareness in their eyes – the moment when they couldn't decide whether or not to offer condolences. Why is it that the bereaved are treated as outcasts? As the girls started to push through the gates in laughing groups in school coats with a jumble of tennis rackets, violin cases and satchels, I always hoped that Pandora would be among the main throng. But she never was. She would come out later, alone and white-faced, and walk straight towards the car.

"It's no good, I can't stand it," she said. "The work's too difficult and none of the girls like me."

"Nonsense, of course they like you. It's your imagination, darling." My false, cheerful voice prattled on with advice and optimistic predictions, but Pandora looked unbelieving and hid in a silent privacy of resistance.

At half-term we were asked to stay in Scotland with Hugh and Antonia Fraser and their family. It was a kind gesture and I accepted with gratitude. We flew to Inverness and were met by a cheerful man with a rugged face, wearing a kilt in the tartan of his laird's clan. We drove along narrow, winding roads, past the castle where Hugh's nephew and his wife Virginia lived, and over a small stone bridge to the dower house, called Eilean Aigas, on an island in the River Beauly – a grey stone shooting lodge surrounded by water, the colour of peat.

Antonia and Hugh gave us a warm welcome. There were two other guests, philosophers from Cambridge. At the first dinner in the shabby, grand dining room with the children at the far end of the table, the talk veered from political and university gossip to a discourse from one of the dons on his interpretation of structuralism. The more I tried to contribute to the conversation, the more banal my words seemed. Without Julian's presence to give me support and self-confidence, I felt inadequate.

After dinner, Verdi's Requiem was played on the gramophone. It was one of my favourite pieces, and I sank back into the faded chintz chair to enjoy the First Movement with its melodies so full of restraint and piety and yet strangely sensual. But towards the end of the Kyrie, when the choral music reached its joyful climax, I suddenly felt tears coursing uncontrollably down my face. I rushed from the room along endless corridors to the guest bedroom. Later Hugh appeared with words of sympathy and a cup of hot milk.

"Have this. I've put a dram into it. Do you nothing but good." He stood by my bed, tall and splendid in his velvet jacket and tartan trousers. "Did you know," he said, "that one of the dons is doing a thesis on the effect of music on the emotions – how certain themes can trigger certain feelings. Of course, we didn't foresee the effect on you when we played Verdi's Requiem, but you certainly proved his point and he's full of remorse."

I found I was smiling. "As automatic as a Pavlov dog," I said. "Tell him not to worry. I'm glad I've been of some use."

The next day, the philosophers swam in the outdoor heated pool, which Antonia told me she had built from the proceeds of her book on Mary Queen of Scots. It was surrounded by a high stone wall crowned with climbing roses. On the flight returning home, Pandora and I swapped stories about the visit, which had broken the routine of our London existence and helped plan our thoughts for the future.

Peter was fighting his own battles. In a long letter he sent me later, he wrote: "I will do everything I can to make your life easier in the next few months and years. I hope that you will help me assert myself to make decisions and play the role that I must in the future. The way life goes, small things are bound to upset people, and we are bound to upset each other, me more than you, I'm sure. I hope and pray this won't ever come between us. Things never have in the past and I feel I need your support more now than I ever have."

Peter was asked when he would be taking his seat in the House of Lords. This he was very reluctant to do, believing that a future Labour Party should abolish the hereditary system. But he was persuaded by me and our close family friend, the peer Eddy Shackleton, that the best way to fight for his beliefs was within the establishment. Yet he made no concessions. He stuck to his lifestyle and would ride to the Lords on his bike, leaving it in the peers' car park and putting on a tie as he passed the top-hatted attendants. He soon became completely at ease with the formalities in the Upper House and began to make a reputation as a formidable speaker and committed Socialist. Whenever I sat in the Peeresses' Gallery, listening to him and watching the tall, authoritative figure of a man, I could hardly believe this was the same delicate child I had worried over in the control tower in Norfolk.

He left the Institute of Psychiatry only when Prime Minister Harold Wilson asked him to join his government. Later Wilson told me of his reluctance. Until then, he himself had held the record of being the youngest minister in the government.

In the meantime, the relationship between me and Pandora didn't improve. On returning from school, she would go to her bedroom and play her stereo at a deafening volume. The room began to look like a corner of a refugee camp.

Cigarettes were squashed into half-empty coffee mugs and the waste paper basket brimmed over with laddered tights. One day I could stand it no longer and, stepping through the pile of dirty clothes on the floor, I tried to create a little cleanliness and order. While sorting out the clothes to be washed, I picked up a plastic bag with a small amount of dark-brown grains at the bottom. Thinking the worst and sick with worry, I telephoned Peter. He suggested we meet for lunch the next day at the Lords. When I told him I was terrified his sister was on drugs, he asked to see the offending article. "Surely not here," I said looking nervously at a purple-robed cleric sitting at the next table. "Why not? No one would suspect us to be examining an illegal substance under the eyes of a bishop." I produced the evidence from my bag and Peter bent down, pretending to do up his shoelace, and smelt it. His eyes were twinkling as he looked up. "Coffee," he said. "She probably doesn't like the Nescafé at school. Serves you right for being so suspicious."

Kerena was in love with Richard, the son of the writer Alan Moorehead. He was already travelling across South Asia by public transport. She joined him later in Western Australia. There she took various jobs to fund the trip. She and Richard traversed the outback, and after visiting Bali, Java, Sumatra, Thailand and Laos, they flew from Bangkok to Calcutta. Crossing India by buses and trains, she told me afterwards that it was the most fascinating experience, given all the different cultures, architecture and peoples. Living rough and mostly on rice and vegetables, they absorbed the true India, which I had never seen, even in my childhood memories.

When I met her at Victoria Station a year and a half later, I could hardly recognise her. She must have lost at least three stone in weight. After staying for a while with Richard's parents in their house in Porto Ercole in Italy, she and Richard took a cottage outside Norwich, where they began their Degrees in Development Studies at the University of East Anglia. She had become more and more involved with the problems of the oppressed peoples of the Third World, ground down and exploited by the great multinational companies of the West. A new generation was emerging from the universities, citizens of the world, passionately anti-nuclear, taking for granted as their heritage the benefits of the welfare state, for which their parents had fought.

The drug culture flourished, creating further rifts between the generations. We happily sipped our gin-and-tonics while being lectured on the virtues of pot. I was fortunate that my children had not drifted into the hard drug scene. I had seen the children of some of my friends destroying themselves on the slippery slopes of addiction.

In trying to pick up the pieces of my life, I started accepting invitations to drinks, dinners and even to a dance. In my eagerness to fight the fear of being alone, I tried to convince myself that it was essential to behave as normally as possible. I was trying to breathe rather than drown. When I went out, I always left a light on, and on returning, I saw it shining behind the curtains. Inside once more, solitude burst on me like a gust of wind, and there was only silence and darkness. It had always seemed to me that the dividing line between the sane and the insane was so fine as sometimes to appear indistinct. I was afraid of falling into the snake pit.

I was hurt by the insensitivity of couples overtly demonstrating their love for each other, the intimate glances exchanged, a kind of collusion above the heads of the crowd – the shared look that put the world back in focus in spite of the raucous voices, the cigarette smoke and the whisky fumes. Whenever I felt the happiness of others, I felt my fall from joy most painfully. I would make my escape from a dinner long before the conventional time for polite departure, refusing offers of lifts.

One night in late summer, I went to a dance in an extravagantly decorated marquee in the middle of Holland Park. I was dancing with a politician who was trying to be amusing while treading on my toes. Julian had been a good dancer; we had danced as one and even enjoyed showing off a little, aware of the admiration of others. Looking round at the sea of animated couples, I suddenly panicked, feeling as if I were stranded on an island. I had to escape, and making some inadequate excuse, I rushed for the exit. Leaving the lights and music behind me, I ran stumbling through the park, losing my bearings in the dark. Falling and picking myself up, the giant trees seemed to be surrounding me like demons. Shall I never find my way? Making for the sound of distant traffic, with my torn dress and soaking feet, I eventually found myself on a pavement, coatless and with no handbag.

"Do you need a cab?" A taxi driver was pulling down his window. I sank wearily into the darkness and only came to my senses when Pandora opened the front door. Looking horrified, she managed to find some money to pay the driver.

The politician I had been dancing with telephoned the next day. "What happened, are you all right? Everyone was worried about you." He came to see me, offering comfort and advice. "You should have a purpose in life – a job that really interests you. What sort of work do you feel you most want to do? Perhaps I could help in some way."

"I'd like to do some interviewing." The words came out without me realising I'd been thinking along those lines. I'd written various articles for the *Evening Standard* while the Editor, Charles Wintour, had even said he would give me a Press Card.

"Interviewing. What sort of people?" Before I could answer, he went on, "I've got an idea. Why don't you travel round the Middle East, Abu Dhabi, Kuwait? The role of women is changing rapidly in that part of the world. It could be interesting. When I was Under-Secretary at the Foreign Office, I spent some time travelling around there. I could give you some introductions."

For the first time in weeks, I felt a flicker of enthusiasm. "But would they accept a woman interviewer, a second-class citizen?"

"Well, it's a challenge, isn't it?" he replied. "In any case, let's throw some balls in the air. I'm a great believer in plurality. Put out lots of tosses and then if some come to nothing, you've always got the others floating. You'll be a great hit, I promise. They like blondes."

These compliments and the assurance of my ability to succeed gave me a disproportionate comfort. I realised that my grief had brought with it a total lack of self-confidence. In my marriage hardly a day had gone by without Julian praising me in some way – my looks, a new way of doing my hair, a special meal I'd prepared. I'd taken it all for granted, but it had become as necessary to me as breathing; it was yet another prop which had been removed. I'd been special in his eyes – therefore I was special. Now, what appeared to be a possible lifeline was being offered, and I began to feel almost excited.

I talked over the Middle East plan with Pandora.

"Yes, you should go," she said. "It'll do you good to do some work. But you won't go straight away, will you? It won't stop us going to Turkey?" This was a plan we'd had for some time.

"No, of course not. I'll probably go in the New Year."

In the meantime an intriguing trip was suggested by George Weidenfeld, who was being extremely supportive. He suggested I travel to Vienna for a few days to witness for myself what the Prime Minister of Austria, Kreisky, was doing to help a number of Jews move from Russia to their homeland. Apparently he had brokered a deal with the Russian Government to allow many Jewish families to travel to Israel, and he wanted the world to know of this goodwill mission. I would be accompanied by Raymond Carr and Susan Crosland and stay in a luxury hotel in central Vienna. We would be looked after by the Viennese Tourist Board.

I jumped at the idea, and when the day came, the three of us flew to Vienna in great anticipation. Our selected hotel was truly luxurious. My four-poster bedroom was adjoined to a high-ceilinged anteroom with an enormous hanging chandelier. The first night, we were wined and dined at a local restaurant, serenaded by musicians. We were told by our hosts to be ready at 5 AM the following morning. The unreality of the situation was beginning to dawn on me, and I couldn't quite believe I wasn't taking part in a Graham Greene spy film.

The facts were all too true. We were driven the next day to the local railway station and told that the train from Russia was due to arrive in one hour. When it steamed up on time, we could hardly believe our eyes. Hundreds of Jews emerged from the train carrying their meagre possessions tied up in bundles. But the most amazing sight of all was that every man had a car tyre hanging round his neck. They had been informed that tyres were the most wealth-creating commodity they could take into Israel.

How true this was, I would never know. But I do know that the goodwill mission was successful and enabled many a family to start a new life for themselves in their beloved homeland. I think we all returned to England having experienced an extraordinary mission of compassion. And certainly I was grateful to George for having made it possible for me and my companions to have witnessed this piece of history.

My closest male friend, Mike Richey, whom I'd known since moving into Wilton Row, was now in his early fifties and running the Royal Institute of Navigation in South Kensington, a part of the Royal Geographical Society. He was deeply religious, and at Downside he had considered becoming a priest. He had been a novice for a year before leaving to join the Navy during the war, serving in minesweepers and later in convoys. An expert navigator, every four years he had taken part in the single-handed Transatlantic race from Plymouth to Newport, Rhode Island, in a tiny junk-rigged boat called *Jester*. My relationship with him had always been one of mutual trust and affection, but now I began to feel a deeper emotional dependence.

Mike and I decided to charter a caique, by chance called the *Pandora*. We were to sail in summer for two weeks from Athens across to the western Turkish coast, ending at Rhodes. My sister Bunty and her three youngest children joined us, while Pandora brought her friend Sarah-Jane Prior, the daughter of a Conservative minister; Peter and his girlfriend Cassandra Wedd completed the party.

Arriving at the Piraeus in Athens, we easily found the *Pandora* with her wide pine bulwarks and twin masts towering above the sleek yachts and a shiny floating hotel. The captain, a small, dark-skinned man who looked like a quizzical bird, greeted us and introduced the crew. He came from Samos and spoke no English, but after a few days we developed a degree of communication. A see-saw motion of his hands denoted strong disapproval of anything ranging from Turkish officialdom to chic Patmos homosexuals. Approval was a philosophical shrug of the shoulders, while an occasional wave and cry of 'bezouki' meant he was feeling gregarious. The crew consisted of a Greek cook, aged eighty-two, who always wore a grubby chef's hat at a rakish angle and spoke English with a strong Chicago accent. There was also the Captain's nephew, a good-looking young man with trendy sideburns who seemed to do everything from hoisting the sails and taking the helm to comprehending the vagaries of the outboard motor on the dinghy.

We all sorted ourselves out in the cramped spaces waiting for us. Bunty and I shared a cabin, the grown-ups were in the salon while the children all slept on deck. As we sailed towards Turkey, we stopped briefly at Delos, Patmos and Samos. Life on board left little time for thought. There were endless practical details to be got through, and the new experiences blunted my pain. We reached Delos, the birthplace of Apollo, in the evening, after the last tourist had left. We wandered round the House of the Dolphins, touched the huge marble lions and walked through the wild mint and rosemary, growing in profusion amongst the ruins. Later, foot-weary but full of wonder, we swam back to the boat. Her masts were silver splints on the full moon.

I began to feel the timeless quality of life on board. There were moments when past, present and future were the same. The sea fused every voyage I had ever had. I longed for this nomadic life to continue forever.

At Patmos, we climbed for two hours up the narrow winding streets to the eleventh-century monastery, stopping halfway at the grotto where St John the Divine was said to have written the *Apocalypse*. Bunty and I weren't allowed to enter the monastery as our skirts were considered too short by the holy fathers, but the girls with their clinging jeans, decorated with symbols of sex and politics such as "Cure Virginity" and "Babies Against the Bomb" were allowed to see the treasures. Mike would have spent many happy hours poring over the *Codex Porphyrianus* and the thirty-three leaves of St Mark's Gospel written in the fifth century on purple vellum, but the captain was anxious to set sail for his home island of Samos, only a mile from Turkey.

Famous as the birthplace of Pythagoras and for its good dry wine, the captain insisted on playing host at the local nightspot. All the inhabitants seemed to be related to him, and ouzo and Samos sec flowed. We visited the Temple of Hero and saw a tiny chapel where the unconsecrated wine was stored in ketchup bottles.

Our main goal was Ephesus. After many delays, we cleared Turkish Customs with the help of a good deal of whisky and cigarettes passing hands. We drove along the coast, the old course of the Cayster River, down which St Paul had been rowed nineteen centuries before. Arriving at the Basilica of St John, we were besieged by small boys selling 'genuine' newly-made antiques and postcards of phallic symbols. But nothing could mar the grandeur of the ancient city and the tiny House of the Virgin Mary, where we attended a service under the eucalyptus tree with the altar a slab of marble resting on two Corinthian pillars. Walking down the long marble Arcadian avenue and looking back at the vast amphitheatre, I saw an emptiness far greater than my own.

Sailing by day and sometimes at night along the Anatolian coast, we explored many bays and harbours – every bay or headland carried signs of the long-dead past. The children were thrilled when a school of dolphins kept the boat company, leaping sometimes so high into the air that they seemed ready to land on deck.

At our next anchorage, Mike explored the underwater walls and tombs of Kekova, long ago destroyed by an earthquake. Once a great Byzantine Riviera, now two miles of sunken quays, a lost mystery, an Atlantis. That night, sitting under the stars, sipping our raki, we agreed this voyage had heightened all our senses. We'd discovered the secret of adventure, the precariousness, the constant surprises of the Aegean, each hour taken on its own merit, its troubles and hopes wrapped within it, with no entanglements of before and after to complicate such a simplified interval of time. We planned another voyage to wander further eastwards and follow where Alexander the Great had journeyed over two thousand years ago. Perhaps there was a future after all.

On our return to London, I found a mass of letters to be answered and forms to be filled, letters from the solicitors and accountants, forms from the Ministry of Labour and the Inland Revenue. In the past there had been secretaries and a chauffeur-driven car. Now I had to relearn Tube and bus routes. I preferred buses, where I could lose myself in the outside world and listen to the jokes of the conductors and the repartee of the passengers. I found the tube somewhat threatening, a race against time, and always the advertisements on the walls and alongside the escalators showing couples – couples handing each other a drink, lighting each other's cigarettes. Couples, always couples.

I began planning my trip to the Middle East, visiting embassies for information and visas. Someone introduced me to a diplomat who had been posted to Bahrain. He was full of advice and letters of introduction, but he was sceptical about the chances of success in my new role as a journalist. "It takes time to gain their trust," he warned. "They will be charming and polite, but you'll find it difficult to pin them down." Meanwhile I read everything I could on the history and important figures in the Middle East, the Sheiks and their advisers.

When my sister Bunty was living at Dacre, she spent her time painting and working on embroidered tapestries of medieval knights and ladies standing in front of other castles, oblivious of the various farm animals and dogs wandering around. Rather eccentrically, she chose one of her sheep to be the Godfather of her son Sebastian. In 1980, she and Anthony moved to the small village of Ryme Intrinseca in Dorset. He had lost nearly all of his money in Lloyd's insurance syndicates, so they were existing on a pittance.

While Anthony was away, she was sleeping alone on the top floor of the house. One night, she thought she heard the dogs barking. While looking for them, she fell down the steep staircase to her death. We had been so close all our lives and I missed her dreadfully. Yet she had crammed more into her life than most people do who live to an old age. She had become famous for her spectacular New Year's Eve parties and her exotic Ascot hats, which were regularly photographed in the popular press. No one realised she had made them herself. Totally in love with her husband, she had created a fulfilling life for the family, and she remained close to her four children until she died.

Her youngest daughter Sapphia had a spell as a boarder in a convent, and as she was rather unhappy there, I had her to live with me at home. Soon she went to work daily at Story Boards, a small firm creating advertising material. Through my friendship with Lord Oppenheimer, I was able to get the boys, Ivan and Sebastian, jobs in South Africa. The elder daughter Amanda married a successful banker, Gordon Grender, by whom she had a son and a daughter. My nephews and nieces would become part of my dear extended family, as now they had no mother to call their own.

My friends continued to include me in their social activities, and I accepted everything and then, when the time came, regretted my impulsiveness. Before leaving the house, I would insulate myself with a strong drink against the evening ahead. George Weidenfeld, who had published my first book, was particularly generous and also gave fascinating dinner parties with influential guests including politicians, writers and visitors from overseas. One night Harold Wilson was a guest of honour, but dinner was kept inordinately late as Marcia Falkender hadn't arrived. After calls to Downing Street, she eventually appeared, seemingly unconscious that her lateness had caused concern. There was much gossip about the relationship between the Prime Minister and his personal assistant, but in the end, it was discounted. Mary, his wife, was a quiet, charming woman, more interested in poetry than politics.

One decision I couldn't avoid was what to do about Christmas. In the past the family had always spent the holiday at the farm. I'd thrown myself wholeheartedly into the preparations, pretending to complain, but really enjoying the last-minute frenetic activities, decorating the tree, the feeling of relief when the tiny lights worked once again and the tattered fairy on top was discovered among the decorations. As Julian would be working until the last moment, the rest of us would drive down ahead. Julian always did his shopping on Christmas Eve, and then he would fly himself down to join us in the evening. He would beg coloured paper from the children and get them to help him wrap. I still kept the note he stuck to his last gift. It just said: "Darling, I can't wrap parcels, but I love you more than ever." No, it wouldn't be the farm this year I thought. How public celebrations hurt the lonely.

I would have liked to flee the country, but I knew I would have to create some sort of occasion for the sake of my children. In the past I'd got the pre-Christmas organisation down to a fine art. Now every tiny errand and decision seemed to be gigantic. One day, shopping for crackers in Harrods, I thought I was going mad. What did it matter whether I chose the red or the gold, presents for all ages, or indeed fireworks with hats and mottos, or useful trinkets and bad jokes? All around me, people were filling their baskets with confidence. I knew I must decide – the shop assistant was growing impatient, but I was beginning to break into a cold sweat and thought I was going to faint.

"I'll come back tomorrow," I said and I started running through the store. Outside it was raining, and there were long queues for the buses. I must have walked home. I can't remember.

In the end, Nuala came to my rescue with practical help and encouragement. She lived close by in Cheyne Walk and was divorced from her MP husband, James. She listened to my outpourings on the telephone late at night when sleep eluded me, and helped me decide who to have to lunch on Christmas Day, and brought her two sons. I also asked Mike Richey, who had often stayed with Julian and me in Majorca, and the children were all fond of him.

He agreed to come up from his flat in Brighton for Christmas lunch. Kerena and Richard came down from

Norfolk, while Peter brought Cassandra, and I added one or two people who I knew would be alone. Exchanging presents, Pandora wrote, "I love you more than anyone in the world", inside a copy of Ted Hughes's *Selected Poems*. Mike gave me Illich's latest book on alternative education. As we sat round the old refectory table, I felt we had at least created some semblance of an occasion. Peter performed the ritual warming of the spoon over a flame before pouring brandy and setting it alight over the Christmas pudding, just as Julian had done. We crossed arms and pulled crackers, put on paper hats and caught the end of the Queen's Speech. Another hurdle over, I thought. Later Pandora told me that none of them had felt like celebrating, but felt I would be upset if they didn't make an effort. The false faces we wear for the sake of convention, I thought. Adults pretending for the sake of children, and children for the sake of adults.

During my evenings alone, I found I would still be watching the clock at the time Julian would have been returning from work, and waiting for the sound of his key in the lock and remembering how I had quickly looked at the expression on his face for signs of his day's doing. Then the light kiss, the carefully prepared drinks, the flood of exchanges, the tiny rituals of a marriage, the luxury of sharing our day's disasters and, like children, keeping a minor success to the end. But the nights were the worst, when the sheer physical yearning would suddenly attack me, like a treacherous intruder, and my senses became so acutely aware that I felt I could almost smell his presence. At these moments, I felt I could never accept what had happened and was only pretending to endure. But there were other times when I found myself looking forwards as well as backwards, and I clung to these tenuous moments of freedom from the past.

China had for many years been closed to outsiders, but in 1975 small groups were allowed to visit certain cities while carefully supervised by the authorities. Nuala Allason had been particularly supportive since Julian's death. When she suggested she and I joined a Serenissima group of ten other people who had been given Foreign Office permission to visit the ancient country for two weeks, I jumped at the chance. We were told to meet at Heathrow at a certain time and there we stared curiously, looking at each other, wondering what the future held in store. After a few days the travellers took on their own individual characteristics. The only person I vaguely knew was a director of Partridge, the antique furniture shop in Bond Street, but the rest of them were complete strangers.

Arriving at Peking Airport was an amazing experience. The people who greeted us were hospitable and charming. All were dressed in identical grey uniforms, and they ushered us into a large lounge and immediately offered us cups of tea and cakes. Not one's usual airport reception. Driving through Peking in a bus to our hotel, I saw the streets were seething with people, mostly riding bicycles, and dressed in the same grey uniforms. The hotel was not exactly luxurious, but large and clean. We were told to meet at 6.30 the next morning on a visit to the Great Wall, the Ming Tombs and the Imperial Palace. Walking along the Great Wall was an exhausting experience, but I was bemused to see how the Japanese tourists merely took endless camera shots to show on their return, hardly raising their heads to see the wonders around them, even in the Imperial Palace, which I found impressive.

That night we were taken to the Forbidden City and later to a restaurant where they served the original Peking 'Yule' duck – plate after plate of duck in all its many manifestations. Moving from place to place in our original small bus, we all got to know each other well and were fascinated in what we were being shown, except for the one cynic amongst us, who predicted that in the near future all would change for the worst. We were flown to Sian where we saw the Monastery and then taken to an opera. The singers were all dressed in colourful clothes and sang songs blessing the wonders of Chairman Mao. Travelling by overnight train on the Shanghai Express to Juchin was a strange journey. The men and women were divided into different compartments and the only loo consisted of a hole in the corner of the last carriage. We passed endless paddy fields with peasants slaving up to their waists in water. This was not on our tourist agenda. But we were shown 'The Garden of Fisherman's Net' and the Learning Pagoda at Tiger Hill.

In all the villages we went through, men would be sitting outside their tumbledown homes and smoking endless hubble-bubbles. In fact, I never saw any of the Chinese without a cigarette hanging from his or her mouth. Back in Shanghai, I watched from my hotel window in the morning as the people walked to their places of work, doing their callisthenic movements – a rule of Chairman Mao's to keep them fit. After flying to Canton where we did some shopping, we were taken by train to Peking, from where we flew back to England.

Rereading Mao's *Little Red Book* on my return – so popular amongst the Hippies in America – I realised he had already declared his purpose.

> If there is to be a revolution, there must be a revolutionary party ... we must have faith in the masses and we must have faith in the Party ... if we doubt these principles, we shall accomplish nothing.

> We must conduct a rectification movement both now and in the future, and constantly rid ourselves of whatever is wrong.

> Classes struggle, some classes triumph, others are eliminated. Such is history... Everything reactionary is the same; if you don't hit it, it won't fall.

Not at that time being particularly interested in politics, I realised later that Mao would prove to have been one of the greater monsters in history. Carrying out his instructions, the Red Guard and hunger put paid to around 40,000,000 people, one of the world's worst massacres. How the wool can be pulled over one's eyes. Yes, we were told about the 'downward transfer movement', meaning that when men became too clever, they should go back to the land and relearn the basics of agriculture, before climbing back to the intelligentsia. But never would I have guessed at the horrors that were to follow and yet, neither will I regret that unforgettable visit.

On my return, I found that Pandora was enjoying St Paul's more and had begun to appreciate its sophisticated approach to teaching. Run more on the lines of a university, the girls were given the responsibility to succeed or fail with guidance, but not dogmatic instruction. Pandora had made a friend at last. "She's the most interesting girl in my form and really clever. She's a Communist and has a habit of always dressing in grey. I really like her. We'd like to throw a party this term. Could we give it at home?"

"Of course, darling, ask her round and we'll talk about it."

Another grey Communist, I thought – oh dear! But I welcomed the fact that at last Pandora had found a friend. The next week she brought her back to Tite Street and it was obvious that my daughter was very much in awe of her. The girl had a quality of controlled vitality and great assurance, and she was exceedingly beautiful with large, unblinking grey eyes, white skin and straight brown hair. Her clothes were all in different shades of grey.

She looked round my large L-shaped drawing room with its white sofas and yellow curtains. "I suppose it will do," she said to Pandora, "but of course, those will have to go." She pointed at the pictures – the Matthew Smith, the Sutherland, the Frinck lithograph. "And I suppose we could cover the furniture with some Indian bedspreads."

"Do you really think it's necessary to move all the pictures?" I asked tentatively.

"Oh yes, absolutely. I'll need to put up my Communist posters."

Pandora was looking nervous. "Oh, that'll be easy," she said.

"How many people are you having?" I asked, "and how about food and drink?"

"We'll think about that later," she said, "as long as there's plenty of red plonk."

"Couldn't it be white?" I asked. "Red stains so."

"Oh no, it must be red," the beautiful girl said firmly.

Goodness, I thought, she pursues her whims with a will of iron.

As the day of the party approached, I asked how things were going.

"Well, we've asked about twenty girls from school, but we don't know many boys."

"It's not going to be much fun without any boys." So I suggested I asked a friend's son, who was in his last year at Eton to come and bring a gang along.

"I'll suggest it," said Pandora, "but I don't think she'll agree. She doesn't believe in public schools." I didn't point out she was at one.

In the end I took matters into my own hands and insisted, "Just pretend they're from the local comprehensive."

The Etonians came to the house on the morning of the party to arrange the music, carry all the pictures upstairs and move furniture. About half an hour before the party was due to start, the beautiful Communist arrived, looking serene in an ankle-length grey silk dress. She put up enormous posters of Fidel Castro, Che Guevara, Lenin and Karl Marx, and flung some old Indian cotton bedspreads over the furniture.

"That's much better now," she announced. "And if we don't put the lights on but have a few candles it will be quite passable. Where's the red wine?"

"I'm afraid I've only got white," I said. A slight flicker of annoyance crossed the beautiful pale face. "Oh well, that'll have to do."

I had asked Mike Richey to come and stay the night for support. He had always been particularly good with the young, but even he found it difficult to break through the generation barrier the girls had erected. In the end, we shut ourselves in my bedroom with some food and drinks.

As the teenagers started to congregate and more gatecrashers arrived, the music was turned up louder and louder, and the screams and moans of the pop singers reverberated through the house. I lay back on my bed, sipping white wine while Mike was sprawled on the chaise-longue and had switched to whisky. As I listened to him, I thought how attractive he was and wondered again why he had never married. Sometimes he showed signs of some deep inner conflict, as if he was waging a private war within himself. At these moments, a muscle in his arm would twitch uncontrollably, and his eyes would express some deep hurt, which he would never allow himself to communicate. He was telling me of a book he had just read – Huizinga's *Homo Ludens*. "He tried to define the role of play in all religious rituals, just as there is an element of ritual in all sport – both being equally important to the human spirit, both essential to living – and defining us as homo sapiens rather than an ordinary mammal."

As I half-listened to him and looked into those troubled, intelligent eyes and at his square, capable hands, I thought of the many months he had spent alone in his tiny sailing boat, pitting his body and mind against the elements, tossed by great waves, bothered by storms. In his faded corduroy suit, heavy-ribbed sweater and square leather shoes, I was acutely aware of his masculinity. I believed myself capable of loving this man. The level in the bottle of whisky was going down and his voice was beginning to slur.

"And now with so much unemployment and early retirement people will have to be taught how to make the maximum use of their leisure. I read the *Anti Mémoire* of Malraux on the last Atlantic crossing. It became a microcosm of the whole world I'd known. How was this enormously sophisticated intellectual, also the man of action who'd fought in the Spanish Civil War and become a great Resistance hero? I found this mixture of commitment and culture so intensely engaging –"

The telephone rang. I looked at my watch – it was three in the morning. An irate neighbour was threatening to call the police. I went into the living-room and turned down the music. The room was in total darkness except for the light of a single candle. All around me was the sickly smell of pot. I became aware of bodies everywhere, some clutching each other on sofas, some under tables, some swaying to the sound of the music and others with joints in their hands, gazing into space. No one took any notice of me. Looking for Pandora, I eventually found her among the heap of bodies on the sofa.

"The neighbours are complaining. You can't make so much noise or they're going to call the police."

Pandora disengaged herself and followed me into the bedroom. Her face was flushed and the pupils of her eyes were dilated. There was a red mark on her neck.

"What's that?" I asked.

"Oh, for goodness sake, it's only a love-bite. And please don't spoil the party – we can't dance when the music is as quiet as that."

But I was firm. "You've got to, or I'll have to throw everyone out."

At last, things quietened. Mike had finished the whisky, and was obviously ready for bed.

"You'd better sleep in the spare room," I said and led him upstairs. At the door, he gave me a clumsy embrace.

"Sorry I got a bit sloshed. Not much help, I'm afraid."

"You're always a great help," I said. "Sleep well."

The next day Pandora slept until noon. She had dark circles under her eyes and was wearing a high-necked sweater to hide the mark on her neck.

"The party was a terrific success," she said. "Everyone said so."

"I'm glad. How did your friend enjoy the Etonians?"

Pandora giggled.

"Well, really it was quite funny – she never discovered. She got off with some attractive Indian guy and they've made a date. He didn't tell her he was a Maharajah's son and in Pop."

We both laughed. And I decided not to spoil the moment and talk of drugs. I'd think about that tomorrow. Like Scarlett O'Hara, I'd always been hopeless about facing unpleasant things and sometimes saw life as a permanent unanswered in-tray, but I consoled myself that sometimes problems, if left long enough, went away of their own accord.

A few days later, Mike telephoned to ask if I'd like to spend the following weekend at his flat in Brighton. "There's nothing I'd rather do," I said and meant it. I arranged for Pandora to spend the weekend in Norfolk and on Saturday morning I took the train to Brighton. Mike met me in his beloved *Deux-chevaux* with its back seat full of sailing paraphernalia. We drove to his two-roomed flat on the ground floor of a Regency Terrace overlooking the sea. The living-room, as compact as a ship's cabin, was furnished with the barest of necessities. It reminded me of a description I'd read of Pushkin's cell. The only concessions to luxury were some pictures by David Jones and three shelves of books. A typewriter stood on a table underneath the curtainless window and a painting by an Australian aborigine hung over the settee.

Throughout the years I'd known him, this was my first visit to his flat and I felt an unusual barrier of shyness between us. "I thought we'd lunch here," he said, and from the corner of the room which served as a kitchen, he produced a bottle of red wine, a cooked chicken, some wholemeal bread and a tomato salad, heavily laced with garlic and oil.

"Would you like it if we gave Jester an airing this afternoon? There's a good north-westerly and I'd like to try her with the new self-steering."

"That would be great," I said, as I watched him set out the simple meal on the bare table. Why do men prepare meals so effortlessly? Plain simple food to satisfy hunger, not consuming time to titillate the appetite? After Stilton cheese and fruit, he made some strong coffee in a jug and fetched a box of Coronas from the cupboard.

"You're sure you won't?"

I shook my head and watched as he carefully prodded the tip of the cigar with a match. "I keep them for special occasions, like this," he said. "Your first visit." I had given him the cigars every Christmas, a yearly ritual and a luxury I knew he would never have been able to afford for himself. I got up.

"Do you mind if I …"

"I'm sorry. It's just outside off the landing – French style. And here's the bedroom – I'll sleep on the sofa."

He put my Vuitton overnight bag on the single bed, the only furniture in the room, except for a narrow chest-of-drawers with a simple carved wooden cross hanging above it on the whitewashed wall.

"We'd better set off soon. You'll need this." He threw me a large anorak. "Might get a bit wet."

Walking down to the Marina and across the intricate maze of jetties, he was stopped many times by members of the sailing fraternity, all with weatherbeaten faces and wearing the yachtsman's unofficial uniform of dark blue leather sneakers and oilskins, some with peaked caps adorned with club badges. He was obviously a popular figure, and they talked about *Jester* as if they were discussing a mutual friend.

"Thought she did beautifully in the Fastnet – not showing her age at all – no need for that face-lift yet."

"Well, I'll probably have to invest in some new sails for her soon. Anyway I'm trying this fancy self-steering gear on her today."

Edging *Jester* out of the harbour was no easy process. Unlike most other small yachts, she had no engine. We missed an elegant ketch by inches. Mike swore to himself and shouted to me to keep an eye on the fenders as he steered skilfully with the help of the junk sails. In a few moments, we had cleared the last boat and were rounding the harbour wall into the open sea. I tucked myself out of the way when he hoisted the sail, and I began to relish the sensation of the cold, salty foam of the waves as they crashed over the edge of the deck. Suddenly the boat tilted at a remarkably sharp angle, and I clutched the rail, pulling myself as high as I could to escape the waves washing over the slanting deck. Mike turned round.

"You OK? Enjoying it? I'll take in a reef if you think we're going too fast."

I thought I'd never seen him so good-looking and relaxed as he manoeuvred his boat.

"No, I'm fine," I said. Looking at him as he handled the wheel and sails with an almost tactile sensitivity, I felt suddenly that I loved this man. I wondered what it would be like to be touched by him in the way he was handling his beloved boat. And then I started feeling exhilaration, mixed with fear, as we seemed to be sailing at right angles to the sea. Revelling in the beauty of the waves as they rose, arched and broke before us, Mike asked if I would like to take the helm for a minute while he adjusted the self-steering. He showed me how to keep the sails filled on the wind and left me to cope, as he disappeared into the tiny cockpit. The wheel seemed to have a will of its own, as I strained to keep the boat steady, I saw an enormous wave approaching and as it broke over the deck, I panicked and screamed for him to come back.

"Don't worry, you're doing fine."

143

But I was terrified and insisted. He laughed, but he took over the tiller.

"I think you've had enough. Just put your head down. We've got to go about."

That evening, Mike took me to his favourite pub – "the only passable real beer around here" – and he introduced me to his friends, mostly professors from Sussex University. Later we dined at a fish restaurant on the sea front. We talked about his latest Atlantic race, and I asked him about how much winning really mattered.

"Well," he answered, "as Graham Greene said, all failure is a kind of death, but no – it's obviously fun to win races, but to me, just getting there, testing one's ability to survive, is enough."

He had had a traumatic experience when *Jester* capsized in a gale and was nearly dismasted, but his worst fears, he said, were those of a collision at night or of being becalmed.

"Once I was becalmed for days on end. I felt the wind would never blow again and I'd remain in that particular spot forever. A pretty weird feeling."

"And what about loneliness?" I asked.

"Surely everyone is alone, ultimately. Rilke, the German poet, said that to enjoy your loneliness you have to endure the pain it brings you."

As we talked, I looked into his unfathomable blue eyes and tried to understand the truth behind the words. For the first time since Julian's death, I was beginning to feel that life might have a meaning again. Mike ordered brandies and coffee, and later as we walked back to his flat, he took my hand in a tight hold. Back in the flat, I undressed in the tiny bedroom and felt my body and face glowing from the exercise and sea air. Putting on my dressing-gown, I walked into the other room. Mike was standing in front of the two-bar electric fire.

"That was the best day I've had for ages," I said truthfully. "I loved seeing you practising your craft."

He stepped towards me and held me awkwardly in his arms. As our lips touched, I felt a pure love between us, and a kiss of such sweetness that I wanted it to continue forever. I led him gently towards the small bedroom, but he stood by the door and mumbled something about plans for the morning. A few moments later, I heard the front door slam, the sound of him running down the steps, and I knew I was alone once more.

Before travelling back to London on the *Brighton Belle* the next day, I had been overcome by shame and despair. How could I have so misread his feelings? My body had cried out to him and been rejected. In the early hours of the morning, after a night of tossing and turning, I eventually fell into a troubled sleep. When I woke, I tried to behave lightly as if nothing unusual had passed between us. But after breakfast, I telephoned London for messages and pretended Pandora had returned early from Norfolk, was unwell and needed me.

Sitting in the train, I looked round the seedy elegance of the old railway carriage with its solid mahogany woodwork and brass door handles, the white lace antimacassars with 'Pullman' embroidered in blue, the Victorian lamp with its scalloped dirty glass lampshade like a crinoline with frilled edges. Inset into the panelling opposite were Japanese-style pictures made of different types of wood. A cockney attendant, wearing a starched white monkey jacket, brought me tea in a Staffordshire china teacup patterned with blue and green leaves. But the swaying of the train made it impossible to drink without spilling half the contents onto the spotless white linen tablecloth. Subdued lighting behind panels of cut glass helped to create an atmosphere of safety, comfort and warmth. The steady rhythm of the wheels went de-dum, do-dum, de-dum and then suddenly do-de-du-do-de-dum with an extra heartbeat. The lamps reflected in the window, raced past station after station and I realised I would soon be there.

Would life always be like this – a series of false starts and terrible errors of judgement?

Ten

Among my mail waiting for me was a letter from Max Stafford-Clark, asking me to join the Board of the Royal Court Theatre. I had worked as a fundraiser for my local theatre with a group of friends including Lois Sieff and Angela Fox (mother of the three thespian Fox brothers), and I had organised various events to avoid the theatre closing down. I agreed to become a Board Member, which I thoroughly enjoyed. The Court meetings were fairly informal affairs. Max was a charismatic chairman, whom I had met briefly years earlier when staying with Sam Spiegel in the South of France. He was now married to Ann Pennington, who had also been a guest. He was brilliant at discovering new young directors and putting on controversial plays such as *Waiting for Godot*. The only musical Laurence Olivier ever played was the lead in John Osborne's *The Entertainer*, an enthralling mixture of the comic and the tragic.

Matthew Evans, the Chairman of Faber and Faber, followed in the same role at the Court, while the artistic director was the outstanding original young Stephen Daldry, who had worked in a circus before joining the theatrical profession. Other Board members were Lois Sieff, Alan Rickman, David Hare, Robert Fox and Alan Yentob. But by far the most popular chairman was Sir John Mortimer. He had the disarming habit of arriving late for a meeting, swinging a bottle of champagne in one hand with his other hand round the waist of an attractive young secretary. Beaming at all of us, he flipped through the agenda of the meeting and asked us for our opinions. But it was clear that he had done his research beforehand, reaching his own conclusions, which invariably proved to be right. His air of affability hid a brilliant mind and it was mainly due to him that the rebuilt theatre turned out to be such a success. He and his wife Penny gave great parties in the country where he lived in the old house of his blind father, who inspired his book, *A Voyage Round My Father*.

One weekend, Mike telephoned and asked if he could stay for a few days. He appeared unaware that anything had changed between us, and he didn't allude to the Brighton episode. A male presence in the house was a comfort to us both, and I enjoyed the ritual of preparing the evening meal for the three of us. Later when Pandora had gone to bed, we would talk late into the night. I curled up in front of the fire with Mike opposite, a glass of whisky in his hand, telling me of an article which had impressed him in the *Times Literary Supplement* or the *Tablet*, or about the book he had been asked to write about his sailing experiences. Whenever the conversation became too personal, he would gently steer me away on another track. The awareness of his physical presence utterly dominated me. When I told Nuala of my innermost feelings, I received in return a warning that I was merely trying to replace my loss with unreal solutions. Gradually a pattern emerged. Whenever Mike had work to do in London, he would stay in the spare room. Soon we took his presence for granted.

One night I went to a dinner party given by one of Julian's old friends. I sat next to the Dutch Ambassador, whose wife Gaby was visiting Paris for the fashion collections. While listening and trying to contribute to the pompous and artificial conversation, something inside me seemed to explode. I longed to leap up and rush from the room. The careful cosmetic faces of the women, their smart fashionable dresses, the preserved conventions to hide real emotion, the platitudes and complacent attitude of the men. The Ambassador was turning to me.

"I suppose you'll get married again very soon – people who were happily married once always do."

Arriving home, I looked up to see if Mike's light in the spare room was still on. It was. I rushed upstairs and found him reading in bed. I sat on the edge of the bed and tried to explain the futility of the evening. He put his arms round me.

"Do you want to stay here?" he asked. "I promise I won't touch you."

The next day, I felt it was time to consider planning my trip to the Middle East. Enough of self-pity and morbid introspection. I knew Mike would always be a strong presence in my life, but I felt it was time to pull my socks up, as my father used to say. Having procured all my necessary visas and introductions, I booked my airline ticket to Kuwait, and I was full of optimism. A friend had written that a woman, Najir Ohman, who was a leading figure in the Women's Movement in Kuwait, had agreed to be interviewed, and I had an introduction to the Ruler of Abu Dhabi from my contact in the Foreign Office. Unfortunately, the timing was not ideal. The previous year, a female journalist had insinuated her way into some male-only domains and on returning to the west, she had written lascivious and libellous articles. Naturally, the Arabs would be suspicious of another female interviewer.

I was worried about the working of my new tape-recorder. I had practised on it twice before I left London, once on Mike, and the second time on Bianca Jagger, who had agreed to be interviewed for Vogue through the introduction of a mutual friend. I was incredibly nervous as I waited for her in my living room at Tite Street and I grew more so as her expected time of arrival became later and later. Almost an hour after we had agreed to meet, she arrived, looking stunning and wearing a white tuxedo suit with a bowler hat, while carrying an ivory stick. After a brief chat, with no apologies for her late arrival, I turned on the machine. Only after my second attempt did I get it to work. She gave me a description of her marriage to Mick Jagger in Bali and said she loved living in London. I knew they had a house in the country and asked her where it was. Hesitation.

"Well, as we have all the car windows darkened, I'm not quite sure of the location."

Trying not to show my surprise, I continued the interview. When I met her many years later at a lunch given by Marguerite Littman, she confessed to me that she had been just as nervous as I was.

A stewardess touched me on the arm. "Will you please fasten your seat-belt? We're about to land."

Driving through the streets of Kuwait, I was disappointed by the towers of concrete buildings, the roads filled with noisy cars, the advertisements for prefabricated homes, the cranes and concrete mixers. I knew that Kuwait was one of the more westernised of the Arab states, but I had also heard stories of picnics in the desert and hawking expeditions. My imagination had taken me to carpeted tents, where unspeakable delicacies such as sheep's eyes and testicles were handed to me by white-robed Arabs, their camels resting in the background under date palms. Little did I know at the time that years later, when I was going out with Hugh Fraser and he took me to Israel, we would be taken into the desert and treated to just such a fantasy. But now, as I unpacked in a newly-built impersonal hotel with its air conditioning on at full blast, I was filled with dismay. Looking though the slit of a window, I saw the silhouette of a dhow. Mike had told me about these local, beautifully-shaped handmade fishing boats. I had an urge for a closer look, and so I wandered out of the hotel for a walk by the sea. After a few yards, cars started hooting at me and a man's leering face looked out and said something in Arabic. I realised I was the only woman walking along the beach and quickly retraced my footsteps to the hotel, followed by a crowd of laughing children.

There was a message waiting for me. Najir would like me to go to her art gallery the following morning for coffee. I experienced a mixed feeling of anticipation and fear. I wasn't in some kind of dream – something would happen. This would be my first interview, already set up in London. Najir Ohman had the reputation of being a unique and controversial figure in Kuwait. Not only did she own her own gallery, specialising in modern art, but she was the first woman chosen to sit on the Board of the Arts Council, which was part of the National Planning Board, a twelve-man think-tank, headed by the Prime Minister.

Entering the art gallery the next day, I had my first introduction to the ritual courtesies of the Middle East. Wearing stylish western clothes, Najir was younger and more attractive than I had expected. A vital, dark-haired woman in her mid-thirties, she fluttered about like a delicate bird. A servant in flowing beige robes, with a white head-piece held by a black cord, carried a tray with an ornate silver pot. Sweet coffee was poured into tiny china cups and biscuits were handed round.

"So you wish to interview me," Najir said. "I'm flattered but I don't think it will be of much interest in England. We're rather behind the times here, I'm afraid, but I expect you'd like to know something about the Harikanisia, our Women's Movement?"

After a few false starts with the recording machine and some faltering questions, Najir told me of her crusade to liberate the women of Kuwait, nine in ten of whom are still veiled and illiterate.

"There's beginning to emerge in the Arab world a strong feeling for a movement which would involve women in the affairs of their country, particularly in education. You see, we live in a completely male culture – they're not used to dealing with women. But we're in a state of flux and the big issue is now not the veil but the Family Affairs Law, an archaic and medieval law which means that women are exploited by men and merely used as property. This is the law which oppresses the Arab women the most. Everything else is becoming secular except this last issue.

"Marriages are still arranged – very few Kuwaiti girls marry outside the family – but it's just the beginning. My mother and father were named for each other – they were first cousins, but had never met before. And the women lived in seclusion. They went outside the house twice: once for marriage and the second time for death. In Islamic law, the man can obtain a divorce by simply saying, 'I divorce you, I divorce you, I divorce you,' in front of a witness, and then it would be *haram* which means a sin for him to see her again without remarriage.

"But you see," she added, "our men have no concept of original sin, no guilt. I would say they are elegantly bisexual."

The telephone rang and Najir went to answer it. Waiting, my thoughts began to wander. In Scotland, they used to say divorce was death. In my own somewhat turbulent marriage, the word divorce had never once been mentioned. We had hurt each other deeply at times, but, like the peeling of an onion, with each hurt and tears and the removal of a protective skin we had reached a deeper understanding and love, until at the end …

Najir had been speaking angrily on the telephone in Arabic, but she put down the receiver and went on saying that she was fighting for political rights for women. To a tentative question, she answered:

"No, none of this conflict is with our religion. It is only the way the Koran is interpreted. In fact, the first mystic was a woman and the first martyr was a woman. We are still totally ruled by males, but something is happening. It's like a bubble all through the Arab world, although we are still thinking in isolation. But maybe, one day."

The recorder clicked to a stop. I realised I had only brought one tape, so I took notes as we continue to talk. I told Najir that my next stop was Abu Dhabi.

"My God, there you will find things even more backward. They make us look sophisticated."

Back in the hotel, I blessed Najir for her unconscious contribution to these first teetering steps towards my rehabilitation. I opened the half-bottle of vodka I had brought with me, and I drank a silent toast to the future. I doubted that I would ever be swept away by the mysteries of the East like the intrepid Isobel Burton and Jane Digby. Yet I was beginning to enjoy my own special Arabian adventure, where women were also beginning to search for new identities.

Another vast concrete hotel threatened with slit windows as a protection against the sandstorms from the desert; streets, crowded with American cars and lorries spilling over with imported foreign workers. Pavements bustled with Arab men in long brown robes and occasionally a veiled and hooded woman. Abu Dhabi had once been simply a palace fortress, two oases and a village. Since the oil had begun to flow, it now had the largest per capita income in the world. It looked as if the monstrous towers of concrete had been put up haphazardly, without plans, askew. Everywhere were cranes and drills and half-completed prefabricated houses and a landscape of advertisements for material fulfilment.

Lying on my bed in the hotel, trying to reach people to make appointments, I was assailed by dismay and frustration. Everyone was polite, but time was irrelevant. "Inshallah, a meeting may be arranged. I will call you back." I had been promised an interview with Sheikh Zayed, the Ruler, who would give me a decision after I had submitted my questions. In the meantime, Sheikha Fatima would be delighted if I would take tea with her the following day at the Palace. I had been told that although the Ruler had several younger wives, Sheikha Fatima was his first and favourite and the mother of his eldest son.

The next day, a smiling young Egyptian girl from the Office of Tourism arrived to accompany me to the Palace and act as an interpreter. Armed with my list of questions to be given to the Ruler, we walked through the hibiscus-bright garden, up steep steps and along marble corridors, and we were shown into the Throne Room. Unfurnished except for rows of chairs arranged round the walls, an ornate throne at the far end and vast chandeliers suspended from the ceiling, it gave the impression of a setting for an early Cecil B. de Mille movie on Babylon. The Sheikha, her ample flesh tightly enveloped in scarlet silk, fluttered her arms as she chattered to the obsequious ladies around her. A hawklike *burqa* hid her expression except for her eyes, heavily outlined in kohl, peering through the slits.

"There is a delegation from Kuwait," the interpreter said. "We will have to wait our turn."

I was aware of a strong smell of incense and sandalwood, and trays of coffee and sweet cakes were constantly passed around. All the women seemed grossly overweight and giggled a great deal. The scene reminded me of an aviary of brightly-coloured, twittering parakeets. Their arms were covered with multi-coloured bracelets and their fingernails beautifully manicured and painted – their only display of vanity. The minutes and hours passed slowly and I looked up at the enormous portrait of Sheikh Zayed hanging over the double doors at the far end of the long Throne Room. He was said to have deposed his brother in a bloodless coup, but that he himself, under the influence of his mother Sheikha Salama, was a peace-loving, generous and just ruler, not hoarding money for himself, but distributing it amongst his subjects. His compelling, fierce eyes set in a long, fine-boned face gazed out of the portrait, the only male presence. Suddenly the great door opened and a young boy of about fourteen appeared and waved to his mother. All the women quickly threw their veils over their masked faces and looked away. The boy laughed and waved again, but he didn't enter the room.

As he ran off, my thoughts turned to my own son. Peter had been deeply distressed at my display of violence in Norfolk, when I had destroyed the portraits of Julian and myself. Later we had talked about it. I had tried to explain my mad motives, and he admitted to feeling guilty for leaving the pictures where I might see them. Luckily, it failed to cause a rift between us.

Dragging myself once more into the present and after what seemed like several hours, I was being presented to Her Highness. More cakes were offered and this time I couldn't refuse. After asking politely about my journey, she said, "There is a friend of your country outside, waiting to see the Ruler. His name is Sir Hugh Bousted, he has asked you to visit him at Al-'Ain."

Sir Hugh was a soldier, author and traveller, also one of the Sheikh Zayed's earlier advisers. I'd read his book, *Wind in the Morning*, and I couldn't believe in this piece of luck. Later, relieved to escape the gilded birdcage, I saw him, a bowed, dignified figure in khaki, waiting patiently in the shining corridor.

"I've been here six hours," he said resignedly, "but this is the Ruler's day for seeing his subjects. They sometimes wait all day for his *majlis* – he cannot refuse anyone."

We arranged that I would visit him at his home in the desert the following day. He would send a Land Rover and his Indian driver. At last, perhaps, a real look at the sands of Araby, or so I thought.

After driving along a four-lane highway, we left the concrete town behind us and took the road to Al-'Ain. Gradually the road became a track. Now all around us was the desert, undulating dunes with the sun beating down and casting vast moving shadows. I carried on a desultory conversation with the driver. He had been with his master for many years and often accompanied him on his travels. I told him I knew India and had been born there.

"Where do you come from?" I asked.

"It's not a place you would know," he said, "not a big place – a village called Kamptee on the bank of the river Kanhan." There seemed to be a blinding flash on the windscreen, as if it were on fire. For a second, I saw another fire: the fire than had terrified me as a child. *Suttee.* I closed my eyes to shut it out.

"Memsahib all right?"

I opened my eyes and saw the anxious expression on the driver's face in the mirror.

"Yes, it was nothing – it must be the heat."

But I was shaking with fear. I must pull myself together. I looked around me. The desert was more incredible than I had imagined. An ocean of sand with ridges running across it like the waves of the sea and just as treacherous. Occasionally a herd of camels, led by a single Arab towards some well, would come into view, while Bedouin settlements sprang like rare beehives out of the sand. The emptiness became a balm to my jangled nerves and disturbed thoughts, leaving an inner stillness and peace. The relentless grandeur made me feel immensely small. My personal grief was insignificant, as relevant as a particle of sand in the desert.

As the mountains of Oman appeared in the distance, we arrived at the hotel where Sir Hugh was waiting on the steps to meet us. We transferred to another Land Rover, specially constructed to drive over the rough terrain of his ranch. As we bumped across the craters and hills, he explained that Sheikh Zayed had given him this house on retirement to look after his Arab stud.

"But," he said sadly, "His Highness is not interested any more. An American breeder gave him a splendid black stallion and now he considers his own breed rather inferior."

He spoke about his life in nostalgic terms, although he was loyal to the Ruler. But it seemed to me that he had been rather negligently treated. The previous night, after his wait for six hours, he had been told that an audience could not be granted. Yet he talked of Sheikh Zayed's compassion and love for his people, of the improvements that had come: free education, medicine and maintenance.

"He has what is known as *hazz* – good luck." He laughed. "That is considered to be the most important quality you can possess in these parts."

He showed me, with pride, the beautiful small Arab mares being exercised. They were made to gallop round a paddock, encouraged by a gentle whip, as the sand filled the air around them. Hugh and I ate a simple meal in the small white house where he lived alone, surrounded by books and photographs of the famous. In a central place of honour was a signed photograph of H.E. Sheikh Zayed bin Sultan al-Nahyan, the Ruler of Abu Dhabi.

"This was his birthplace, you know."

Yes, I knew that, and I knew the Sheikh did not come here any more. That was the price of a life of service. On my return to Abu Dhabi, I was not surprised that my request to interview Sheikh Zayed had once again been postponed, so instead of waiting at my uninviting hotel, I decided to fly back to England.

At home I found a host of minor problems, which temporarily alleviated the major one. I felt that my journey had not been successful. I had failed to get the promised interview, but at least a magazine published an article on the Women's Movement in the Middle East, and I was interviewed on the BBC wireless. And there was a message to telephone the Prime Minister James Callaghan at once.

Eleven

When I was put through to Downing Street, Callaghan said he had failed to contact my son Peter, and as he was doing his Government reshuffle, he asked if I thought Peter would agree to being moved to the Northern Ireland Office. I was speechless for a moment. Peter and Cassandra, I knew, had gone to Ithaca in Greece to explore some of the remoter spots, and they were completely out of touch with anybody else.

"Would he have to go there very often?" I asked, knowing of the dangers in that country.

Callaghan replied, "No, not too often."

"Would this mean promotion?" I enquired.

"Yes."

"In that case, I'm sure he'll agree," I answered.

When Peter and Cassandra arrived at the main port in Ithaca and stopped for a coffee, he picked up a five-day old copy of the *Observer* and read an article commenting on the Government's reshuffle. His name was mentioned, but without details of his new job. He immediately went to the main post office and found four telegrams waiting for him. The first one was from the Embassy in Athens, asking him to contact them immediately. The second was from the Department of Trade and Industry. The third was from the Northern Ireland Office, saying, "Please contact your private office urgently," and the fourth was from me, saying, "Congratulations, darling – you've been promoted." So he realised he was being moved, but not to the job he'd been given.

Luckily Peter took it in his stride and failed to berate me for taking control of his life. He flew in an RAF jet with Roy Mason, the Secretary of State for Northern Ireland, and he was told he would be the Minister of State in the Northern Ireland Office responsible for Education, Sport, the Arts and also Minister of Health and Social Services, based in Stormont Castle. Those were demanding jobs and meant being separated from his girlfriend for long stretches at a time. I once visited him in Stormont Castle, expecting it to be very grand, but instead found it had been divided up into small, dreary offices and living-quarters. He established a reputation as a popular, fair and competent minister, with excellent relationships with his civil servants and all sections of society. But his major achievements were increasing the number of teachers, closing inadequate schools and hospitals, modernising provisions for the mentally ill and providing Northern Ireland with world-class sporting facilities. As a result of his initiatives, a Bill making it possible to set up integrated non-sectarian schools passed into law. Apart from the whole range of public duties, he was also intimately involved in security issues. These included secret and top secret meetings and negotiations with businesses and American politicians over internal investment decisions.

It was inconceivable that I could ever again visit Formentor and Casa Melchett for the summer holidays, so I began to rent houses abroad. In 1977, Lord and Lady Kleinwort decided to let their beautiful villa, Casa Lo Sbarcatello at Porto Ercole, Italy, for a month. Pandora and I drove there from Chelsea in my small Honda. Arriving much later than I had planned, we were met by a rather cross-looking Italian couple, Enno and Monserrat, the housekeepers. After Enno had reluctantly cooked us some pasta, we found two bedrooms and fell asleep immediately. I learned later that our rented villa was built on the coast, where St Paul was said to have landed after his voyage from Ephesus and where he wrote his Letter to the Congregation.

The next day, we explored the house, beautifully furnished in an old-fashioned English style, and wandered down through the terraced gardens to the sea beyond. After a few days, Enno had completely thawed and cooked us delicious meals under the verbena-covered terrace. I had asked some friends to stay, and Pandora said vaguely that some of her chums might look in on their way through Italy. Prince Bernhard and Princess Beatrix (or 'Mummy' as she was known) of the Netherlands were our immediate neighbours. They owned a large rather ugly modern house, surrounded by a high stone wall. A yacht was permanently moored opposite the villa.

A few weeks after our arrival, our guests and Pandora had all gone down to the village to do some shopping. I was in the middle of washing my hair, when Enno knocked at the door and said some boys were asking to see me. Wrapping a towel round my wet hair, I looked out of the window and saw four bedraggled barefooted young men standing in the garden. One was dressed in dirty dungarees and the others in what looked like cast-offs from Oxfam.

"Are you looking for work?" I asked.

"No," the one in overalls said tentatively. "Pandora said we might stay here a few nights as we're passing through Italy."

"Oh dear," I said. "I'm afraid we're completely full up, but there's a large barn if you don't mind sleeping on some make-do mattresses."

"Oh, that'll be fine," he said.

Putting on a dressing-gown, I went downstairs to meet them. They politely held out their hands.

"Hi – I'm Nick Coleridge," said the first.

"And my name's Craig Brown," said the second, "and this is John Scott."

"And you're?" I asked the fourth boy.

"Guy Lubbock," he said. "I think you know my parents."

"Yes, of course," I answered, feeling rather foolish at my initial reaction. Never judge by appearances, as the saying goes.

In the end, they stayed a week, and we all became great friends. Dinners on the terrace were hilarious, with Craig being his cleverly humorous self and making up rhyming couplets about my guests. One included Edna O'Brien, who would entertain us after dinner by reading poetry in her soft Irish brogue.

Alan and Lucy Moorehead owned a villa opposite, perched high up on a forested mountain, overlooking the harbour. Alan had had a bad stroke and had only two favourite expressions. One was "bloody awful," and the other was "on and on and on." They owned a much-loved parrot, who would delight in repeating "bloody awful." I had always been a great admirer of Alan and his writing, and I was sad to see him reduced to this state, although, I must say, he made a great effort. Lucy, who some said was an even greater writer but had kept very much in the background to look after the children, came into her own and created a cheerful atmosphere for friends and family.

Geoffrey Keating, an amusing Irish bachelor, also had a house in Porto Ercole. He was one of the few people I had stayed with briefly soon after Julian's death. Among his guests had been Jonathan Aitken, and one night Geoffrey had taken me aside and said, "You two should have an affair – it would do you good." I knew Geoffrey too well to take umbrage, but he could be outrageous at times, especially when drunk, which was all too often.

Around the corner from Porto Ercole, Sunni Agnelli, the Mayor of Monte Argentario, had a beautiful villa where she gave long dinner parties with interesting guests – mostly politicians. She was challenging and charismatic, and she would take hold of my arm and say, "You sit next to me," and to the others, "Just sit anywhere you like." Later she would become a Senior Senator and serve in the Italian Parliament.

Just past her house was a famous nightclub called La Strega. On arrival, one was handed a cocktail called Passport to Paradise. It turned out to be lethal, and as the dance floor was on a slight slope with the rocks beyond reaching the sea, dancing became a hazard. But it didn't deter the young, and

Pandora and her friends danced with gay abandon on many a visit.

I took Lo Sbarcatello for a second August holiday, this time sharing it with Elizabeth Harris, who was about to marry the financier Peter Aitken, before she eventually married her true love, Jonathan Aitken. We all admired the way she spent ages applying fake tan, but never went sitting in the sun. Parviz Radji, the elegant ex-Iranian Ambassador to London, was one of my guests, and Lizzy Spender, the poet's daughter, was a frequent visitor. She was madly in love with the handsome Parviz and was staying with Geoffrey Keating across the water. But luckily, it came to nothing, partially because Lizzy did up her dresses with safety pins, which were always flying open, deterring the fastidious Parviz. Eventually she married the brilliant Barry Humphreys, always outrageous as Dame Edna Everage, and she couldn't be happier. Barry was a total bibliophile and had collected so many books that they had begun to sink into the floor below. His answer was to buy the lower flat and so all went well and the shelves were restored.

Back in London, I found that Peter and Cassandra had decided to set up a home together in North London, and on the fall of the Labour government in 1979, he was free to follow what had become his true passion – conservation. He was first President of the Ramblers Association, and he chaired a coalition of all the Wildlife Organisations. He also covered the Environment on the Labour Opposition Front Bench in the House of Lords.

I suppose the only really serious argument we ever had was on a walk round Battersea Park, when he told me that

Cassandra was pregnant. Even if it was a son, they didn't intend to marry. He didn't believe in making vows in church or in a registry office that he could equally well make in private. He didn't believe in God, disliked organised religion, thought many aspects of marriage demeaned women, and didn't believe in the hereditary principle. Having been brought up in the Church of England, I believed that my religion was part of my national heritage; it gave me an inner strength in spite of the fact that I was not a regular churchgoer. But as we walked round the park, this was not what we discussed in depth. I felt that, in spite of his own convictions, he should at least give freedom of choice to a son, who might one day disagree with him and might wish to carry on the Melchett name and all it stood for. Peter argued that if he wasn't strong enough to convince his own son of his belief, he wouldn't be much good as a father. As we circled the park, round and round went the arguments, which I knew Peter would win in the end, as he always did. But I was convinced it was my duty to put the case as strongly as I could for his dead father and, indeed, for his unborn son. I don't know how long we walked and talked, but it was growing dark and the gates were closing. And that was the last time the issue of hereditary title was mentioned between us. Cassandra had a daughter and, two years later, a son. Peter is a model of the 'new age father' and is adored by his children, who seem to have adopted most of his beliefs and philosophy.

Later that year, Anne and Gordon Getty asked me to stay with them at their house in San Francisco for a Gala they were giving for Princess Margaret. I had never visited San

Francisco, but I had heard how beautiful it was. I decided to go as I was fond of Anne, although I'd hardly met Gordon who was known to be a bit of an eccentric and extremely reclusive. After changing planes in New York, I arrived at the house late in the evening and totally exhausted. A butler showed me to my room and I was relieved to find a note from Gordon saying that Anne was in New York awaiting the arrival of the Princess and would be away for two days. He suggested I had a quiet supper on a tray, and that the next day he would put a car at my disposal to explore the city. A maid unpacked my luggage and after delicious scrambled eggs and caviar, I fell into a deep sleep.

There was no sign of Gordon the following morning, but a chauffeur-driven Cadillac was waiting to take me round the city. The first place I wanted to see was the famous Golden Gate Bridge. I decided to walk across it, which I was told afterwards was something people rarely did. When the winds were really strong, people had been swept all the way to Alcatraz in the sea below. The car was waiting for me on the far side, and after doing a bit of shopping, I returned to the house. The large living-room had a splendid view overlooking the yachting harbour, and I realised that a table laid for one was awaiting me by the tall French windows. By this time I was feeling slightly dismayed by the strange lack of hospitality from my host. But later, when I was resting in my bedroom, I received another note from Gordon, asking me if I would like to join him for dinner. He would like to show me Chinatown. Would I meet him at 7 o'clock?

The evening turned out to be one of the most extraordinary of my life. Gordon had asked Placido Domingo to join us together with a famous American opera singer. I had met Placido before in London when he was staying at Claridge's with his wife, and I had found him to be a great charmer. We set off for an unpretentious restaurant in Chinatown and as the champagne flowed and the fortune cookies popped, the atmosphere became more and more relaxed. After dinner, Gordon suggested we return to the house, and he took us to what he called his private den. It was a small windowless room in the basement, wholly lined with gramophone records. Gordon was well-known to have a great singing voice and to be a brilliant pianist, but only rarely would he be persuaded to sing or play in public. More champagne was produced, and Placido was examining row upon row of records, arranged round the walls like books in a library. Miraculously, Gordon could find any record without any kind of list, for he had a photographic memory. He suggested we should all let our hair down. Placido would play the piano, while he, Gordon, would sing arias. The famous American opera singer and I would dance. And dance we did until the early hours.

The following afternoon, Anne arrived and life assumed an air of reality. Princess Margaret and her lady-in-waiting were staying at a nearby hotel for some reason, and she was expected for the gala dinner that night. Anne rushed around arranging flowers and finalising plans. As we lined up to greet the Princess before dinner, Gordon stood at the end of the row. Inexplicably, just before he was due to greet Her Royal Highness, he suddenly disappeared and was not to be seen again for the rest of the evening. Anne was completely unthrown by this and made no comment. The unexpected was to be expected. She was used to his eccentric behaviour.

The great and the best of San Francisco society began to encircle the rooms set aside for the gala evening. The scent of the white lilies was almost overpowering and the women's jewellery glittered like the real diamonds they were. I found I was seated at dinner in between the famous film actor Rock Hudson and a prominent businessman. I spent most of the meal talking to Rock, whom I found attractive and charming and showing no sign of his later death from AIDS. In those years, men didn't 'come out' about their sexuality, especially if they were built like beefcake.

After dinner, there was a cabaret and then the dancing began, which continued until the early hours. When most of the guests had departed, Anne persuaded Princess Margaret to play the piano. After only the slightest hesitation, she responded by playing all her favourite songs, ranging from Noel Coward to Elvis Presley, and we gathered round the piano to join her. She was indefatigable. With a cigarette hanging from her mouth, she was obviously enjoying herself hugely and impressed us all. She then began to accompany herself by singing word-perfectly all the well-known hit songs. I think it must have been around two in the morning that her lady-in-waiting reminded her of appointments the following day. She left reluctantly, and Anne and I sat down for a final drink. I congratulated Anne on the success of the evening, although I couldn't help contrasting it with the night before in Gordon's den.

Returning on a flight to London two days later, I suddenly felt extremely ill and tried to make a dash to the

Ladies. But I never made it, because I fainted in the passage and passed clean out. It was the first and last time this has ever happened to me and was the nastiest of experiences. I later put it down to something I had eaten earlier that day, when we lunched at the Four Seasons Restaurant. But the stewardess took my name, and I gathered I would be put on some sort of list of 'susceptible passengers'. Not that I have ever been subjected to any queries on any flight since then; except on the ridiculous security measures taken at airports today, when you may have to remove your shoes and your belt, and have your lipstick confiscated, I can't remember ever having been too much of a bomb threat.

After my father died of a heart attack in 1967, my mother Wendy lived in a flat at the top of a high-rise block in Brighton overlooking the pier. She had a whippet called Misty, whom she adored – the only reason to get her to go for a short daily walk. Whatever the weather, she always wore her platinum mink coat, which I had given her and was her most treasured possession. She made friends easily and one was George Melly's mother, who visited her regularly. Unfortunately, her drinking habit had become steadily worse, but luckily she had a good neighbour, who dropped in to see her every day. She was totally gullible. When a young man she had met on her morning walk asked if he could visit her, she immediately accepted and let him have a look round her flat. He admired her few antiques and said he was setting up an antique shop in the old Lanes. When he asked if he could borrow a small Chippendale desk to put in the window, she immediately said yes. Of course, she never saw him or the desk again.

Once I got a frantic call from her to say she had lost her precious mink coat. I rang the neighbours and they searched the flat everywhere, only to find it hanging on the peg in the bathroom. When I was in London, I would try and visit her once a week, and she would always cook her wartime recipe of boiled chicken and rice laced with brandy.

One day the neighbours rang me in a panic to say that Wendy had had a bad fall and needed treatment. When I arrived at the hospital, I discovered she had broken her arm, but luckily not seriously. I realised it was time to bring her to London and get her settled into a care home for the elderly. While she stayed with me at Tite Street, I became aware of just how much her health had deteriorated and started searching for a suitable home. I found most of them decidedly depressing, with elderly patients in a far worse condition than Wendy. Eventually I was recommended a small privately-run care institution near St George's Square, where the Matron seemed cheerful and friendly. I knew that in my rather nomadic life, I couldn't keep her at Tite Street, especially as she had now become a serious alcoholic. I admit to a slight feeling of guilt as I left her with her few possessions in the care of the smiling Matron. My weekly visits became more and more stressful, as I realised my mother was in poor spirits and seemed to be kept under heavy sedation. Once when I arrived, she was in tears and deeply unhappy. Without hesitation, I told her I was taking her away and after packing up her suitcase and passing a gaping Matron on the stairs, I bundled her into my Honda, which was parked outside the so-called Home.

In the end, I rented a small flat not far from me in Chelsea and I engaged a series of part-time nurses to keep a daily eye on her. We encouraged her to switch from her favourite gin to watered-down whiskies. She would spend her days sitting by the window listening to the radio with her darling Misty at her feet. As she seemed to take against the part-time nurses, I had the brainwave of engaging young babysitters. She had always been fond of the young and they, in their turn, became devoted to her. We kept the whisky hidden and rationed her intake, which seemed to keep her happy. Always small, she seemed to have diminished in size, but she still wore the platinum mink coat when she was reluctantly persuaded to take a short walk to Burton Court Gardens. I was abroad, when my Filipino maid rang me to say my mother was dead. She had died peacefully in her sleep, and after her funeral we had her ashes laid to rest in Chelsea Old Church by the river.

As I no longer wished to visit the farm in Norfolk for Pandora's school holidays, I rented a small cottage in Bembridge in the Isle of Wight. My great friends Michael and Christine West had a beautiful house there, called the Garland. Mike had retired from the Army, and their daughter Carinthia would often spend time there when she wasn't leading a glamorous life in Los Angeles. She had become a close friend of Mick Jagger and The Rolling Stones. She took many photographs of them which started her career as a professional photographer. Pandora and I would spend some weekends at Bembridge, and somehow crossing in the ferry and landing on the island seemed a great escape. Mike would often join us and my love for him was as strong as ever, although I now knew it could never be fully reciprocated. My friend Nuala also had a house on the island near the beach, and her two sons, Julian and Rupert, introduced Pandora to their young peer group. I was glad to see her emerging from her shell of grief, and she and I regained the closeness which had existed before Julian's death. Prince Andrew often stayed in a cottage in the same street as ours, but Pandora's lot found him rather boring. I would go for long walks by the sea and sometimes, when the tide was at its lowest, I could walk as far as the nearest fort.

One day, we had a near disaster. Pandora and her friend Tatiana Jenkinson decided to take a small Mirror dinghy out to sea. I was having lunch with Mike, and we suddenly realised they had been gone for over two hours. Later, we started looking out for them but they were nowhere to be seen. Finally, looking through binoculars, we spotted the dinghy upside down in the Solent. Apparently, it had capsized, and they were clinging on for dear life. We called out the Air Sea Helicopter, and the pilots lowered a rope ladder to rescue them. It was a particularly hair-raising business for both girls, as Tatiana was a poor swimmer and couldn't have made it to the shore.

Twelve

In London, Peter was making a name for himself in the House of Lords. As a Lord-in-Waiting, he represented Her Majesty the Queen at a range of meetings and functions. At the Department of the Environment, he was called to chair a Government enquiry into the controversial area of pop festivals, leading to legislation still in force. He also ensured that some of the first wildlife protection laws were passed. At the Department of Trade and Industry, he was responsible for small firms, working with Lord (Harold) Lever on Government policy.

Later he chaired the first national body representing over thirty nations, non-governmental wildlife and environmental groups, and he secured agreement of all the groups and the necessary funding. In the Lords, he led the Labour Opposition on the highly controversial Wildlife and Countryside Bill, seeing through major amendments and working closely with a number of eminent Conservative back-bench peers. He introduced the system of protection for the British leading wildlife sites, which changed official attitudes to ecological protection. This was to form the basis for the European Habitats Directive. As a result, he was asked to be President, Chair or Board member of many of the major wildlife organisations in Britain, from the most established of them, such as the World Wildlife Fund and the Royal Society for the Prevention of Cruelty to Birds, to the more radical ones, such as the Friends of the Earth and the Ramblers Association. He was also a member of the Select Committee of the House of Lords on Science and Technology, as if the preservation of nature needed something more from him.

He and his partner Cassandra had bought a home in Kentish Town, and in 1981 Cassandra had a daughter, Jessica, who was adored by her parents and grew up to be a beautiful and highly intelligent blonde who became a brilliant lawyer. Two years later, their son Jay was born, and, true to his beliefs, Peter had them both educated by the State system. They spent weekends at the Norfolk farm, which Peter had turned into a wildlife sanctuary. The garden is now left to grow weeds, and moles are encouraged to drill holes. Butterflies flutter about the profusion of wild flowers. Nature has taken over from a little order. I must say that his organic methods have greatly increased the number of wild mammals and birds. He has provided footpaths for walkers and their dogs, as long as they keep away from ground-nesting birds.

When I first went again to Courtyard, I was horrified to see my beautifully manicured lawn awash with wild flowers and molehills, and all the beds that had been full of shrubs and roses left abandoned. But Peter explained to me that the farm now had hares and autumn skylarks and lapwings and golden plovers and curlews returning in great number. There were more songbirds trilling in the fields and hedges.

The farm had been praised in many agricultural books for its forward-looking methods. So, as usual, I agreed to disagree. Now I love my infrequent visits, especially when walking through the marshlands to the never-ending beach beyond.

I was beginning to go to more parties and dinners and was constantly photographed and described in Nigel Dempster's column as 'The Merry Widow'. I was extremely upset by this description as I felt anything but merry, but I was making an effort to resume a normal life. After my sister Bunty had gone, her husband Anthony, devastated by her death, had turned to me for comfort. He had always been a clever and amusing man apart from being extremely handsome. He would often accompany me to parties, as Mike Richey was not exactly a party animal. My other close male friend was Hugh Fraser. His wife, Antonia, was now living with Harold Pinter. She had temporarily moved out of Campden Hill Square where Hugh still lived. Shortly after being deserted by Antonia, he had narrowly missed death. An IRA bomb exploded outside his home, killing his next-door neighbour, cancer specialist Professor Gordon Hamilton-Fairley. Hugh had his friend Jackie Kennedy's daughter Caroline staying with him at the time, as she was taking an arts course at Christie's. Some thought the bomb was meant for his car, as the blast happened when he regularly drove Caroline to work. That day, he had been delayed by a long telephone call. His brilliant neighbour's death in his place appalled him.

When Pandora reached twenty-one, I decided to throw a party for her. We thought we'd make the theme 'Black and Gold' and held it at the Orangery at Holland Park with an extended marquee and a raised platform for the Pasadena Roof Orchestra. I actually sold my tiara to pay for it. My friend Elizabeth Anson, who ran Party Planners, helped with all the interminable details involved in holding a ball. She created a glittering black and gold atmosphere, with the ceiling of the marquee hung with a midnight sky-spangled drape displaying a myriad of stars arranged in actual constellations. The round tables were covered with gold lamé surrounded by gold chairs. A couple of Ambassadors and many friends agreed to give dinner parties beforehand, which meant that everyone arrived well-fed and in good spirits. I gave a dinner in the Orangery Restaurant to get things going.

The interior decorator and manic socialite Nicky Haslam wrote: "Arriving guests, Katie Asquith, Diana Phipps, Princess Alexandra, all wearing black and gold were greeted by their hostess, Sonia Melchett, a blonde and molten gold classical column; her scintillating daughters – gilt-headed Kerena (soon to be married to Alan Moorehead's son Richard) in rippling black silk, and Pandora Mond, just twenty-one, her raven hair and flashing eyes weaving circles round her star-spangled black *faille* dress. They greet a clutch of Ambassadors, Spain's, Italy's, the Philippines', Belgium's. Leonora Lichfield, Gioconda Cicogna, Pamela Harlech, Edward Heath, Paul and Ingrid Channon, the Pinters and George Weidenfeld. The atmosphere hums with anticipation and as the orchestra starts up, the dancers take the floor, Arianna Stassinopoulos, Ian and Caroline Gilmour, Fitzroy and Veronica McLean, Benjy Fraser, Nenna Eberstadt, David Ogilvy, Cosmo Fry, Sapphia and Amanda Kinsman,

Lindy Dufferin, Emma Soames and Marcia Falkender. The black 'n deckers and gilt 'n sterners are dancing away under the fantasy stars until a real dawn breaks and all except the memories fade ..."

Soon after Kerena and Richard returned from their Far Eastern travels they moved to a cottage in Norfolk, where they lived for three years and both secured their degrees. But apart from the beginning, this was not a particularly happy period for my daughter. Although being highly intelligent, Richard could be difficult to live with – after returning home late after joining fellow students at the local pub I would get tearful telephone calls, and I felt useless in my inability to help the situation. When they moved back to London, Kerena took an MA at the School of Oriental and African Studies, and they eventually got married in 1980 in the old village church at Ringstead, close to Courtyard Farm, where we celebrated by sitting on hay bales round trestle tables in the barn. They went to Ireland for their honeymoon, and their daughter Lucy was born the following October. But sadly, soon after this, the marriage ended. Richard returned to Mali in West Africa to work for the World Bank and on various projects connected with providing medical aid supplies to the underdeveloped countries. Kay (as we all called her) rented a flat in Wandsworth and returned to working with Mike Richey at the Royal Institute of Navigation. Peter let her have a cottage on the farm which provided her with a weekend escape.

His partner Cassandra was a strong feminist and engaged in various anti-nuclear activities. She had worked on the underground newspaper *INK* in the early 1970s, which led to her qualifying as a book designer and artist. She illustrated works by writers such as Arnold Wesker and John Berger as well as books like *Marx for Beginners* and *Cuba for Beginners*. At the same time, she did freelance work for the Anti-Slavery Society under Jeremy Swift, then Caroline Moorehead's husband. In 1985, she and her daughter Jessie went on 'Babies Against the Bomb' demonstrations. I never found that politics in any way affected my friendship with Cassandra, for whom I have a deep admiration. Always a splendid partner and mother, her strength of character, kindness and beauty were perhaps sometimes overshadowed by Peter's more vaunted exploits.

Pandora was now studying art at the Ruskin College at Oxford and living in a small rented house near Blenheim, which she shared with a girlfriend. We had given up our Bembridge weekend cottage, but still occasionally stayed with Mike and Christine West at The Garland. My London life had become socially active, and 'The Merry Widow' was endlessly appearing in the William Hickey column. My two regular male friends were my brother-in-law Anthony and Hugh Fraser, both of whom wanted to deepen our relationships. But much as I admired them both and needed their friendship, I wasn't in love with either of them and treasured my independence. But when Anthony asked me if I would like to join him in a trip down the Nile in a cruise boat, I was immediately tempted. I had never been to Egypt and was full of curiosity. I don't think I can describe the trip better than Anthony in a poem he wrote me on our return.

There were lunches at Luxor
and dinners at Mina
and canters on camels
across the Medina.
There were visits to temples
and burial places
and outings in gharries
that ended in races.
There were saffron and backsheesh
and dark Moslem faces
and markets with carpets
and crocodile cases.
A stately Nile steamer
A Nubian crew
A neat little cabin
A fabulous view.
There were Cheops and Isis
and Rameses two.
But best of all – for
me there was you.

I was still giving parties at Tite Street and making new contacts. One evening David Frost arrived with a Ugandan Princess, Elizabeth of Toro. Idi Amin had put out a story that she had had sex at Kampala Airport. She was endlessly thereafter libelled in Private Eye as in 'the Ugandan position'. No one believed the story and it was totally untrue. She became a close friend and was strikingly beautiful. Although her tribe was at odds with Idi Amin, she was later made Ambassador to the United Nations assembly. One evening, she brought her mother, a nun, to visit me. Elizabeth was always trying to encourage me to stay with her in Uganda, but somehow I found the prospect daunting. Our friendship lasted, however, and she would always come and see me on her rare visits to London.

Another new friend was Sharmini Thiruchelvan, who came from Penak in Malaysia and was well known because Annigoni had painted her frequently, although he only did the Queen once. Apart from her beauty, she was also extremely hospitable. When in England, she gave parties in her house in Paddington with delicious food, cooked by herself. Another striking lady was Maharani Ayesha of Jaipur, who I had originally met when Julian and I used to go to the Maharajah's parties in Grosvenor Square. In those days, she was very shy and always kept in the background. But after her husband's death on the polo field, she blossomed into the grand Maharani, with an international reputation. Sadly, along with many other high-ranking Indians, she was imprisoned by Mrs Ghandi under the false accusation that they had hidden jewellery and treasure in the walls of their Palaces. They were not told how long their imprisonment would last. When I managed to find out her address, I wrote to her regularly. I invited her to stay with me at Tite Street *when*, and not *if*, she was released. She told me later that, when she heard a plane fly overhead, she prayed she would one day be able to travel to England, but she had only a faint belief in the possibility.

In actual fact, her imprisonment lasted for two years. On her release, she contacted me and took up my offer. She lived with me for three months, sleeping in what used to be Pandora's small bedroom on the top floor of the house. I was hardly aware of her presence, as she had become very reclusive. Every morning, a maid would arrive from her sequestered house at Ascot with a newly-pressed sari. While Her Highness was in prison, the maid would press the saris daily to keep them in pristine condition. After we'd had a short morning chat, the Maharani would wrap a floor-length black cloak around her and go to her various meetings. Sometimes we would have a quiet meal in the evenings, but she never enlarged on her experiences under house arrest. Two years later her house in Ascot was restored to her, and her son, the present Maharajah, was reinstated in the Palace at Jaipur. Near the palace, Ayesha was given a lovely small house called The Lilypool. One day, she invited Pandora and me to stay with her there. This was Pandora's first visit to India and she was horrified by the sights in Bombay of the maimed and begging children wandering the streets. When we arrived at Jaipur, Ayesha welcomed us with her usual charm. To help her diminished income, she had set up a small factory behind her house to make rugs to sell in England.

Pandora and I were taken on a tour round Jaipur and given the customary elephant rides. Ayesha told me that her son wanted to give a party for me. She was particularly pleased, as she hoped this would create a rapprochement between them. They had quarrelled, when she had tried to advise him about the furnishing of the Palace, and he had, since then, not allowed her entrance. It didn't work out as she had hoped. The grand dinner was held on the vast lawn outside the Palace. It was a particularly lavish occasion with each guest having an individual servant to look after their every need.

Each August I rented a house in Italy for the summer. Now that Judy and Johnny Vesty had bought Casa lo Sbarcatello, I had to look elsewhere. Twice I rented houses on the sea at Ansedonia from Johnny Agnelli, the head of the Fiat motor industry. The nearest town was Orbetello on the way to Porto Ercole, where Woodrow and Veruska Wyatt and their daughter Petronella regularly took a house in the hills nearby. Their guests were usually politicians and writers such as the Norman Lamonts, the Peter Lilleys and the historian Andrew Roberts, so there was no shortage of friends in the vicinity.

I would always try and mix the friends I invited with old faithfuls, Pandora's group and a few new acquaintances. The most regular guests would be Derek Granger, the very social Norman Lonsdale and of course Anthony Kinsman and Hugh Fraser (although not at the same time). Ludovic and Moira Kennedy came one year, although Moira with her red hair (not dancing in her *Red Shoes*) and pale complexion, couldn't spend much time in the sun. My friend Marianne Javits, the wife of the Senator, visited and was a great life-enhancer. Antoinette and Marino Guerrini-Maraldi had a flat in the port, and they would often ask a few of us for a trip on their large speedboat. We would visit the island of Giglio where, in 2011, tragedy occurred when the liner *Costa Concordia* hit the rocks before crashing on its side with the loss of many lives. My memory of these holidays tends to blur into one of blissful escapism. Although, of course, it wasn't always like that. We usually had a living-in cook, but not always. So there was a lot of organising and sometimes cooking to be done. People visited from other parts of Italy, and some of my friends would venture inland to explore the various hill towns and ancient ruins. Once, Clare Ward and Tony Lambton brought over their house-party from their magnificent villa near Siena. Luckily, Hugh was staying at the time, and as they were good friends, the day proved a great success, with much political gossip.

Once, for a change, I took a farmhouse in the Tuscan Hills. It had a small swimming pool with a beautiful view. Pandora's friends, Nick Coleridge and Craig Brown, John Scott and Guy Lubbock all stayed again. This time, the boys were fully shod, but just as much fun as before, and after-dinner conversations struck sparks of delight. Unfortunately two friends of Pandora's from Ruskin College were also staying, and after the day when they were meant to leave, they decided to stay on, but to lead separate lives from the rest of the house party – even taking over the kitchen at unlikely times. After a few tactful hints from me as to departing, it was obvious they had decided to be thoroughly bolshy. Mike Richey said he would see to their going, but he failed miserably. Only when Guy Lubbock got them into his car on some pretext and drove them up the long drive past the village to dump them and their belongings (which he had carefully put in the boot of the car) at the side of the main road, did we manage to see the backs of them. But this was a rare occurrence, and luckily our summer holidays in Italy were a great success. I love Italy, and if I didn't love England so much, this is the country I would choose to live in.

Once I drove down to visit Mario D'Orso, who had a house on the sea beyond Naples. He had Princess Margaret staying with him, and there were always paparazzi hanging around and trying to photograph her. She loved swimming, which she did regularly before breakfast, to avoid the press. Mario had a visiting brother who was a Communist, but in spite of this, he and the Princess got along very well. Later Mario went into politics and became a minister in the Italian Government, before the *bunga-bunga* parties that were to come.

Thirteen

Ten years after the death of my first husband, I met my future one. It was at a party in Chelsea given by a visiting American, Eileen Finletter. At the far end of the room, standing with his back to the wall, was Andrew Sinclair. I had twice seen his film *Under Milk Wood*, written by the poet Dylan Thomas, and read several of his books including *Gog* – a strange bardic novel, so I felt somewhat in awe of him. As with most well-known people I admire, I was shy about approaching him. In this case, seeing he was on his own, I went up and said, "I know you're Andrew Sinclair and I've seen one of your films twice." It seemed only natural that we began talking. "Usually," he said, "most people have only read my first novel *The Breaking of Bumbo*. Not the best." We moved to the buffet table and stayed together for the rest of the evening. I was given a lift home by my friend the broadcaster Richard Kershaw, who had brought me. Later, Andrew told me that he thought we were a couple and put me out of his mind.

We met again at a party given for my birthday by my friend, Edna O'Brien. To my chagrin, Andrew completely ignored me, spending most of the evening talking to the beautiful Antonia Fraser. She had recently left her husband, the MP Hugh Fraser, for Harold Pinter, who had been Andrew's neighbour in Regent's Park. But just before leaving, he put a small black ebony rabbit in my hand and wished me luck and a happy birthday. I have carried it with me ever since.

I was hoping that Andrew would contact me, but in vain. Now I know he has a horror of the telephone and was busy rebuilding his house in Hanover Terrace. I read his regular book reviews in the *Sunday Times* and watched him on Ned Sherrin's television programme. In the meantime, I was working for the Social Democratic Party at its Headquarters in Cowley Street, I worked as a fundraiser and chaired the Alliance Ball for several years. But I felt strongly that it had its limitations, as it was the only occasion where supporters of the SDP and the Liberals met. I wrote to David Steel and David Owen to suggest that there should be an Alliance conference similar to the Conservative and Labour Party conferences. This, I felt, would present the nation with the image of a united Alliance ready to run the country with a common manifesto. David Steel replied that he would not be opposed to a joint conference of some kind, preferably for the candidates, but David Owen's two-page reply was directly opposed to the idea. So much for trying!

Pandora, now aged twenty-four, was having an exhibition of her paintings at Gallery 10 in Brook Street, and I decided to ask Andrew to the opening. He fetched me from my home in Tite Street and later took me to dinner at Wheeler's in Soho, where he had once had a flat in the square there. We seemed to have an immediate rapport. He was flattering about Pandora's work, which he rightly realised had been influenced by Francis Bacon and Edward Munch, on whom she had written her graduate thesis at the Ruskin at Oxford. Andrew was a keen amateur artist himself. In fact, Grey (Lord) Gowrie later told me that, when they were at Eton together, he thought that Andrew would choose painting as his career. When Andrew took me home, he refused my offer of a drink and said he would call me.

A few weeks later, he asked me to a first night at the National Theatre, as he was reviewing for the wireless programme *Kaleidoscope* a play there, which he had to comment on immediately in a van parked outside the theatre. Later at my house, we talked about our past lives, and before he left he leant towards me and reached out to put the palm of his hand on mine. Touch Hands Day became a yearly celebration in our future marriage.

Before I met Andrew, I had been seeing a great deal of Hugh Fraser, who wanted to marry me. Much as I loved and admired him, I was alarmed by the thought of our different interests and personalities and spending time at his Lodge, The Island, in Scotland, which I had visited several times. Antonia had made it very comfortable, decorating the main living room in the Lovat tartan. The building was surrounded by a moat, in which the hardier guests would swim. Paul and Marigold Johnson rented a cottage on the estate. As well as a leading editor, Paul was a great walker and also a good landscape painter.

On one visit, I had asked Hugh if we could visit Cawdor Castle, famous from Shakespeare's *Macbeth* because of the witches' prophecy that he would become Thane of Cawdor before being the King of Scotland. But Hugh said the Frasers and the Cawdors had fallen out several generations ago. "But perhaps we'd better bury the hatchet," he said, and I got my wish to meet the handsome Cawdor, who showed me round his ancient home and spectacular gardens.

When Hugh's marriage had broken down, he moved out of his house in Campden Hill Square and took a flat in Kensington. One day he told me he was going to ask Antonia for a divorce so that she could marry Harold Pinter. But when he arrived at his old home, he found Harold alone watching an international Test Match. He offered Hugh a glass of champagne, and it was only at the end of play that he remembered why he had come. Back with me at Tite Street, he said, "I've divorced Antonia – will you marry me?" He had planned a river trip to Greenwich to see an exhibition about the Duke of Wellington. Wandering round the show, I knew the answer would have to be 'No'. I had already fallen in love with someone else.

Although I had continued to see Hugh intermittently for the odd lunch or dinner, I was adamant that I could never marry him. He took the rejection philosophically as was his nature, but his health was gradually deteriorating. In the March of 1984, he was admitted to hospital where he was diagnosed with lung cancer. Whenever I went to visit him, he would smile and then turn his face to the wall. He died in hospital. I flew to his Highland home at Eilean Aigas for the funeral. It was an icy cold day for the few mourners, only his family and closest friends. Antonia had thoughtfully brought a flask of whisky, which she handed round. Later there was a Memorial Service for him, attended by royalty, politicians and friends, at Westminster Cathedral. He had been a popular, controversial and respected member of the House of Commons for many years and will be remembered for his generosity and grace.

In a memorial *Festchrift* booklet to Hugh Fraser by Lord Goodman, the following tributes were written by some of his friends and colleagues. Andrew Devonshire wrote: "I deeply loved Hugh and mourn his passing every day that goes by. In my life I have had far more than my share of the good things but very high among them I count my lifelong friendship with Hugh."

And Eunice Shriver, John F. Kennedy's sister: "He came to America several times when my brothers were running for President, victoriously when Jack won in 1960 and tragically when Bobby was killed in 1968. He caught on very quickly to the essentials of the American political system, and the articles he wrote about these campaigns showed that he understood the candidates, the issues and the idiosyncrasies of the American electoral process. We shall miss Hugh, but his influence on all of us will remain. We shall never forget the lessons he taught us by his life: Truth, Joy, Kindness and Courage conquer all."

Jonathan Aitken wrote: "Some parliamentary deaths pull at the heartstrings. Hugh Fraser's was one of these, for the sudden loss of a courageous, dashing and independent spirit robs the whole House of one of its most colourful characters ... Hugh's great friend, President Kennedy, once defined courage as grace under pressure. This was a quality Hugh had in abundance, and it mingled well with his native Highland romanticism, blending Hugh with a strong, strange, singular and sympathetic character whose memory will be cherished across the valleys of the years."

In December, Andrew asked me to stay for a few days at his flat in Paris by the Luxembourg Gardens. We met at the Closerie des Lilas by the Observatoire. Strolling through the fallen chestnut leaves of the park, I felt happier than I had for the previous ten years. Andrew's first wife, Marianne, still lived in Paris, but their marriage had ended in a *ménage-à-trois* with Derek Lindsay, a fascinating and eccentric writer, with whom she eventually lived. In recounting his past, Andrew told me of his years in Hollywood, rewriting film scripts. He said, on the slippery slope from Harvard to Hollywood, he never knew which direction was right. When successful, he lived in the grandest hotels, and when broke, in a small cabin on Malibu Lake, furnished with *bric-à-brac* bought from Salvation Army stores. He loved the United States, especially the wide open spaces of the West. He insisted we should go there soon and visit some of his old haunts.

The following month, we flew to New York, where my old friend Sam Spiegel had offered us his apartment. The great film producer of *Lawrence of Arabia* once came to a party at Tite Street, bringing with him a young girl, dressed in what looked like a shabby nightdress. Sam took me aside and said, "That's Helen Mirren and one day she will be one of our greatest actresses." How right he was.

In Sam's Park Avenue Apartment, I was slightly overcome by his enormous bed with its mirrored ceiling and walls covered by famous Impressionist artists; also a hot-tub Jacuzzi big enough for a naked fivesome. We were looked after by a butler who was the spitting image of Charlie Chaplin.

One night in New York, Andrew took me to the restaurant on top of the Twin Towers. I looked in amazement at the helicopters flying like dragonflies below me, while the Statue of Liberty was a tiny doll in the river. When he asked me to marry him, I think he knew what the answer would be, and we celebrated with champagne. How lucky we cannot look into the future. The table where we were sitting would in some twenty years' time be a mass of rubble and grief.

Arianna Stassinopoulos (now Huffington) gave a celebratory party for me with her usual lavish hospitality, together with her family and a bunch of luminaries. Flying to Los Angeles a few days later, we stayed with Carinthia West and Ian Gordon. We visited David Hemmings at Malibu Colony. He had starred in Andrew's play *Adventures in the Skin Trade* and gone on to make *Blow-up*. Actually, I found Malibu disappointing, entering the houses on stilts through a dreary back passage, while the view from the front was of a beach much smaller than I'd imagined. "You've just missed Paul Newman jogging," said David's son with pride. Not that I minded too much. To me, Los Angeles is a soulless city, particularly as walking is more or less impossible and limos a necessity. But a visit to the Getty Museum – the largest misplaced Roman villa in the world – was a great event, as was the Chateau Marmont Hotel and the Avenue of the Stars with its handprints in concrete.

After a few days, we hired a car and set off to see the Grand Canyon. The drive was entertaining, but as it was becoming dark, Andrew said his eyes were giving up. He thought it better if we stayed the night in the car and carried on the next day. I was against the idea and, though I'd never driven in the States, I took the wheel and we carried on. Following behind the enormous lorries with their coloured lights from top to bottom was one of the most frightening experiences of my life, but love gives one courage. I was determined to reach our destination, the hotel on the edge of the big drop. The next day was clear and sunny, but we heard that all further visits to the Canyon were being cancelled, as snow was closing in and disappointed tourists were being stranded for miles around. We had been lucky.

There are many ways to see the Canyon – some friends had gone on muleback down the trails. Norman Mailer took his sons by canoe and had some exciting moments rowing against the rapids. We walked down the Hermit Trail on the West Rim, named after Louis Boucher, one of the more eccentric of the American frontiersmen. He and other prospector miners discovered that tourists would give the Canyon a priceless value far beyond digging for minerals.

That afternoon was the climax of our trip. Goethe had once said, "It is impossible to look at the most beautiful sight in the world for more than fifteen minutes." But he hadn't spent thirty minutes in a helicopter diving like a bird through the crags and caverns of the Canyon, which reach up like jagged spires a mile high into the sky from the winding snake of the mighty Colorado below. This portion of the earth's crust has been elevated over a mile above sea level and the 277-mile river, rushing by gravity to the sea. Perhaps nowhere on earth is there such a view, stretching back 200 million years.

Our helicopter pilot was a nonchalant version of Steve McQueen, a match stuck onto his lower lip, cowboy-booted and wearing dark glasses. He teased us as he flew like a Kamikaze pilot towards a mountainous ridge of sandstone, only to swoop at right angles down towards the river, then up into a vast limestone gorge carved like a Greek amphitheatre. There is another Canyon, many times larger, but it's on Mars. We were dazzled by this total impact on our senses, so utter as to blot out all thought. It made me feel the intensity of my life and love measured against the mightiness of the Canyon's perennial existence.

Coming down to earth the next day, we set off west, cruising along the highway at the compulsory 55 mph, or 'double nickels', to save petrol crossing the Colorado Plateau. We stopped at a shack and a sign, "AT LAST – A DRINK IN NOWHERE – BURRO INN", and there a drunk Sioux tried to sell us his Indian cigarette lighter for a dollar to buy a beer. Then, winding over rocky mountains which seemed to contain minerals of every colour, we hit Jerome, clinging to the side of the hill and looking at first sight like the film set for every authentic Western. It was, in fact, founded in 1870 – a prosperous mining town with a population of 15,000. Early in the 1900s the mines ran out and a board went up which read "JEROME – POPULATION 15,000". A line was drawn through it and the number became 10,000 – in turn, another line, and the figure 5,000 – then 1,000, finally 50 and this was crossed out and underneath was written simply – "GHOST TOWN". In the Sixties hippies moved in, and now the board says "STATE HISTORICAL MONUMENT".

Standing by the Grand Canyon

(Right) Kerena after her wedding, in front of the portrait of Sir Ludwig Mond

Andrew with me and Sir Richard Eyre in New York after the gala production of *Richard III*

Pandora and Nick go horse riding as newlyweds

After our wedding in Tite Street

(Right) Merlin and Shula get married

Christina and Bamber Gascoigne with Cassandra Wedd

Taken by Dominic O'Neill at my riverside party

(Left) Lizzie Spender and Barrie Humphries

(Right) The Earl and Countess of Dudley

(Left) Angharad Rees and David McAlpine

(Left) Sir Christopher Lee and Lady Lee

(Right) Sir Peregrine Worsthorne and Lady Soames

(Left) Viscount Bath

We arrived at Cameron and stopped for a coffee at the Indian Trading Post. It was a sadly deserted-looking place with its few wooden shacks. Apart from a Pentecostal church, it looked like a huge junk yard. The only other inhabitant was a bulky rancher, sitting as if in a trance – like a cardboard cut-out. On his lapel a button stated unequivocally "Your Bed Needs Me". He half opened one mean blue eye in our direction. We moved on.

Reluctantly we drove towards our final destination – a date for lunch with Walter and Lee Annenberg in Palm Springs. Walter had been a popular American Ambassador in London and a great host in his Regent's Park Embassy. He now lived on an estate called Rancho Mirage on the corner of Bob Hope Avenue and Frank Sinatra Drive, which a friend described as "a place that God would have had if he could have afforded it." Each plot was a square acre of guarded paradise.

After driving me in a canopied buggy round his miniature golf course centred by a pink pagoda, we were joined at lunch on the terrace by Norman St John Stevas, who was teaching nearby. 'Mother,' as Walter called his wife, then offered to show us their superb gallery of French Impressionists, which even had matching Monet haystacks on either side of the fireplace.

When we flew back to London and my house in Tite Street, Andrew sold his Nash house in Hanover Terrace and made himself an office on my top floor to continue his writing. He was also travelling to Norwich once a week to teach American history and literature to post-graduate students at the University there. He was keen for me to meet his mother Lily, who lived in Bath. He had told me little about her, and I was surprised, when she opened the door of her flat, to see a small, stocky, figure with piercing blue eyes, even brighter than those of her tall son. After the briefest introduction, she began to demand that Andrew perform a few chores around the flat, such as hanging pictures and mending bits of broken furniture. It was amazing to me to see this strong man bend to her will of iron. When I told her I had been to the Royal School at Bath, she suggested we drive there as it was only a mile away. I was astonished to see a medium-sized, uncompromising building, which I remembered as being a daunting and huge mansion. But age shrinks memory and ourselves.

After we returned from Bath, we planned a trip to France to see the Loire Châteaux and the Dordogne. It was an enchanting experience. The sheer beauty of Azay-le-Rideau, surrounded by water; the fascinating Chambord with Leonardo's double helix staircase; Cheverny, perfect in its symmetry; the four alchemic gardens of love at Villandry; the fairy-sweet splendour of Chenanceaux astride the river, almost too miraculous to be believed; the black Virgin and child at Rocamadour; the Beynoc feudal Castle at Périgord, perched as an eagle at roost above the town. We ended our pilgrimage at Avignon, where the bridge across the Rhone was never finished, but you can still dance upon it.

Our wedding on 25 July 1984 was a simple affair with only our family and closest friends there. After the service at Chelsea Registry Office, we were blessed at Chelsea Old Church by the Reverend Leighton Thomson. Our guests back at Tite Street included my old friend Eddy Lord

Shackleton, Jean Galitzine, Dominique de Borchgrave, Nuala Allason, Edna O'Brien, my three children, Peter and Cassandra, Kerena and Pandora, and Andrew's brother Ian and his mother. Andrew had asked two of his best friends with their wives, Bamber Gascoigne and William Plowden. As Best Man, Bamber was going to make a speech, but when he stood up, he said that it was only by chance he had read in the *Evening Standard* in a piece by Nigel Dempster of his wedding role. Andrew had forgotten to ask him. Anyway, with his usual charm, Bamber was unperturbed and proceeded to be both amusing and charismatic. I was in a state of bliss, but I heard afterwards that one of my girlfriends had muttered, "I give it a year."

The following day we went to France to stay for a week at La Voile d'Or at St Jean Cap Ferrat. But our real honeymoon was a month later, when we flew to Rhodes and chartered a small twin-masted yacht, the *Carespa*. We met our bearded Australian Captain Frank and his wife Rosemary. The rest of the party consisted of my niece Sapphia and her boyfriend and Andrew's sons, Timon and Merlin. We sailed across to Turkey with our first stop at Fetiya – a long string of a town dominated by three Lycian tombs carved into reddish-brown iron-pregnated rock. Since my last visit seven years before, it had changed greatly. The old aggressive Turkish officialdom had gone, and we were met everywhere with friendliness and charm.

After a hot and steep climb to see the tombs, we ventured inland to explore the deserted city of Minara, built in the bowl of a mountain. A vast towering rock, honeycombed with oblong Lycian graves, loomed over a perfect Greek theatre. That night we sat at a café, sipping *raki* and cracking pistachio nuts, as we watched the old men smoke their hubble-bubbles. The next day we were guided by a school of dolphins, as we sailed by the wild Anatolian mountains. We anchored at the tiny port of Kas with its two-storied white houses and slender minarets and its crowded restaurants with men playing backgammon and modern Ataturk Mahjong.

When sailing before with Mike Richey on the caique *Pandora*, I had visited Kekova, one of the most spectacular sights on the southern Turkish coast. Andrew and I decided to set off with a local boatman in a small dinghy to visit the underwater city. Two miles of sunken quays, open rock cellars and chambers, underwater stone steps, scalloped hillsides – Poe's Ulalume and his City under the Sea. We wandered round the plundered Lycian tombs on the mainland, and then we took the steep climb to the Ghibelline castle. The fanged battlements contained the smallest theatre in the world – eight little ascending stone semicircles overlooking the harbour. At a tumbledown shack sporting the sign LIMEAN RESTAURANT, we ate an assortment of red, yellow and grey fish grilled over charcoal and we drank the local Kavak wine. But our boatman was looking at the sky. "Sea … problem," he said, and it was.

As we voyaged back to the *Carespa*, the waves broke over the hull of our little dinghy, but our brave pilot crashed, then surfed the sides of the billows, and then he tacked until our safe return. A superior sort of water skiing. The timeless quality, the essence of life on any size or type of craft, had asserted itself. On our gentle sailing westwards towards

Marmaris, the *meltemme* held off, and we anchored at many a sheltered haven along the coast – every bay or headland carrying a sign of the past. The best, however, was when the *Carespa* was edged slowly into a tiny inlet, Skoffa Bay, with still navy-blue water reflecting the mountains around us. The boys searched on the beach for fossils and pieces of alabaster and amphora. That night on shore under the pines, we ate tuna and sea mullet, charcoal grilled with tomato salad, and we drank red wine – a feast fit for Poseidon. A child serenaded us on a *saz*, a type of mandolin. As we boarded, we were followed by cries of 'Gule Gule', ('Go laughing'). Later we slept deeply, drugged by brine and sun and lulled by water lapping on the pebbles.

In the morning, we explored the ancient city of Caunus, which had been ravaged by fire. The huge Roman theatre, which could seat 5,000 people, had Turkish prisoners excavating for the archaeologists. The two harbours are now cotton paddy fields and a marshland for egrets, overlooked by the battlements of a Crusader castle. Every civilisation has looted the stone blocks of the previous ones to build something new.

The *meltemme* was rising with white caps covering the bay, so we sailed back to Marmaris, that cheerful port with Turkish flags flying above the little fort. Kelim rugs were hung out in zigzags for sale, with leather goods and gold jewellery sparkling among restaurants selling fish balls, sea bream, red rock-cod and bass. Hundreds of yachts formed an armada in the harbour, which housed the Bavarian and Austrian Yacht Club, not seen around here since Barbarossa's First Crusade – and *he* drowned.

Our charter ended, as it had begun, at Rhodes. The Aegean seemed to me to offer the essence of adventure, solitude, the precariousness and the constant surprises of every hour spent there. There seemed no entanglements, but only the hope to complete such a simple interval of time.

Fourteen

Back in Chelsea, Andrew and I soon settled into what was to become the future pattern of our married life. By day, we would go our own ways and give each other the space of separate rooms. In the evening we would meet up for supper. Andrew was continuing to write diligently and I was working at the National Theatre and catching up with family and friends. My children had already shown me how happy they were about my remarriage. Thankfully, they all got along with my husband. Being the youngest, Pandora had found it more difficult but, having left Oxford, she was being pursued by a bevy of boyfriends. Soon she found herself a Notting Hill flat, which she shared with her friend Nicky Shulman, elegant and fun as always.

Andrew was reticent in talking about his life before we met, but gradually, by degrees, I managed to learn the salient facts. He and his brother Ian, who was two years older, were born in Oxford and lived in a house in Polstead Road, near where Lawrence of Arabia had written of his exploits. His father, a Colonial Police Officer, was stationed in Africa's Gold Coast, too dangerous for children to go out there before the discovery of penicillin. Andrew was born in 1935, and his memories were not of blitz and ruins, but of shortages of food when rationing was introduced. He had always wanted to be a writer, even at an early age, covering his bedroom walls in scribbles with his mother's lipstick. Both boys attended the Dragon School, and one of Andrew's memories was of playing rugby with Antonia Pakenham, who fought with vigour. He had a photographic memory until he was twelve, and at the age of six he had his first story published in the school magazine, which told of a small boy starving to death.

Unfortunately for Ian, his elder brother, Andrew eventually overtook him academically and got a scholarship to Eton as a Colleger after the war was over. Their mother had returned to the Gold Coast, where soon she and Zinc – as his father was known – got a divorce. For she had fallen in love with a handsome lawyer called Patrick Eve. He had previously been a major in the Coldstream Guards, when he had looked after Winston Churchill at Chequers and had guarded Buckingham Palace. Andrew's holidays were spent with step-relations, who didn't want to be bothered with him, and so his room at Eton College became his home until he won a History Scholarship to Cambridge. He told me he was writing bad poems, although one was printed in a defunct magazine called *Truth*, while also trying to write short stories. He edited the school magazine and, as the Keeper of the mixed Wall, he was put into Pop, a self-elected group of school prefects who dressed in gaudy waistcoats and disciplined the rest of the school.

Before going up to Cambridge, Andrew had to do two years' National Service in the Army. His stepfather had always wanted Andrew to join his old Regiment. So Andrew became an Ensign in the Coldstream Guards, and after surviving the training camp at Caterham, he was posted as an officer to London; this meant living in Wellington Barracks close to Buckingham Palace, which he guarded along with St James's Palace, the Tower of London and the Bank of England.

When his stepfather died, his mother had returned to England in a distraught state, needing Andrew's comfort. Ian, who had been at Rugby, was unable to be of help as he was doing his National Service behind the Suez Canal, where Andrew would shortly be directed. For during his first year at Cambridge and still in the Reserve Army, Andrew was called up to resist Colonel Nasser's grab of the Suez Canal. He refused to go. Instead, he set off to fight for the Hungarians against the Russian invasion. As a child of the British Empire, the intervention at Suez struck him as imperialism and murder, while the Hungarian revolt against Russian control seemed in the just cause of liberty and human rights. But he never reached Budapest owing to the pleading and intervention of his mother. He returned to Trinity College with his tail between his legs. Luckily, he was not court-martialled.

As he said, it was fortunate that he had taken a moral position against the state, for it provoked him into writing his first novel *The Breaking of Bumbo* in five weeks of the Cambridge long vacation at the age of twenty-one. He wrote it as a tragedy, but its many readers fell about laughing at his satire of his Brigade of Guards background – the debutante dances and Royal Garden Parties, Trooping the Colour, the Ceremony of the Keys, the manners of London Society and the Officers' Mess. The short novel was an immense success, written at the time when the so-called Angry Young Men were kicking their way into the Establishment, while Andrew felt he was kicking his way out. He also got a Double First in History at Cambridge, and graduate work in America lured him across the Atlantic. He was given a Harkness Fellowship to do research on Prohibition. He studied under Oscar Handlin at Harvard, where he met a beautiful French girl, Marianne Alexandre, whose mother Denise taught French at Brandeis University. She had come to hear one of his lectures. Eventually they were married by a Massachusetts judge after an obligatory blood test; two strollers off the street were their witnesses. Then they travelled across America from coast to coast in an enormous white Buick, a free gift of the Fellowship, with Jonathan Spence, later Professor of Chinese History at Yale – fellow voyagers sharing the experiences and dangers of the honeymoon on the road.

They returned to England to live in a small apartment in Soho Square. Andrew had been asked to become a Founding Fellow of the new scientific institution at Cambridge, Churchill College. His social history of Prohibition was published and was received well and gained him a doctorate. A career as an American historian opened up. After two years at Churchill College, he spent a year in the United States in San Francisco among the Beats, writing *The Emancipation of American Women*. Then he returned to England to lecture on American history and political philosophy at University College, London.

He and Marianne were soon to meet a charismatic friend of Kenneth Tynan. He was to change their lives forever. He was known as Deacon because of his solemn style and bleak wit. His real name was Derek Lindsay, and he had written a book called *The Rack* about his years in a Swiss sanatorium, while recovering from tuberculosis. I remember being enormously impressed by the book myself, when I read it on publication. Deacon was smitten by the beauty of Marianne and gave her his address and telephone number, an almost unknown occurrence, and she and Andrew became some of the few people that Deacon ever saw. To say he was eccentric was an understatement. His home was his hermitage and proved his biological determinism. On the wall of his bedroom, he maintained the cross-section of a live ant colony, so that he would be reminded of a superior organisation for living. His stories were told with a deprecating humour that confirmed his incurable pessimism about the human race. When I met him with Andrew years later, I was also beguiled by his strikingly saturnine good looks and gifts as a great raconteur of comic gloom.

Marianne and Andrew moved from Soho to the river in London's bombed dockland where they had discovered six derelict houses in Narrow Street. They bought some for a song and kept one for themselves. They also managed to buy a small flat in Montparnasse. But as Marianne became more and more involved with Derek, Andrew decided to write his first long novel, *Gog*, which involved his tramping some two hundred miles without any money along the old right-of-ways across the Borders between England and Scotland. Although he was only playing at being a tramp, the experience was all too true. As he said, an empty belly is no forgery, and sleeping on a moor soaked to the skin is no lie. *Gog* took three years in gestation and another two to write. He ended the book to find he had lost his wife, as Marianne had moved into Derek's north London home. For company, he had an Abyssinian cat called Mishkin, which would sleep on his bed, waking him in the small hours by walking across his face, or leaping through the manuscript he was reading.

His life changed when he was chosen by the executors of the Dylan Thomas Estate to adapt for the stage Dylan's unfinished novel, *Adventures in the Skin Trade*, starring a then unknown actor called David Hemmings, who soon took the lead in *Blow-up*. Tennessee Williams saw the play and pronounced it the best in London. Andrew was then selected to write an original screenplay for a fortune, which he accepted. It was called *Before Winter Comes*, starring David Niven, Topol, John Hurt and Anna Karina, and directed by J. Lee Thompson, who became a friend. Although offered various professorships in history, he decided to concentrate on film and literature. He became a script doctor for Columbia and CBS Films and spent two years travelling between Hollywood, New York, London and Paris. In his own words, he was "overpaid, overrated, overseas and under the weather."

Then another political crisis changed his life, the failed revolutions of 1968. He was in the Beverley Hills Hotel, when Marianne called him from Havana. They had been briefly reconciled the previous year, and she told him she was pregnant and had run away to Cuba to present the child to Fidel Castro and the Revolution. But she had lost her nerve and needed escape. Could Andrew get her out? Their telephone calls were being monitored by the American Secret Service. 'Baby' to the eavesdroppers seemed the code word for 'bomb'. Andrew was being followed by American and French agents, before he flew out to Cuba to rescue Marianne. She had made friends with Eldridge Cleaver and some refugee Black Panthers, who had even become an embarrassment to Fidel Castro. Eventually, he decided to deport them together with Andrew and Marianne. This broke all airline regulations, as she was now eight months pregnant. The baby boy was born in Paris and baptised Timon Sinclair. But although his mother could give up the Cuban Revolution, she couldn't give up her love of Deacon, and Andrew was unable to live under his shadow any longer.

He sold his dockland home and within a week bought a vast Nash terrace house in Regent's Park on a short lease. It was six stories high and had a mews at the end of the garden. As William Golding, a frequent guest, once said, Andrew needed a lot of space to write in. His immediate neighbours were Harold Pinter and his wife Vivien Merchant. His Hollywood career had ended suddenly after his Havana caper – the moguls wanted nothing to do with those who meddled with revolutionary countries. He used all his screenwriting money to start a company, Lorrimer Publishing, to buy the rights of classic screen plays such as *The Blue Angel*, *Greed*, and *The Third Man*. The list grew to sixty titles and sold across the world, teaching how to construct a scenario to all the new directors of the Spielberg generation.

The book *Gog* was always meant to be a part of a trilogy – the story of the struggle of the people against power, of Gog against his half-brother Magog, both nicknamed from the twin giants of ancient Britain who used to guard the City of London, mythologically built by King Ludd. *Magog* was to be a novel about the corruption of power, about a man who joined the Establishment, and about the decline of England in the three decades after the end of the Second World War. Andrew felt he was, himself, half Gog and half Magog, the anarchic fighters for liberty and self-expression. It seemed to him that this was a struggle for some people throughout history that could not be resolved, even in the book intended to complete the trilogy, *King Ludd*. But although he eventually did finish the project, various important events intervened in his life.

Always being a lover of the cinema, he bought the rights to Dylan Thomas's radio play *Under Milk Wood* and made a film of it, directing the three biggest stars of the time – Richard Burton, Elizabeth Taylor and Peter O'Toole. There was magic in the film and a trick, the use of a panning camera which slid between shots so that the sequences appeared as continuous as the words in one wave from the living to the dead, from dream to reality, as if all were in a single sea of imagination. The film was an immediate success and opened the Venice Festival in 1972.

By a strange coincidence, I had seen the film when it came to London's St Martin's Lane theatre. I was enraptured and even returned to see it a second time, little realising that I would one day marry the director. But the success of *Under Milk Wood* was also Andrew's undoing. He was offered other subjects and had to take financial risks. On one occasion, while trying to shoot a modern Faustian legend with Oliver Reed and Orson Welles in Athens, the English stock market crashed and the producer fled. Films were no longer his *forte*, but his ruin.

He married again, Miranda Seymour, fresh from the counties, and apparently the sort of debutante that he had pilloried in *The Breaking of Bumbo*. They stayed together for ten years, filling the emptiness of the Nash house and giving him another splendid son, Merlin, who grew to love his French half-brother. The disaster that Andrew's friends had predicted for his second marriage was a slow one, the story of a woman trying to escape from his shadow and live as a writer in her own right. This, indeed, she accomplished, and she is now a successful writer and reviewer.

To keep financially afloat, Andrew wrote biographies of Jack London, John Ford, the film director, and J.P. Morgan, which meant spending time doing research in America and leaving Miranda and Merlin in London. But he also wrote a biography of Vicky, the eldest daughter of Queen Victoria, later the Empress of Germany for ninety-nine days. For this he was permitted to enter the Royal Archives at Windsor Castle.

Andrew and Miranda had bought a ruined Venetian villa in Corfu in the middle of the island with a view overlooking the valleys beyond. At the bottom of the garden was an ancient Venetian well, which was listed under Government protection. The villagers would walk down the path to fill their pitchers with the pure waters, which created an almost biblical scene. I grew to love the villa, as Miranda had, and I concentrated on creating a syringa-covered terrace pergola, under which we ate all our meals. We spent many a happy August there, filling the villa with our friends and family.

Both ancient wisdom and an Orthodox blessing guarded our house in Corfu. Twice we were awoken in the dark by a true nightmare. Above us, the sound of dragging and squealing on the roof tiles, hidden by the concrete ceiling of the bedroom. Nothing to be seen in the morning. Then our gardener came with his shotgun to Andrew. "Kirios, come!" They went to see a beautiful vision. A red and gold and green python, fifteen foot long, was coiled on the path to our Venetian well, where it lived in the chamber below and feasted on the grey squirrels that climbed our pergola. Taki raised his gun, but Andrew pushed it down.

"Don't," he said. "The snake is far wiser than we are."

He was referring to our friend William Golding's last book, *Pythia*. The python was the spirit of the Greek god Apollo and spoke prophecies through the Pythia, the priestess at the divine shrine at Delphi. Our place was now protected for us.

Then there was the old curse of Kombitsi. The three houses there had been abandoned by their owner, a Venetian Count, because his son had died. Those who rebuilt them were meant to pass away, too – and three of the new owners had. Andrew had survived a thunderbolt through the engine of an Airbus flying away from there, so he decided to have the place blessed. He had bought a thirteenth-century wooden Spanish statue of the Madonna and Child, and he decided to build a roughstone shrine to her under the stairs to the second floor bedrooms. As the local priest and villagers were completing the ceremony to end the curse, the bare feet of the naked oversleeping Merlin appeared on the stairs. Hardly the wings of an angel, but that's how these blessings may be.

Apart from our immediate family, our most regular visitors were Tarquin and Zelfa Olivier, Jean and George Galitzine and Mike Richey. Luckily, Mike and Andrew got on well, as I was sure they would. Mike loved his Chinese rigged sail boat *Jester*, just twenty-six foot overall, slung on an unstaged hollow wooden mast, and without an engine. He had bought it from its designer Blondie Hasler in 1964, by which time she had completed four singlehanded passages across the Atlantic and a patrol of Loch Ness in search of the monster. In the twenty-four years Mike had owned her, she had completed another six transatlantic voyages. One eventful voyage from Bermuda to the Lizard in 1981 included an attack by killer whales off the Grand Banks and a knockdown with the loss of the self-steering gear in the Western Approaches. In 1986, on the way back from Nova Scotia, the boat was overtaken by a storm of unusual ferocity some 300 miles west of Ushant, finally rolled over and was dismasted. She continued the passage on the deck of a banana boat and took considerable damage, which had to be made good over the winter.

Yet, on 15 July 1988, Mike took off from Plymouth. He could not have anticipated what lay ahead. *Jester* effectively sailed herself, and although a reef or a sail and the self-steering gear would have to be adjusted, there was no deck house and life on board became a matter of eating, sleeping, cooking, navigating, and much of the time reading. In

Mike's own words, "There is little to hinder concentration. I generally kept several books going at once, at least one for study rather than recreation that will probably last the whole voyage. On my birthday, the sixth of June, it was a hot day and I spent most of the time shifting restlessly between Teresa of Avila, Proust (the perfect stand-by) and Leigh Fermor's entertaining account of his early years. As usual my diet consisted in the main of spaghetti, rice, lentils and beans with a good supply of onions and potatoes, lubricated as necessary with wine.

"I have always found flat calms deeply depressing, partly because they seem to intensify the feeling of isolation that is always just below the surface; and because there seems no evidence why they should not go on forever, leaving one abandoned and floating aimlessly about the ocean. I suppose a perfectly balanced man, knowing that there is nothing he can do about it, would take advantage of the situation to do all sorts of things about the boat. But I have found it difficult to preserve enough equanimity even to read. One evening later in the voyage, I saw two large fins about twenty yards ahead of the boat and had at the last moment to seize the whipstaff and put the helm over to avoid collision with two whales on the surface, apparently oblivious of our presence. I scooped past them a few feet away. One of them started to follow the boat and then gave it up. It shook me slightly, even though they probably live on shrimp.

"About forty-eight miles from Newport, the wind piped up to about Force 6 or 7 for a few hours during the afternoon. After an infernal afternoon, I wrote in the log,

212

'virtually hove-to under a single panel of sail in appallingly confused seas bursting all over the place in quite alarming peaks, the gale quite suddenly ceased and we proceeded northward under two and later three panels of sail.' On the 13th we were heading toward Labrador. 'Extreme discomfort aboard,' I noted in the log. 'For the past three days every stitch of clothing soaked, every towel dripping, the matches won't strike. If only,' I wrote, 'we could have a fine day to dry everything out.' Morale seemed to have been sagging. By evening the wind had got up again and by midnight it was blowing a full gale from the south-west. I went down to a single panel and then, under the self-steering gear, to bare pole. 'Some of the breakers quite frighten me,' I wrote in the log. 'They come at you hissing, generally just across the wave train, and carry you along for a while, generally on your beam ends. There was not much I could do but wait hopefully for the storm to pass.'

"Surveying the scene from the control hatch, I saw a plunging breaker coming at us from the port side and said out loud, 'Oh hell, here's a knock-down,' as indeed it proved to be. The boat was smashed down to starboard and carried along with mast below the horizontal until we had passed and the weight of the ballast keel brought her upright again. She was full of water with floorboards, books, chairs, sleeping bag and food all floating free. More importantly, the starboard sidehatch had been stove in, totally demolished. The boat was now open to the seas. I became convinced the boat could well founder and that I should need assistance to sail on. I activated the EPIRB. Soon an aircraft from the US Coast Guard Rescue Service flew overhead and I switched on the hand-held VHF on channel 16. I reported the damage and asked whether any ship in the vicinity would be able to offer a tow or hoisting the boat on board. The pilot announced that the MV *Nilam*, a bulk carrier some twenty miles away, was prepared to help and was closing in. When a second aircraft arrived, we went through the extent of the damage again, and I emphasised that the boat could well founder in a gale. I suggested that the ship, when she arrived, should provide me with some water, if possible, some tins of food, and some stout canvas with which to effect a temporary repair. When MV *Nilam* came alongside, she dropped over the stern three barricoes of water, some tins in a large plastic bag, and the canvas. I told the pilot there was no chance of picking up the drop without getting rid of the liferaft and then cast it off, manoeuvring astern of the ship to recover the stores.

"At this stage, the possibility of abandoning *Jester* had never been contemplated. I asked the aircraft pilot to get me a weather forecast for the next seven days to my next landfall, Halifax in Nova Scotia. He said, because of the deteriorating weather situation, both the Canadian Coast Guard in Halifax and the US Coast Guard Centre in New York strongly urged me to terminate the voyage now. This came as a blow. I asked for a few minutes to consider the matter, but I found it very difficult to think with a plane circling overhead and a 60,000-ton ship standing by, and after forty days on the sea on one's own, a balanced judgement was almost impossible. I agreed to accept the Coast Guard's advice and the transfer was effected, the master manoeuvring his ship with great skill. I thanked him profusely, and he told me he would attempt a tow, although he had little hope of success. It was a quixotic gesture, for at that speed a boat of *Jester*'s size could but be towed under.

"In due course, I was given a cabin facing aft and some dry clothes. After a shower, I watched *Jester* through the scuttle at the end of her long tow. I suddenly realised she was getting smaller. I had taken a quick turn on the king post with a hawser far too large whilst getting aboard and, I suppose, it had jumped.

"'That's that,' I said out loud, without emotion, for there could be no going back. But as I watched her recede into the distance, looking as trim and pretty as ever, I realised how much I had loved her. Men personalise their boats as no other artefact. I felt I had failed her, that I should have stayed with the boat. It was one of the unhappiest moments of my life, and a passage occurred to me from the sad soliloquy at the end of Joyce's story 'The Dead', 'Better pass boldly into the other world in the full glory of some passion than fade and wither dismally with age.' *Jester* had been if anything a passion."

Some months later Mike came to spend a few weeks with us in Corfu. He put on a brave face over his great loss, but one day on the terrace he opened out his heart to Andrew and there were tears in his eyes. A lost ship is a lost heart.

I loved Kombitsi, but in the end we decided to sell it as the expense of keeping two homes was proving impossible. Also, try as I could, I had never learnt to speak Greek. Andrew spoke Ancient Greek and was under the delightful illusion that this could be understood by the locals. Much to his surprise, this was not the case. In the end a young hippie from California (a nephew of Lady Porter) bought it on the condition we left everything exactly as it was – even Andrew's worn clothes. Someone told us that when they paid a visit to the villa a couple of years later, nothing had changed.

Fifteen

I have always been a great escapist. Having sold our villa in Corfu, we spent many happy holidays staying at various properties belonging to the Landmark Trust. We stayed twice at the Gothic temple in the grounds of Stowe school. A folly, built by William Kent, it had one great high room which was beautiful, with the light coming in at strange angles. It had two bedrooms in one of the towers with a tiny kitchen in another tower. The Trust had left all the necessities, you just had to take your own linen and as there was no television or telephone, there were no distractions. Andrew finished his book *King Ludd* there and also began to write a biography of Sam Spiegel. I was also writing *Someone is Missing* about the death of Julian, something I had never before been able to contemplate.

Another favourite place was Luttrell's high Tower on the Solent with one room on top of another and views over to the Isle of Wight. Marconi once lived in it and invented radio communications there. One of his first messages was to Queen Victoria before her Diamond Jubilee. We could buy fresh fish direct from the local fisherman, and I particularly enjoyed it because, loving bathing as I do, I could go for long swims in the nearby sea. In fact for me, the feeling of weightlessness and joining a natural element is perhaps the best escape of all, making one feel part of that great ocean which never ends.

The Trust owns many odd places – a converted station, a stone pineapple and even a whole remote island off the South-West coast. The strangest place we rented was a Tudor Castle on the Dorset shoreline. One day, looking out of one of the slitted battlements, we watched a nuclear submarine come into view on its way to the harbour – a sure sign of the horrors of so-called civilisation. But one of our favourite occupations was climbing over the surrounding rocks of the castle and picking samphire, as in *King Lear*, and cooking it for our supper. And there Andrew scattered the ashes of his dead mother.

The most historic place we took was 26 Piazza di Spagna on the Spanish Steps in Rome, where Keats had lived and died. There also Shelley composed *Prometheus Unbound* before he went to Livorno to charter a yacht and was drowned on the voyage south. The flat was extremely atmospheric with various *memento mori* hanging on the walls. But it was rather dark and the noise made by the crowds clambering down the steps towards the Trevi fountain and the flower-sellers could be disturbing.

Andrew wrote me a sonnet there, not to be compared to Keats, which ended:

When youth in jeans with Sonys lounges loud
    We sit above in peace, piazza lights.
Her mouth is Duccio. In one pink cloud,
    We live Assisi-long, Giotto-bright.
If all roads lead to such in Italy.
Then here we move to live, to die, to be.

My three children were all leading full lives and I didn't see as much of them as I would have liked – happy as I was in my second marriage. After being Opposition Front Bench Spokesperson on the Environment for three years, Peter had taken a leave of absence from going to the House of Lords, but he was the Chairman of Community Industry, which was a Government-funded organisation employing 8,000 of the most disadvantaged young people throughout England, Scotland and Wales. He was also a Trustee of the World Wildlife Fund from 1977 to 1984 and President of the Ramblers' Association for another four years. Even more, he was Patron, Vice-President or Council member of numerous environmental organisations involved with wildlife, conservation and nature.

In 1985, Peter and Cassandra and their two young children took a picnic to the American Airbase at Sculthorpe in Norfolk in order to join an anti-nuclear protest. Cass and Pete tried to cut the wires surrounding the base and were arrested. They made anti-nuclear speeches at their trial, but were merely given fines. As the part-time Chairman of Greenpeace in the early nineties, Peter led a successful protest against Shell dumping the Brent Spear oil platform on the bottom of the ocean. This was due to the bravery of the peace activists, who were prepared, under appalling conditions, to climb and board the oil platform and stay there until the protest was successful. Since then, no oil rigs have been discarded in the ocean.

The same year, he took a leave of absence from the House of Lords, becoming full-time Chairman of Greenpeace the following year and Executive Director the year after.

Hereditary peers had stopped sitting in the House of Lords unless elected by their fellow peers. Peter did not stand for election. He appealed against the Government's approval of the Thorpe Nuclear Plant at Sellafield in Cumbria without holding a public inquiry. The judge rejected the appeal, saying that the Government acted within the law, after authorisation was given to discharge radioactive substances into the Irish Sea. The 2.8 billion pound project cleared its final hurdle following fifteen years of fierce debate. Greenpeace sued on financial and environmental grounds as reprocessing spent fuel was uneconomical and would increase the world's supply of bomb-making plutonium and the incidence of human cancer. Peter pledged that Greenpeace would fight on. Action could include attempts to block rail, road and sea shipments to Sellafield. Looking back, we know that Thorpe Plant was indeed uneconomic and is now closed.

In 1999, just before Peter left, Greenpeace asked for volunteers to cut some genetically modified crops at a farm close to Courtyard in Lyng, near Dereham. A mixture of people appeared and were all given white overalls. They included a vicar of the Church of England, a beautician, a forester, and a young science graduate. Peter believed the crops contained genetically modified maize and would pose a danger to other natural crops.

With a farm tractor and pulling a mower, he and the volunteers began cutting the crops. They were soon arrested and taken to Norwich Police Station. Peter appeared before the magistrate along with the twenty-seven others on the charge of criminal damage and theft of maize from the Lyng farm. Releasing the rest, the magistrate remanded Peter in custody for two nights and three days. Peter said afterwards that it was more comfortable than being on a Greenpeace ship and, of course, after Eton, nothing seemed too bad. The prisoners serving the food said they couldn't guarantee it to be non-genetically modified, so they advised him to go on hunger strike.

As the original trial had been for theft, and there had been a hung jury on that charge, there was a retrial on a second charge about nine months later. I attended this – a daunting experience to see my son once again in the dock. But when the verdict was given, Peter was found not guilty of the offence. As he left the court, the crowd outside shouted, "Good for you, m'lud." Peter was not averse to publicity when he was able to put forward his views, and he was endlessly on radio and television and in the Press. When Valerie Grove interviewed him for *The Times* in 1993, she did so at the Headquarters, an urban backwater in Islington. Peter was waiting for her in a wild garden with frogs in the pond, butterflies, sparrow-hawks and kestrels.

"A precious little spot," Peter remarked, almost deafened by birdsong. "Unimaginably on this very site, chemicals were tested on animals. When we first took over the building, a terrible slaughterhouse stench lingered. Some in ICI said three years ago that Greenpeace is ridiculous and unrealistic. The world can't wait around for ten years to see if their hydrocarbons work or not. Two years later, the first fridges rolled off the production line in thousands. And now it's a worldwide commercial business. A new factory in China uses entirely Greenpeace technology. We work with companies to make things happen. It's internationalism. It's commitment to honesty and non-violence – these are the things about Greenpeace which are so precious, really." Valerie left him, as he was off to Glastonbury for the Festival and to hear the Boomtown Rats.

These duties left him little time for his true loves – first his partner Cassandra and then running the farm which Julian and I had bought in Norfolk, and which he had inherited on his father's death. He made the farm into a charity, and his two sisters got some capital from the deal. He and Cass always spend their holidays together, usually staying in small hotels in Cumbria, climbing and sailing on the lakes. Cass, a strong feminist, is a good artist and photographer, winning the prize at the South Bank Photo show called *Make Believe*. She also set up and ran a charity in the Kentish Town Women's Workshop with activities and courses and established an innovative after-school collection service for working women. She took part in demonstrations against the Poll Tax which she refused to pay, and she appeared in court where she made a speech condemning its unfairness. It was later abolished. By this time, Peter had become Chairman of Greenpeace in Japan and also a member of its International Board.

Kerena had always been passionate about volcanoes. Studying the effects of natural disasters at the School of African and Oriental Studies, she visited the largest volcanoes in Australia, Indonesia, Malaysia, Laos, Thailand, India and Sri Lanka. Three years after her divorce from Richard, she married the television pundit Adam Boulton in 1986, and had two daughters by him to join Lucy, Hannah and then Blaise. Sadly the marriage didn't last, and my daughter divorced again. With her love of music, Kerena started to take singing and piano lessons once more and sang in the local choir. She had a great capacity for making and keeping friends and joined three other women on walking expeditions in both England and European destinations.

Pandora had rented a charming mews house off the Portobello Road with her current boyfriend, Nicholas Wesolowski. He worked long hours on 'The Floor' of the Stock Exchange in the City. They had Will Self as a tenant, and Joan and Laurence Olivier's children lived opposite. They soon decided to get married and wanted the wedding to take place in Norfolk. They chose the smallest church in the county, some ten miles from Courtyard Farm, in the middle of a large field. They decided to dress in Edwardian riding habits with Pandora wearing a long skirt, top hat and veil and riding sidesaddle. All the immediate family attended, and we celebrated through the afternoon.

After returning to London, Pandora was able to get on with her painting and had several exhibitions. The first was at Leighton House, where she won the Lord Leighton Award. Her next major one was at the Bartlett Gallery in the West End. After a few years, she and Nick moved to Devon with their child Ludovic, who was only ten days old. Their first home was a tumbledown house called Foxhanger near Taunton, which they converted while they lived in a nearby caravan, as Julian and I had done in Norfolk. As they both loved hunting, they joined the Devon and Somerset staghounds. Two years later their second son, Alexander, known as Xan, was born. Rather like my own premature arrival in India on the steps of the hospital, Xan arrived in their hallway before the midwife could reach them.

After a few years, they moved to a National Trust property called Combe Park on the North Devon coast, where stags could often be seen wandering across their lawn. It was an idyllic life, as Nick was able to work from home as a Hedge Fund Manager. Although Peter totally disapproved of hunting, this never interfered with his love for his sister. In fact, in spite of their differing ideologies, my three children have always remained close and supportive of each other. I am thankful for this when I hear of the rows and sometimes complete estrangement between the children of some of my friends.

Andrew's book, *The Red and the Blue: Intelligence, Treason and the Universities*, was well reviewed by Malcolm Bradbury among others. He exposed the connection of the Cambridge secret society, The Apostles, with the spy ring that gave nuclear material to the Kremlin. Such a revelation did not make him popular at his home university. He also wrote a musical of *The Blue Angel*, for he had worked on publishing the original screenplay with Josef von Sternberg himself. He claimed that he had included the iconic performance of Marlene Dietrich, who was a puppet on his strings. Starring Stephanie Lawrence, Andrew's version opened in Bristol and Brighton to full houses, but it never reached London because the producer went bust. As the last line went, "Kill the lights".

Merlin had passed all the necessary exams to enter Eton, but when he went for his interview with his potential housemaster, instead of answering the questions he was asked, Merlin took it into his head to tell a string of jokes about frogs. Soon afterwards, Andrew received a letter from the housemaster, ending "in spite of your distinguished career here, I never want to set eyes on your son again." In spite of this setback, Merlin obtained a place at Westminster School, where he remained for five years as a weekly boarder, spending most weekends with his mother. Timon was also with his mother, living in France, and studying at a lycée. His holidays were spent with Marianne and Derek in England.

Andrew and I took the chance to fly round the world. He had been asked to give a series of lectures in India. We stayed a couple of nights with J. Lee Thompson and his wife Penny in Los Angeles. At the airport, I left my handbag, containing our passports and all our travel documents in the small bus taking us to our hire car. I thought our adventure had been brought to an abrupt end but, unbelievably, the handbag was discovered intact, and we were able to continue our journey to Australia. After a brief stay in Sydney, we visited Bali, where we luxuriated in our hotel which consisted of a series of chalets with their own swimming pools. Ours spouted its waters from an elephant's head. We only ventured out to see the ballet performed by enigmatic young girls accompanied by a twenty-six piece gamelan orchestra, the men sitting cross-legged behind their gongs and drums. Straight-backed, the girls fluttered their double-jointed figures like butterflies. They jerked their necks from side to side and danced with the extremities of their bodies, using only their eyes to express fear and surprise. As they performed their ancient rituals, they were like animated dolls, their small breasts bound in gold; children with painted faces and trained dancers' bodies, beautiful but soulless. Jogjakarta in Java we found oppressive in spite of the dour magnificence of Borobudur.

After a short stay in Bangkok we flew to what was to be the highlight of our travels, Burma, to spend a week with 'The First Inhabitants of the World'. That is what the name Burma means, and what the Burmese consider themselves symbolically to be. In 1986, Burma was controlled by Ne Win and the Army and the brave, lovely lady Aung San Suu Kyi was soon to be put under intermittent house arrest, but this was unknown to us at the time we could spend there would be one week. We were met at Rangoon Airport by our guide Pansy. Small, with almond-shaped brown eyes, her hair swept back in a tight bun caught by an ivory pin and softened by a fringe, she wore the uniform of all Burmese guides, a pale yellow muslin top and a deeper gold *longyi* with bands of blue at the hem and white flip-flops on her feet. Carrying a neat brown shoulder bag, she had the attitude of a gentle school teacher. She took us to the Strand Hotel, which after our luxurious suite overlooking the river in the Oriental at Bangkok, was a come-down. But the old colonial building, with its high ceilings and fans slothfully whirring, had its own particular charm. The paint was peeling off the walls in pastel colours of pink and green, but the broad wooden staircase was waxed daily and our bedroom and bathroom were large and comfortable.

We wandered out that first evening to visit the Sule Pagoda, said to enshrine a hair of the Buddha. Obviously a popular gathering place, people were chatting, kneeling

226

in prayer or throwing money into the cans attached to an enormous spinning wheel to bring them luck, good health and love. Small alcoves enclosing *Nat* gods surrounded the pagoda. These thirty-seven demons and spirits had to be appeased with gifts of flowers, money and food placed on special altars to avoid their wrath. The state lottery was in full swing, and you could buy a prayer and have it intoned by a priest who had an amplifier to make the words appear to come out of the mouth of the Buddha statue.

With a coach and driver to ourselves, Pansy took us the next morning to see the greatest sight in Burma, the Shwedagon or Golden Dragon Pagoda. We approached the monument by walking up the covered stairway, where two giant mythological figures reminded us to remove our shoes. As we reached the Terrace, we were stunned by the beauty of the golden dome, a hundred metres high and topped by a jewel-encrusted spire, gleaming in the sunlight. We were surrounded by pious Buddhists repeating their Three Gems: "I take refuge in the Buddha. I take refuge in the Dharma. I take refuge in Sangha." The hundreds of lesser Temples and shrines, all dedicated to Buddhas or *Nats* or the guardian animals of the eight-day Burmese week, made an incredible kaleidoscope of spice and colour, tracery and aspiration. Those born on that auspicious weekday were washing the stones. "It is their act of merit," explained Pansy. There were stalls where you could buy flowers for offering to Buddha. Each of us placed some in the shrines of our birth signs, on the Lion and the Garuda Bird. Some holy men were sitting cross-legged in front of a divine statue, intoning prayers with their heads as if in a trance and watched by an admiring crowd. "They have been fasting for many weeks," Pansy told us. Before we left, we paid a few kyats to a squatting man with a cage of sparrows. This fee allowed one small winged creature to fly free from his prison.

Next on the programme was a visit to the Chauk Htat Gui Pagoda, where there is a vast reclining Buddha, white-faced and blue-eyed, apparently a donation from a glass factory. The monks at the nearby monastery welcomed us, and one asked us into his hut and showed us with pride his brightly-coloured lights, which twinkled gaudily round the head of his Buddha. A young smiling boy in a bright red robe brought us tea, lumps of rough cane sugar and a mixture of nuts, rice and papayas. Having seen the washing-up in a ditch outside, we ate nervously, not wanting to offend. The novices start at seven years old, and at twelve they can choose whether to stay on and become priests or return to the secular world. But many people enter a monastery for a few years during their life, and one feels that for all the Burmese, Buddhism is not so much a religion but a code of morality, in an evolutionary process through many states of spiritual development until the goal of Nirvana or oneness is reached. Karma is central to the doctrine of rebirth, not fate as it is sometimes described. Each rebirth results from the acts of merit one has performed in the previous life.

The next day, leaving at five in the morning, we flew to Pagan. There we saw the true pace of Burma, the bullock cart. Pairs of venerated cattle slowly pulled the two great cartwheels which also turned the wheel of life that Buddha used, while the driver squatted until he reached his destination. But our transport that day was a pony cart with bags attached under the horse's tail. Everything had its use in Burma.

On our sightseeing tour, we visited a market and a lacquer workshop, where we bought beautiful red mottled lacquered bowls and plates. All the girls had cream-coloured dabs painted on their cheeks and foreheads, which gave them a slightly tribal look. This turned out to be the bark of the sandalwood tree. They believed it would lighten and smooth the skin. I gave myself a facial later on with some bought in the market, mixing the hard block with water, and it made my skin feel like velvet.

Yet the peak of our time in Pagan was a visit to the holy Mount Papa, said to be thrown on high by an extinct volcano. After a two-hour drive across the dusty plain, we approached the solitary peak with its fairy-tale complex of monasteries, spires and pagodas. Papa was the centre of *Nat* worship, and at the Lion and Dragon gates, before we were to start up the steep, winding and sometimes precipitous covered walkway, we gazed in wonder at the thirty-seven life-size statues of *Nats* being offered kyat notes, coins and flowers. About halfway up, we made our own act of merit. We bought a tiny pewter bell with a heart-shaped clapper to hang on one of the gold-spiked domes. We were told it would clink for ever and ever, a memorial to our visit. At the top, feeling dizzy from the rare air, we saw sacred monkeys squatting by sitting Buddhas, and we decided the journey would have been worthwhile for that view alone. After having visited the Grand Canyon, we thought that we had seen the weirdest and most wondrous marvels of red stone and clay. But we both agreed that Pagan outshone even their majesty.

We flew on to Mandalay, where no flying fishes play, because it is upriver and inland. We did see the Mahamuni Pagoda, famous because it contains one of the true Buddha effigies. We walked to the top of Mandalay Hill, which had over a thousand steps, and we were delighted to hear from our guide that we beat our previous Foreign Secretary, Lord Carrington, to the top by five minutes. That afternoon, we drove over the Ava Bridge, the only one across the Irrawaddy, through Amarapura to the Sagaing, which some consider to be the centre of the Buddhist faith in Burma. With its five thousand monks, it is the ultimate retreat for meditation. Gongs and pagoda bells rang out as we climbed the highest pagoda, the Soon U Ponya Shin, to watch yet another dramatic sunset.

Yet it is Pagan which is imprinted on my mind and in my soul forever, the mighty ruins of a huge civilisation rising from the yellow plain, and the thousands of temples which still survive and are lovingly tended. That was an experience I will continue to absorb long after our Burma journey. Now that Angkor Wat, which I was lucky to see, is plundered, Pagan appears to be the greatest wonder of the Orient. We left with the ease we had arrived and a last plea from Pansy, "Please give my regards to Lord Carrington and your Royal Family."

With their generosity and tolerance, dignity and patience, only vicious when aroused by their enemies, the Burmese are good *Nats*, not quite of this world. Their virtues seem greater than ours, their lack of greed, their generosity and their waiting. For the Burmese the performance of all their daily acts of merit are not just attempts to buy a ticket to a higher plane of existence, as Mr Pereira was trying to do in Norman Lewis's classic account of his Burmese travels, *The Good Earth*. They enjoy their giving and their escape from selfish daily preoccupations.

As we travelled, Andrew and I drew ever closer. Sharing the same tastes in music, art and theatre, we realised we might have brushed against each other in theatres, galleries or concert halls a long time ago. Our chance meeting had been just in time. In his state of despair, Andrew had been thinking of starting a new life in America. He regretted our mutual friends' inept failure at bringing us together much earlier. This gave an urgency to our love and a heightened awareness to every shared moment. At the beginning of my grief for Julian, I had recognised the same intense consciousness. Although Andrew and I were fascinated by each other's past, it was the present and the future which absorbed us. I had heard someone say that loving meant losing one's liberty. The reference must have been to a different emotion. Before we met, I had felt chained inside my own skin. The prison of suffering I had experienced was only a minuscule part of the pain of mankind. Perhaps to tell of it was self-indulgent. But I believe that the only real tragedy is to give up hope, to give in to despair, a sin of the Catholic faith.

The final part of our trip was to end in India, where Andrew was to give a lecture in Delhi. But he insisted we travelled on to Nainital and visit the hospital where I had been born. We stopped at Udaipur on the way to my birthplace. As we drove through the noisy, dusty streets, nothing seemed to have changed since my childhood. The stacks of fruits, nuts and spices, the thousands of bicycles, the cows allowed to wander freely through the traffic, bullock carts pulling sugar cane, the bright saris of the erect women carrying water jars and bundles on the heads. The life of India was on the road in continual frenzied movement. Our driver told us it was Purnima, the Festival of the Full Moon. As we crossed the bridge over the River Ganga, we watched the thousands of Indians flocking to the banks for the ritual washing away of sins.

My mother had painted such a romantic picture of Nainital, high in the Himalayas, that, when I saw how run down it was, I was bitterly disappointed. There was a BBC television crew shooting a film about Jim Corbett, the mighty white hunter and local hero, whose claim to fame was the single-handed killing of man-eating tigers. The Swiss Hotel was very full, but the charming old proprietor had kept a room for us in a tumbledown annexe. An icy wind blew through the broken fan-shaped panes of glass above the door. That night with the full moon shining through the dusty broken panes, we clung together for warmth in the freezing room.

The next day, we found the green-gabled Ramsay Hospital on a steep hill overlooking the lake. I wanted to find the record of my birth and to know the exact time for my horoscopes and for fortune tellers. But the old Registrar in his seedy blue tunic was doubtful if he could find anything. In the small office, there was a Dickensian chaos, thousands of papers piled higgledy-piggledy in alcoves, on shelves, in boxes or buried in drawers. Birth and death certificates, all mixed up together. But eventually, with a triumphant flourish, he produced a piece of faded paper. "Female infant – born on steps of hospital to Mrs Graham, wife of Capt. R.H. Graham, RAMC, stationed at British Station & Hospital, Agra." Sadly, no hour of the day or night was inscribed. Maybe I would never be able to discover my future in horoscopes, but we both felt a strange sense of fate. Andrew had taken me back to where I had been born. Now we could continue our journey into India and each other.

After having resigned from the Royal Court, I was given a farewell party. My years there had seen the growth of some of the most charismatic young actors and directors, and it is still considered the most *avant-garde* theatre in London. The tiny Upstairs Theatre only held about eighty people, but it put on some controversial and futuristic plays, which usually transferred successfully to the main venue below. I had thoroughly enjoyed working there and was slightly daunted by the idea of my move to the National. However, my good friend Lois Sieff had made the same move three years earlier, and she was my guide and mentor and showed me the ropes.

When I joined the Board, it was under the chairmanship of Sir Max Rayne. He and his wife Jane had been friends of Julian and myself for many years. The Artistic Director at that time was Sir Peter Hall, and he would briefly join in on the meetings. Dame Judi Dench was on the Board, as was the director Nicholas Wright, Tom Stoppard, Richard Eyre, Sir Peter Parker, Lady Plowden, and Sir Derek Mitchell. The theatre had been designed by Sir Denys Lasdun. Most people found the building a concrete monstrosity, but inside it functioned perfectly well. With its three theatres, bookstalls, restaurant and cafés, all the people who worked there were full of praise.

Max was a forthright chairman with strong views. He had an ongoing battle with the Government for their lack of funding for the Arts and our theatre in particular. A charming and brilliant man, he would plough through the agenda with great thoroughness for a couple of hours. One change he pushed past the Board was for the theatre to have 'Royal' prefixed to its name. Many members were against this, but Max eventually had his wish crowned.

Four years after I joined the board, Lois Sieff and I organised a gala in the presence of the Queen and the Duke of Edinburgh to celebrate the 25th anniversary of the theatre. The play was Peter Hall's acclaimed *The Tempest*, and the evening was sponsored by the *Evening Standard*. I had run galas before, but this had to be particularly special, and Lois and I got together a high-powered committee of fifty people, including Lord Olivier. Luckily, the evening was a complete sell-out and raised much-needed funds for the National Theatre Foundation, which helped to support the Studio Theatre and the educational programme as well as coping with cases of hardship within the Company. I was very touched to receive a personal letter from Max Rayne ending, "the party was quite the finest of its kind and I believe it will set a benchmark for all such occasions in the future. Certainly I shall never forget it."

When Max retired as Chairman, he was succeeded by Lady Soames. Before occupying the post, she came to see me at Tite Street to ask my advice as to whether she should serve. When I asked her how much she knew about the theatre, she replied, "Not much because Christopher hated going to plays." However, she proved a quick learner and an excellent chair. Knowing that council meetings had previously taken rather a long time, she arrived on her first day brandishing a rather large round nursery clock, which she set for exactly one hour. This was always the schedule. She had insisted on having an office in the building, and she soon got to know the names of all the people who worked there, as well as the Council Members. When plays were taken abroad, she always accompanied the cast, and soon she learnt more about the workings of the theatre than I had believed possible. With her Churchillian sense of humour, she was also extremely popular.

Richard Eyre had now taken over from Sir Peter Hall as the Artistic Director, and he and Mary made a truly remarkable partnership. He wanted to stage *Richard the Third* starring Ian McKellen in New York. He asked me if I would go ahead and make all the arrangements. I spent three weeks in New York, setting up a Committee and organising fundraising. I was greatly helped by my friend Nan Kempner, a director of Christie's and a popular socialite. The play was to take place at the Brooklyn Academy of Music. Andrew joined me in New York and spent his time seeing his agent and publishers. His latest book, *War Like a Wasp: the Last Decade of the Forties* had been published in London by Hamish Hamilton to great acclaim, but he was almost better known in the United States than in England. It was great to have his support and luckily the play turned out to be a success.

After the last night, we celebrated with Richard Eyre and the cast in a nearby restaurant.

In the November of 1987, Queen Noor asked us to spend a fortnight in Jordan. She had been introduced to me by Julian's god-daughter, Carinthia West, who had been to school with her when her father Mike was stationed in Washington. When Queen Noor was on her own, she didn't live in the main palace, but in a charming summer mansion by the sea. We were met at Aqaba by a palace official and taken to the King's Suite at the Holiday Inn Hotel. The Queen said she would put a car at our disposal to visit all the sites and would give a dinner for us a few days later. The next day, after a cold sea swim, we were collected by a driver who took us to see the great Canyon Wadi Rum, made famous by Lawrence of Arabia. After showing us the enormous crevasse, he took us to tea in a tent with some Bedouin. A speedboat trip had been organised to ferry us to Pharaoh's Island to see its ancient castle. We picnicked on board and on the return we had the fright of our lives. An Israeli gunboat had decided to track us, as they often did, and we were knocked all over the cabin as our skipper zigzagged the waves to avoid crashing into the Israeli craft.

That night we dined with Queen Noor at her summer palace. She had her American sister staying, and afterwards we sat beside a bonfire on the beach to the delight of her children. Under control, we were taken the next day to the Forum Hotel in order to see the greatest sight of all, Petra. We decided not to take the offered mules, and we walked through the Siq, the vast crack in the sandstone cliff, and up to the Dier Monastery. It was an extremely strenuous climb to reach the top, which we were determined to do. This may have been a mistake, as my knee hurt coming downwards, which proved much more difficult. As my leg was too painful, Andrew set off alone the next day, and I was given a massage by the Assistant Manager of the hotel, but I had to call a stop to that, as it was becoming a bit too personal. We continued to explore Jordan, driving down the King's Highway, visiting Jerash, Pella, Karak and the ancient mosaics of the Holy Land at Madaba, but Petra was supreme. Andrew was moved to write another poem about a beauty impossible to describe:

Slivers of colour pick
    The spectrum bare –
Rainbows in cave and nick
    Make gaudy lair.

The wind and sand throw odds
    To shape each slope
And scarp away for God's
    Kaleidoscope.

Vision divine of Blake
    Imprinted is –
Each cliff and rock and flake
    Infinities.

Dazzle of hue, so grim,
    Frantic and worn.
Time fritters man. Praise Him
    That we are born.

To see blaze and veil of light,
    High sacrifice,
Dark Siq and Wadi bright
    And paradise.

With her in Petra is
    A sight of bliss –
A Heaven too soon is this –
    First obsequies.

When King Hussein and Queen Noor visited England in September the following year, we gave a party for them at Tite Street. They were two hours late, as the traffic had delayed their return from a visit to their daughter at University. I was getting very nervous and could see that Harold Pinter was trying to persuade Antonia to leave. Luckily, they arrived full of apologies and charmed all our guests. In the morning, Andrew received a long letter from His Highness, apologising for their later arrival and thanking us profusely for the dinner, and he went on to write: "In answer to your question as to how one succeeded in leading three million people, all I can say that it was the confidence, trust and support of the people of Jordan that enabled us to weather many storms in a turbulent part of the world and to stand for justice, peace, stability and progress for all Arabs and a better future for generations to come. If many people in the world have been kind enough to recognise our dedicated attempts, it is a reason for our deep appreciation and gratitude. I have personally only striven to be able to live with myself in all I have done, and sought only to be remembered well, hopefully by Jordanians, Arabs and others long after I have gone. I hope that you and Mrs Sinclair will know by now that both Noor and I are always happy to receive you amongst us as honoured guests and friends." And the letter was accompanied by a beautiful present of an inlaid ivory and mother-of-pearl backgammon set, a true work of art.

When I married Andrew, I soon realised I had married a polymath. He would normally have one or sometimes two books published every year as well as writing reviews for *The Times*. His publisher was usually Christopher Sinclair-Stevenson and they became close friends. Andrew is not a particularly social animal, and I think if it wasn't for the fact that I am fascinated by people, he would be content to be alone with me and just keep in touch with his closest friends. Apart from writing, on which he will spend several hours a day, his other great interest is making musical boxes. When living in Paris he had collected everything from postcards to memorabilia, usually from before the First World War. He has had several exhibitions, and in the catalogue of the Redfern Gallery in Cork Street, his foreword stated: "We have collected the important things in our lives from the beginnings of our cultures. From the ancient burial tombs to the Baroque Cabinets of Curiosities, which have led to modern museums, we have put our fond and found trophies in boxes, large and small. In the tradition of the French *automates* and Surrealists and the American Joseph Cornell, Andrew Sinclair shows us a fantasy history of his century as well as of his life and times." In the end, he found that making boxes proved more personal than creating movie sets or writing books. I didn't mind when he stopped to collect interesting pebbles from the numerous beaches we visited, but I remember getting rather annoyed when I saw a tiny ivory elephant I had brought with me from India nestling in one of his creations. Luckily, he is never bored and never boring.

He persuaded me to start writing again, and with my passion for travellers, I began to write *Passionate Quests*, a book about five remarkable women: Clare Francis, a single-handed trans-Atlantic sailor, before she became a well-known writer; Elaine Brook, a mountaineer who later married her Sherpa; Christina Dodwell, an intrepid lone voyager; Dervla Murphy, an adventurous traveller and cyclist, sometimes accompanied by her small child; and Monica Kristensen, who led a three-man team and twenty-two huskies when attempting to follow in Amundsen's footsteps to the South Pole. I became totally involved with the women I wrote about and made some friends for life. But it was a difficult passage for me. I found it completely absorbing and, even with a tape recorder, very time-consuming, particularly with Dervla Murphy, who had written so many fascinating books herself. Since then I have stuck to short stories and some journalism. Until this book, of course.

My close girlfriends are very important to me and hardly a week goes by when I don't have lunch and a heart-to-heart with one of them, either at their homes or in a restaurant. Dominique de Borchgrave, a Belgian Countess, who had lived most of her life in London, was one of my dearest. She was excessive, highly intelligent and mad as a March hare, dancing to the moon. There was never a dull moment when we spent time together. Before Andrew and I married,

Dominique and I had been to a party in the country given by Bubbles Rothermere, and when we arrived back at Cadogan Square, we were told there had been a bad fire in her flat and it was uninhabitable. While it was being repaired, she came to live with me at Tite Street, staying in the same room Ayesha Jaipur had found refuge in years before. In spite of the chaos she created, we became even closer friends.

I suppose the friend I have known longest is Jean Galitzine, as we were both working together after the war in Germany in the Control Commission. Her husband George had worked for Julian in the steel industry, and Jean and I have a great deal in common. When her daughter Katya got married in St Petersburg, Andrew and I travelled there for the wedding, together with Kerena and Pandora. Through a great deal of hard work, Jean had managed to get an old Galitzine palace restored and turned into a superbly stocked library, which had been opened by Prince Charles. Books had been donated from all over the world, and it became quite a centre of the life of St Petersburg.

Another dear friend was Angharad McAlpine. As Angharad Rees, she had acted in Andrew's films *Under Milk Wood* and *Dylan on Dylan*. She will always be remembered for starring in the television series *Poldark*. When her marriage to Christopher Cazenove ended, she lived in a large flat in the Bayswater Road and gave amusing and delicious buffet parties. She had two sons, Lynford and Rees. Sadly Lynford, the eldest, was killed in a tragic motor accident when travelling home from his university, which left her heartbroken. Luckily, she later met the great constructor David McAlpine, and their marriage proved a brilliant success. Our friendship meant a lot to me, and when we met for lunch, we would always start with a glass of champagne – maybe followed by another. Her death of cancer at an early age was a terrible shock – one of the most sympathetic and beautiful women I have ever known.

I don't normally drink at lunch, as it makes me sleepy, but I love sharing a glass of wine with Andrew before dinner in the evening. Whatever we read about the dangers of alcohol, I'm afraid I find it oils the wheels of life and makes one unwind. Being basically a shy person, I don't think I could manage socialising without the odd drink. But I do try and have two or three dry nights a week. When I was discussing drinking problems with Melvyn Bragg, he said he didn't know how I managed it, but he confessed that he went on the wagon for a week every month. I've always been neurotic about my weight and have a strict rule to stay between 9½ and 10 stone. If I do go over my limit, it sends me into paroxysms of self-disgust, and I immediately go into a reverse gear until I can fit comfortably into my favourite jeans. I used to spend the occasional week at a Health Farm, but the expense seems out of all proportion, and now I use my local gym and swimming pool.

Every year we were invited to stay with Ricky and Sandra Portanova at their majestic Villa Arabesque in Acapulco. The first time we arrived, I could hardly believe my eyes. After the security gates were slowly opened, we approached the place past a herd of enormous concrete camels, all facing in different directions. With a Mexican staff dealing with our car and luggage, we were seated in a tiny tented railway, which took us down the cliff face to the level of our bedroom. The villa had eighteen suites, all built into the side of the rock, with a waterfall tumbling past a swimming pool which overlooked the Pacific. There were no corners or straight lines – all was curved or arched in the Moorish fashion. Guests could walk up or down beside 'Sandra's River', flowing over blue mosaic. Ignoring the pool, they could swim in the sea below. That first time, we were given the Jungle suite, where white lamé elephants with jewels in their foreheads trumpeted mutely above our double bed, while a huge lion rug on the floor lay ready to scratch our naked feet. We were told that Ricky had created this fantasy with a resident Italian architect over a period of thirteen years.

Sandra was a wonderful hostess and immediately made one feel relaxed. She was beautiful, with looks like the star Ava Gardner. But I had to be careful not to admire any dress or jewel she was wearing or she would immediately whip it off and give it to me. She turned every meal into a work of art – always in a different part of the villa – sometimes in a cove or a tented alcove. Each meal had a different theme with matching napkins, glasses and centrepiece of curious designs. Her guests were sometimes friends from London, the Michael Yorks, Joan Collins, Bobby and Didi Buxton, Simon Howard from Castle Howard, where *Brideshead* was made as a television serial. Film stars looked in, Tony Curtis, Kirk Douglas and Sylvester Stallone, also Roger Moore and the charming opera singer Placido Domingo.

When Frank Sinatra came to stay, however, he didn't know what he was letting himself in for. Ricky had made friends with a small basking shark, caught by a local fisherman. Pools had been built in the rocks to catch the deluge down the cliff. Ricky had put the shark in a pool and fed it with steaks and cutlets. It became his constant companion in his late nights. But Sandra thought it was cruel and wanted Ricky to release it into the ocean. For days, she brooded on how to separate the new companions. One night after a particularly delicious dinner of ceviche of shrimps, clams and conch marinated in lime, followed by langoustines and quail and mango sorbet, she and Ricky took Sinatra to meet the friend in the rock pool.

"Why don't you turn him loose?" asked Sinatra.

"But he is my guest," replied Ricky.

"What would you take to release him?" asked Frank.

Now Ricky knew that there was one thing that Sinatra would never do. He would not sing at private parties.

"Sing for your supper," Ricky said. "And the shark goes free."

Sinatra scowled. Then he looked at the shark, now floating like a tea-tray with a carving-knife on top. Round and round it skimmed the small pool with nowhere to go.

"You've got it," he said. "I sing and he swims."

So Sinatra sang at the dinner to the guests that night. And when his songs were done, Ricky turned on the pumps until a flood spilled over the cliff top. Then he pressed the switch for the release gate, and a cascade flushed the rocks and the pools, scooping the shark down to the sea inlet below.

There were tears in Ricky's eyes.

"I know he will come back, he is my friend."

"No," Sinatra said. "He needs the sea and other sharks."

244

For three days, the few swimmers in the sea would paddle back to the beach because a small shark came up to put its nose in their hands, as if they had something to give. But on the fourth day, the shark did not appear, and never did again.

Among its other splendours, Arabesque boasted the only private paddle-tennis court outside Marbella. In this outdoor game, a cross between squash and racquets, the balls could bounce off the back walls before they were swatted back over the net. Once when we were staying, Henry Kissinger would come over to play with such aggression that he might have been bombing Vietnam. Sandra gave him a lookalike doll, complete with a tiny paddlebat, and his tall wife Nancy a golden bracelet set with rhinestones. Talking to Andrew, he was generally gloomy about the state of things, particularly pessimistic about Gorbachov and *Glasnost*. Nothing would change in Russia.

He would prove wrong about that, as he had been about the war in Vietnam. He still believed that America could have won the war with another hundred thousand more men and the bombing of Hanoi. Too little was done too late, because of domestic opposition. His most significant remark was, "Nixon – or should I say *I* – decided to mine the port of Haiphong." His accent was still Germanic and guttural. When he was forging American foreign policy, he was kept off the media in case the people thought a European was representing the country.

The most traumatic happening while we were staying at Arabesque was in 1995. Every morning, our breakfast was brought to us in our gilded tent, and with it a Mexican paper translated into English. On this particular day, the headlines

245

stood out like a bad omen. "Queen's Bank Bankrupt". The article went on to describe how a rogue trader working in Singapore had somehow managed to bankrupt the main part of Baring's Bank. My shares left to me by Julian comprised the main part of our income, so the headline made quite an impact. Andrew and I looked at each other. "Well, I suppose we could always hire ourselves out as Butler and Maid," I said. "Or take in boarders like the Queen may have to do at Buckingham Palace."

When later we wandered down to the pool, we found all the guests looking away from us in silence. The nervous laughter that greeted us was decidedly insincere. Later, when I telephoned London, I heard that my shares were in a separate part of the Bank, and I would suffer no loss. But the other guests couldn't understand the way we had taken the news.

Great wealth creates thieves. Lawyers intervened to deal with trustees and bankers and even family affairs. Ricky began to slip into the paranoia of his younger brother Ugo, unfortunately a schizophrenic who became a ward-of-court. Ricky had cause. There was a mysterious fire at his mock-Regency mansion in Houston. And there his groom was mistaken for him and had the back of his head blown off by a rifle shot through the window. There was a poisoning attempt at a major London hotel. One year Andrew and I were both struck down by a temporary paralysis in our legs from toxic food or water. Soon after our stay, we heard that many of his staff of seventy had been fired.

Ricky's growing mistrust could well have been also related to his and Sandra's health. In 1999 Sandra was told she had an inoperable brain tumour and had only three or four weeks to live. Ricky flew to be by her side and fell ill himself. He would not eat and chain-smoked in spite of his damaged throat. An observer said, "He let himself go and died." Sandra was never told that Ricky had gone, but she lapsed into a coma and passed away soon afterwards. Their wish had been to leave their fortune to the orphans of Acapulco, but this was not done by her brother, who inherited Arabesque and the estate. The generosity of spirit of the Portanovas matched their noble hospitality – there will never be a couple quite like them.

One year when we had left Sandra and Ricky, we decided to visit Peru, as I was avid to see Machu Picchu. We stayed for a couple of nights with Emanuel and Gwen Galitzine, George's brother and his wife, in Lima where Emanuel was working. We visited the Gold Museum, where Andrew bought me a ring and earrings. The next day, we flew to Arequipa, which we found disappointing, but we had a delicious dinner washed down by Pisco Sours, vodka made with grapes. Everything in Peru is a bit chaotic, and when we tried to get to Colca Canyon, the bus didn't turn up, but Andrew made friends with a charming man called Mr Holly, who took us in his blue Jeep to Toro Muerto Canyon to see the petroglyphs, the stone tombs of the long dead in the desert. We were told the Shining Path guerrillas might be there, but they were not. We then left for the very high Cuzco and its mighty Cyclopeian masonry, where we drank coca tea to survive the breathlessness. We took the train to Machu Picchu, although we could see little through a swirling mist over the mountains. At dawn, we did see the Sacrifice

Stone pointing towards the sunrise. And we climbed from the Inca city up the pinnacle of Huayna Picchu. The steep winding path was so narrow that a German tourist had fallen off the day before. Near the top, I pushed the tiring Andrew through a hole in the Altar Shrine. We reached the top to admire the spectacular scene, but goodness knows how we scrambled down. Later we got the *altiplano* railway, which went on forever until we reached Lake Titicaca, where we took a boat round the floating islands, built on balsa and tortora reeds, which could be used for thatch, bedding or boats. On the far side of the lake, there had been a railway all the way to La Paz, but it was gone to rust, so we had to take buses to see Tiahuanaco with the most ancient stone arch in all of South America, the cradle of its old civilisations. From La Paz, we flew back to London, but we found it difficult to leave these fascinating cultures and return to the modern realities at home.

Sixteen

Soon after we returned to London, there was a party at the Redfern Gallery to celebrate the publication of Andrew's biography of Francis Bacon – *His Life and Violent Times*. Apart from our family, there were many friends – Patrick Procktor the artist, Freddie and Sandy Forsyth, Jane Asher and her cartoonist husband Gerald Scarfe, Bamber and Christina Gascoigne, Bron Waugh, the Oliviers and Verushka, Petronella and Woodrow Wyatt. Stephen Spender said that he used to drink regularly with Bacon, a lifelong friend. "We would meet for dinner and get horribly drunk. It was a kind of sacred thing, getting drunk with Francis. I do not drink very much but I knew that, if I went out with him, we would be ranting until three in the morning. He would be very good until three and then he would proceed to tell you what he really thought about you."

While researching the book, Andrew saw Bacon many times, mostly in his tiny studio in Kensington. He believed him to be the greatest living painter and the most important British one since Turner. He felt he shared the aloof intuition of the French romantics like Baudelaire. "He had the nihilism and gaiety of certain eighteenth-century minds. Nature was threatening and monotonous, noctambular urban life was his territory. Like Samuel Beckett, Bacon was 'an artist of endgame'."

I well remember the last time Andrew and Bacon met. It was at Groucho's club. He told Andrew that the visual imagery of Eisenstein's films of *Strike* and *The Battleship Potemkin* had much influenced his paintings, particularly those of screaming faces, especially those of the Popes. They discussed Aeschylus, and Bacon quoted a favourite line, "The Reek of Human Blood smiles out of me." He rebuked Andrew for writing in his book *War Like A Wasp* about the culture of the 1940s, that he had said, "The Reek of Human Blood spills out of me." He added, "Spills is so weak and it ruins the metaphor." Profound and discerning he was, however much he tried to disguise it. Andrew told me that although eighty years old, he looked like a pantomime Principal Boy. "His spiky hair was brown with Kiwi boot polish, he wore a loose shirt with britches, tucked into high glossy boots." They drank four bottles of champagne in four hours, paid for by Bacon from a roll of fifty-pound notes, his weekly allowance from the Marlborough Gallery. He despised money and only used it for lovers, friends and gambling. At the end of the session, Francis sprang to his feet, leapt upright as if on spring heels, and made for the exit, leaving Andrew at Groucho's decidedly the worse for wear. He told me that when trying to make his way home, he managed to get into the Tube on a downward moving escalator, but he sat down on the step, unable to rise. A kind commuter lifted him up before he was caught up in the machine. Lurching eventually back to Tite Street, he took to his bed to sleep off his last encounter with the great artist.

I had had my portrait painted several times, though luckily not by Bacon, and when Felix Topolski did my portrait, it was in his underground studio in one of the brick arches beneath Waterloo Bridge. Soon after the Bacon incident, Felix's son Dan and his wife Suzie gave a party in their flat in North London. This was an extremely jolly affair, and we left after midnight. As Andrew was helping me into our car, a black girl came screaming down the street, pursued by four black hoodies. "Help me," she cried and Andrew did, pushing her into the rear seat. He then turned to face the avengers. He stuck his thumb out in the side pocket of his jacket to look like a hidden pistol barrel. The hoodies halted their pursuit, yelling obscenities at him as he backed against the car. He had seen too many gangster movies, but so had they. "You've got two minutes," Andrew said. "The fuzz is coming." The shouting gang offered him crack and mayhem, but all Andrew said was, "Now you've got one minute," and slid into the driving seat and shot away, taking the still-shaking girl to her destination. Andrew always acted on impulse and perhaps had seen too many films, but it always frightens me that one day he will overdo the pretence.

We had started what was to become a yearly event, and that was to give a Christmas party for all the members of our joint family and close friends. For those who lived in the country, it was usually the only time they all met up together. Decorating my small golden Christmas tree, surrounded by crackers and a lot of twinkling candles, was something we both dreaded and loved in equal measure. Andrew was always in charge of the holly and collecting the helium-inflated gold balloons. The smallest children got presents and the rest had quantities of pink champagne and canapés. This was the only time Andrew saw his brother, Ian, who lived in Devon and rarely visited London.

Many articles had appeared over the years in various magazines about my attributes as a famous London hostess – some way over the top, but pleasing nevertheless. One piece written about me was by Nicola Shulman for Nicholas Coleridge. "Sonia Sinclair has been well known as the best and kindest London hostess. When she throws parties at her house near the Chelsea Embankment, she fills the room with politicians, actors, writers and royalty, but always makes sure that the less distinguished guests are enjoying themselves." She continued in the same flattering style. But what I liked about the piece was the approbation of kindness. I believe that some people who throw parties, be they lavish or small, feel that one should be pleased to have been asked at all and leave it at that. I have been to parties where I haven't even spoken to the host or hostess, let alone been greeted by them.

Many of our friends gave annual parties, usually during the summer months. One to be anticipated was the Spectator Party, originally given in their offices in Gower Street. A number of the Great and the Good, politicians and writers and journalists, crowded together in the small garden, sometimes escaping to the upstairs floor. The atmosphere was crushed and electric. Spilling over onto the pavement outside as the noise escalated, the political and bitchy arguments grew in intensity. Cabinet Ministers and occasionally Prime Ministers would come and go. A 'must' in the social calendar.

David and Carina Frost's annual cocktail party was given in the communal garden opposite their house in Carlyle Square. Always patrolled by the police because of the attendance of various members of the Royal Family, it was surrounded by endless photographers. David greeted one at the entrance. Extremely loyal, he asked all his old friends as well as his famous new ones. It was always a very animated gathering, where we met people to party together with later.

The sisters Jayne Rayne and Annabel Bailey each gave grand and lavish annual balls. Jayne's occasions were in her large house in Hampstead with its unique collection of works of modern art and a Henry Moore sculpture in the garden. We sat at round tables for dinner and then danced to a live orchestra afterwards. I found not having place names at dinner rather disturbing and always tried to arrange to get a friendly group together beforehand. Placements are a lot of work for the host or hostess, but well worth it in the end. It is all very well to go to a dinner and not know the man next to you, but when there are hundreds there, why not try to select your own?

When Annabel was married to Jimmy Goldsmith, she gave splendid buffet dinners at her house on the edge of Richmond Park. Princess Alexandra also had a house in the Park, and she was a great friend. Klaus von Bulow was always there, as Annabel and Jayne were two of the few people who believed in his innocence at the murder trial when he was accused of killing his wife. Annabel had one large seated table for her more important guests, but the rest of us had to sink or swim. The buffet was particularly lavish and we danced afterwards in a covered and floored marquee. I once saw Mick Jagger standing alone at the edge of the crowd of guests.

When Princess Alexandra was married to Angus Ogilvy, they gave extremely friendly and unpompous parties. I was fond of Angus and I remember once telling him how much I admired the garden. He immediately took my arm and led me across the vast lawn to show me the spectacular view from the edge before rejoining his guests.

Another regular entertainer in her Chelsea house, Shusha was born Shamsi Assar six years before Iran's occupation by the Soviet Union and Britain during the Second World War. Her father was a Muslim theologian who had been appointed Professor of Philosophy at the University of Tehran under the anti-clerical Reza Shah Pahlavi. Shusha adored him. After studying at the French Lycée in London at the age of seventeen, she won a scholarship to Paris to learn French literature and train as a singer. She sang in nightclubs patronised by the fashionable and the wealthy. Encouraged by Jacques Prévert, she started recording Persian ballads, *chansons* and old French folk songs. In 1961 she came back to London and married the explorer Nicholas Guppy, by whom she had two sons, but the marriage was not a happy one and was dissolved.

Shusha found solace in Sufism, a heterodox doctrine that believes in the unity of all creeds. Her career as a singer and writer really took off. At her concerts, where she played the guitar to the accompaniment of a small orchestra, all hues of intellectual London came together from Sir Alfred Ayer to Roger Scruton. Andrew and I went to hear her sing her *chansons* in a church in Hammersmith. She shared the platform with Andrew's friend Ted Hughes, who recited some of his poetry. She died of cancer, aged seventy-two, surrounded by friends. I will never forget her.

Ted Heath asked us several times to his luncheon parties in his splendid house opposite Salisbury Cathedral. The walls were decorated in handmade Chinese wallpaper, which had been given to him when he was Prime Minister. Unlike his rather taciturn demeanour in the House of Commons, he was an extremely genial host. After pouring glasses of champagne, he would proudly show his guests round his vast garden. We would then sit down to a four-course lunch accompanied by generous pourings of delicious wine. Often late in the afternoon, we were allowed to leave for home. Before that, with heaving shoulders, he told of conducting an orchestra in Spain and having to visit the Royal Yacht *Britannia*, moored in Barcelona. Coming up the gangway he was greeted by Prince Philip drumming his fingers on the railing. "Fiddle, fiddle, fiddle, fiddle, Heath," the Prince said, "what else do you do?"

Before he was sent to prison in the United States, Conrad Black and his wife Barbara Amiel gave many cocktail parties at their home in Phillimore Gardens. Andrew enjoyed these more than me as he and Conrad had two great interests in common – one was Franklin D Roosevelt – Conrad wrote a biography of the President – and the other was Napoleon. They would stand a little apart from the guests and discuss at length their views on the two great men. While in prison, Conrad gave history lessons to his fellow prisoners, while Andrew had done the same inside the Walls of Academe.

Princess Marie-Christine and Prince Michael of Kent became friends of ours soon after they married, and we were invited down to their country house, Nether Lypiatt, for the day. Marie-Christine had been an interior decorator, and the house was immaculately furnished with great style. Wandering around the large gardens, we could imagine why Marie-Christine loved the place so much and was so saddened when they had to sell it.

Marie-Christine and Michael gave the best of the yearly cocktail parties in their garden behind Kensington Palace. Rain always seemed to threaten, but they were usually lucky and the sun shone on the gilded tumblers in which champagne was served. They had a loyal gathering of friends, particularly to celebrate Prince Michael's birthday. Marie-Christine, looking beautiful and often dressed in floating chiffon kaftans, always stood at the entrance giving us a warm welcome, whilst Michael, appearing with his trimmed beard as the image of the late Tsar of Russia, shyly waited amongst the throng of guests to be approached. Not always getting the praise they deserved from the press, they were generous and good for the Royal Family, and received no grants, so they had to make their own way.

For many years, I had belonged to a Health Club at Dolphin Square, where I would meet friends to swim and lunch. They had a good spa there and gave excellent massages and beauty treatments. I also went to the gym and ran on the treadmill, when I was feeling particularly masochistic. One day in the early 1990s, as I was leaving, I saw on the opposite side of the road an enormous blue tarpaulin had been erected and on it the name "Savills". Full of curiosity,

I visited their premises in Sloane Street and asked what was going on. They told me a four-storied block of flats was being built and asked would I like to see the model? Although not a brick had been laid, they said they had sold nearly all the flats. The only one I liked overlooking the river already had had an offer on it. Discussing it with Andrew, we thought it would be a good time to move from Tite Street, as the children now all had their own homes. Luckily, the people who had put an offer on our preferred flat withdrew, and we immediately took the plunge and put Tite Street on the market.

For the next year, wearing our hard hats, we would accompany the builders as Berkeley Homes started the construction. The most difficult part was not selling our Chelsea home, but getting rid of our many belongings which would not fit into the new flat. Being a magpie at heart, Andrew had more trouble than me. Luckily he had a small cottage in Normandy and transferred many books and belongings abroad. When the builders reached our flat on the fourth and top floor, we were able to make a lot of alterations, such as taking out doors to leave more open space and cladding the rafters to give a really high ceiling. I had seen the octagonal ceiling in another penthouse, beautifully hand-painted, and I managed to get hold of the artist. She turned out to be a charming small girl, who was heavily pregnant at the time. But she bravely climbed up ladders and decorated our ceiling in the same pattern – all free style without using any stencils. We had underground parking and a porter on duty day and night, so we felt we had made the right move.

Next to the flat was a grass tennis court, where we played regularly, and beyond that was the Westminster Boating Base, which owned a fleet of small dinghies. I never tired of seeing them sailing past our windows, often overturning and being towed back to base. When we had lived in our new flat for a few years after 1997, we decided to give a party in the Boating Base. It was a perfect venue with a large room surrounded by glass and built on stilts overlooking the river. After our first party, *Hello* put in its weekly diary, "Although Andrew and Sonia Sinclair have a spectacular view of the Thames from their penthouse apartment, they took over the nearby Westminster Boating Base for their summer party. Among the 250 guests were the Marquis of Bath, Lord Lamont, actors Peter Bowles and Alan Bates, Sir Richard and Lady Eyre and Lord and Lady Weidenfeld." Of course, we also had all our children and close friends. This was to be the first of many annual parties.

On 30 August 1997, just after our move to the flat, a tragedy occurred which was to affect the whole nation. Princess Diana was killed in a mysterious motor-car smash in a Paris boulevard tunnel.

Flowers were scattered outside the walls of Kensington Palace, where she had lived, and a bank of bouquets was built up from tens of thousands of bunches of lilies and single roses with many loving notes upon their stems. Although Princess Diana had been a wayward figure, much criticised by some, such as Christopher Soames, I had always been a great admirer. I only met her on official occasions when she had supported a few of my charitable galas, but I always felt she had been a wonderful mother and had successfully brought up her two sons in as normal a way as possible. She allowed them to take part in the same activities as other children with the same freedom. I decided I would like to pay my respects and with Pandora, I drove and parked my car as near to the Palace as we were allowed. Carrying our flowers, we walked the rest of the way and laid them amongst the cornucopia. Diana will never be forgotten.

John Julius Norwich also gave a yearly party at the Mayfair Hotel, in aid of the Duff-Cooper literary prize. On one occasion during the speeches, an elderly gentleman, rather hard of hearing, was heard expressing dismay that Baroness Jay had been elected a member of that male bastion, the Literary Society. He was swiftly reassured that the lady in question was in fact Baroness James, alias the crime writer P.D. James, and calm was restored.

I had always been a great admirer of Victoria Glendinning, and when she asked me to contribute to her book *Sons and Mothers* describing their experience of the natal bond, I accepted with alacrity. Although it was listed as the most reviewed book for two weeks, the response was varied. Newscaster Jon Snow regretted he would never have the chance to know his mother. The reviewer found it unexpectedly tender, progressing from the wry account of the discovery at the age of eight that his mother wore a wig to the heartbreaking present sadness of her Alzheimer's. When she dies, he wrote, "my thoughts of her will wake up and cry." The reviewer continued: "It's hard to imagine any reader, son, mother or otherwise, not identifying with and perhaps learning from this admirable collection."

Although I continued to write the occasional short story and travel pieces for monthly magazines, I could in no way compare my literary efforts to those of my husband. Andrew would settle down regularly after breakfast, using the main living room as his office, and write all day, breaking only for lunch. His publisher Christopher Sinclair-Stevenson had now become his agent and continued to be his close friend. After we left Tite Street, he had already written thirty books including biographies of Jack London and Francis Bacon, the *Albion Triptych*, *War Like a Wasp* and his books about patronage and the arts, *The Need to Give* and *Arts and Culture*. He had also written on Jerusalem and the Grail. When he wrote *The Discovery of the Grail*, Piers Paul Read wrote in *Literary Review*, "Andrew Sinclair tells us in this comprehensive and scholarly book, a holy bowl or magical vessel is found in pre-Christian myth, for example in Mesopotamia, as well as in early Nordic and Celtic rites. Sinclair suggests that the significance of the Grail is that it symbolised a personal approach to God that bypassed the sacramental and sacerdotal structures of the Roman Catholic Church." In this long review, Read ends, "more significant to me is the Jungian interpretation of the myth. Jung saw the Holy Vessel as a womb – the vessel of virtue in the Virgin Mary that receives the Saviour, the Source of intuitive wisdom in the female psyche, and the perennial quest of the male. But this is just one of the many ideas described in Andrew Sinclair's fascinating book."

Andrew had also written *The Sword and the Grail* and *The Secret Scroll*, which he also made into a film for television. This told the story of how the mysterious and condemned Order of the Knights Templar brought their treasures and secrets to the Ancient Scottish Rite. And so these mysteries were passed on to the Masons of all the world. These two books meant that Andrew had to do a great deal of research, in Scotland, Venice and America. I would often accompany him to Scotland, which I loved, and we would stay in Rosslyn Castle, which belonged to the Earl. He had been to Eton and then became a policeman and eventually a Commissioner in charge of guarding the Queen at Windsor Castle. In Rosslyn Chapel, then a dank and mouldering ruin, Andrew discovered the broken Templar tombstone of an early St Clair. This led to the finding of dozens of forgotten Templar graves along the Borders, and told of the continuing importance of the Order in Northern history. I suspect that Andrew's marriage to me was detrimental to his career, as it seemed to some in the literary circles of the time that he was moving into a different world.

For a change from taking our winter holiday in Mauritius, we decided to go to St Barts. People were always telling us that the island had the best climate, best beaches, best food, no racism, no crime. But I had some niggling doubts – a Caribbean island with no indigenous population, so significantly small (eight square miles of craggy peaks) where Columbus didn't even bother to stop, though he did name it after his brother? But we decided to chance it and stayed for two weeks at the Isle de France Hotel on Anse des Flamandes beach, fifteen minutes from the airport. So far so good, our garden bungalow at the hotel was an oasis of peace and quiet. Even the free fruit juice minibar and teasmade were hidden away, and the beach boys served rum *planteurs* by day and night.

261

The first shock came when we strolled down the mile-long sandy beach with the pale turquoise sea lapping on the shore. But it wasn't lapping – it was pounding, and only by taking our courage in both hands did we have the swim for which we had travelled halfway across the world. People don't go to St Barts to swim. The Wizards of Wall Street in Ralph Lauren shorts and their wives in understated costume jewellery come to enjoy the sun, the laid-back atmosphere and the food, and they talk to friends about the futures market and past takeovers.

We, too, had come for the renowned French Creole cuisine, and I had my list of recommended restaurants – the only trouble was to reach them, and this meant hiring a Jeep to take you over the one-track unmade roads and round mountain hairpin bends. I had been told that people would telephone from New York to book at the beachside restaurant in the La Fayette Club on Grand Cul-de-Sac. At lunch, it was only half-full, and a beautiful model drifted among the tables, showing off the choicest beach clothes, but totally ignored by the clientele. We ate a mouth-watering lunch of stuffed crab and crayfish, washed down with *vin rosé* at £20 a bottle, and we tried not to flinch at the bill. All the menus include *mahi-mahi* or *Dorado Coryphaena*. It is actually dolphin fillet under another name, just as in Israel, a rare dish of pork is called 'white steak'.

We visited the chic Eden Rock Hotel, perched like a tiny fairytale castle out of a pop-up book, on a promontory jutting into the Baie de Saint-Jean. There you can swim in calm waters sheltered by a coral reef. And if you don't mind the endless noise of the small planes landing and taking off from the nearby airport, this is the spot to head for. Here as elsewhere, rock stars come to be private and then get annoyed when they are ignored by the sophisticated locals. But why carp when we could walk to our local bistro La Langouste at the Hotel Baie des Anges? This was run by Annie (Ange) whose family originally came from Brittany, but had lived on the island for more than 200 years. The Creole cooking was mouth-watering, especially the green peppers stuffed with minced octopus and the aromatic fish stew topped with puff pastry. Walking back, shoeless, along the head to our hotel, the crashing waves seemed less threatening and under Sagittarius, we decided to keep an open mind about St Barts, and not fire too many arrows at our happiness.

Back in London, we learnt that Woodrow Wyatt had died. Before becoming Chairman of the Tote, Woodrow had pursued careers in politics and journalism. While in the Army, he had become a Socialist, convinced as an officer responsible for the welfare of his men that capitalism offered no solution to social problems. He was selected as a Labour candidate shortly before the 1945 election, beating Roy Jenkins for the nomination and becoming the second youngest MP in the House of Commons. After two failed marriages, Woodrow married Lady Moorea Hastings, the daughter of the 16th Earl of Huntington. I saw a lot of them at this time, and in spite of Moorea's dislike of the idea of having a baby (it would be so ugly!), she actually gave birth to Woodrow's first child, a son called Pericles.

Woodrow had lost his seat in 1970 and sought a career elsewhere, building up a successful local newspaper business and introducing new printing technology into England for the first time. Although he was totally opposed to the renationalisation of steel, this did not get in the way of his friendship with my first husband, and he often used to telephone Julian for advice on various issues. Woodrow's fourth and last marriage to the Hungarian Verushka, widow of Baron Dr Laszlo Banszky von Ambroz, proved to be enduringly happy and produced a daughter Petronella. Woodrow became a close friend of Margaret Thatcher and used to tell me that he rang her nearly every day to offer advice.

He kept a daily diary under lock and key. After he died, two extremely controversial journals were published. He had left very little for Verushka, and he added a codicil to his will that the money from the Journals would be her inheritance. These were entertaining and informative, but they stirred up many a hornets' nest. The historian Paul Johnson, writing in the *Daily Mail*, called it "the most disgusting book of the year, which puts lies into the mouths of innocent people like my friend Sonia Sinclair. In the diaries, Mrs Sinclair allegedly confides to Lord Wyatt that she annoyed Paul Johnson by telling him that Woodrow had the most influence with Margaret Thatcher. Lord Wyatt quoted Mrs Sinclair to the effect that Mr Johnson bridled at this suggestion, saying: 'I see her once a week'."

During Woodrow's life, when he was Chairman of the Tote, he and Verushka gave sumptuous lunches in the Tote Tent in the Royal Enclosure, actually made of brick. Guests sat at round tables, eating lobster and drinking champagne, and they could place their bets at the same time. It was the only time I really enjoyed going to Ascot, which became rather tawdry as the years progressed. Instant celebrities flaunted their flamboyant costumes and their thighs, when none could match the breeding and beauty and longer legs of the horses. But then, the paddock was always more striking than the promenade.

Seventeen

At Christmas, we gave our usual party for family and close friends, and a few days later travelled down to stay with Pandora and Nick at Foxhanger in Devon. There across the stony stream, the stags would storm the oak woods in the rutting season. We were joined by my niece Sapphia, her son Alex who was a year younger than Xan – Pandora's second son – and her boyfriend John Million, a maths teacher. This became a yearly occurrence, later at Combe Park, and then after their move to Bentwitchen near South Molton on the verge of Exmoor. The rest of my family all gathered in Norfolk. This was a happy arrangement and suited us all. I loved the traditional paraphernalia of Christmas. My job was always to peel the sprouts, lay the table and decorate it with the crackers I had brought from London. We drove to the local church, usually arriving as the first hymn was being sung. Andrew also loved the Christmas ritual, which he had never had in his childhood or in either of his previous marriages. He taught the boys chess, which they soon mastered to give him a game. Later we all gathered for the festival at the farm in Norfolk. Peter and Kerena's children all had partners so we would often be around twenty in all. Pandora, Nick and their two boys would join us from Devon and Cassandra would play us her flute after lunch.

Sometimes Mike Richey would join our Christmas family parties. Since the tragedy over the loss of *Jester*, the Observer Trust had a replica built to take her place and, although Mike never again crossed the Atlantic in her, he would often sail to France or Ireland to visit friends. I still considered him to be my closest male friend, and when in London he would come to the flat for a *tête à tête* lunch, always starting with his favourite dry martini. He also joined us on our summer holidays.

When we stopped taking houses or staying with friends at Porto Ercole, we rented villas in Corfu from our friends Count and Countess Flamburiari. We never returned to visit our old villa at Kobitsi – it would have been too nostalgic. We once visited Jacob and Serena Rothschild, who had a grand villa a little to the north facing Albania. Jacob was worried that the Club Mediterranée, a few miles down the coast, would disturb their quiet existence, and so he built a swimming pool beyond the villa to ensure his guests could swim in peace. We also had friends, Kitty and Frank Giles, who had a small charming home with wonderful access to the sea. This was the house years later that was rented by the blind MP David Blunkett and Ms Kimberley Fortier, the deputy publisher of the *Spectator* magazine. This visit was to create an ongoing press scandal. When Ms Fortier produced a son, David Blunkett was convinced that the infant had been conceived on Corfu, a claim that was not made good.

In September when we returned to London, we were unaware that the biggest disaster of our lifetime was about to occur. On September the 11th 2001, two aeroplanes hijacked by Muslim suicide extremists, crashed into the Twin Towers in New York. We had become engaged there. This was our eyrie. And now it was a bombhole of disaster and mass grieving. America had not been attacked for more than a hundred years on this scale. This catastrophe would lead to a global war against terror from Afghanistan and Iraq to Somalia and Yemen. Although these threats were distant, almost every week was troubled on the news, from which there was no escape. The memory of the dead lives as a personal tragedy and political affront that still infuses America.

That same year, a loss occurred in my family. Fifteen years after Kerena's marriage to Adam Boulton, he left her for Anji Hunter, who at the time was one of Tony Blair's political advisers. The divorce which followed left her devastated in spite of the deep love and support from her three daughters and her immediate family. At the time Lucy was twenty, Hannah was fourteen and Blaise only eleven years old. Kerena remained in the same house in Kentish Town with her daughters and threw herself into her music. She studied singing, French and Italian. Luckily, she had a mass of supportive girlfriends and went on tours abroad, often to volcanoes, walking up to fifteen miles in a day. Kerena also took a job teaching French at a children's school for a year and then decided to take a degree at Birkbeck College. This involved her in the study of French culture and history; but she threw herself wholeheartedly into the research. As Andrew often told me, work is the antidote to misery.

He had been writing his Scots epic novel *Blood and Kin* over some years. This book deals with the Sinclair clan as servants of the British Empire until modern times. Beginning with the Highland Clearances, the crofter Sinclairs fight in the Indian Mutiny, the Boer War and both World Wars. These are the soldiers and engineers and colonial officers who straddle the world to keep the flag flying. Partly a family history, including the traumatic shooting of his grandmother by his grandfather in South Africa, the Sinclair clan are fully investigated. The book was published in September 2002 and compared in the *Times Literary Supplement* by Alan Massie even to Proust and Tolstoy. *Blood and Kin* is a moving tribute to the Scots' diaspora.

Andrew's son, Merlin, now married his girlfriend Shula Goldberg. They were perfectly matched. Shula was as extrovert as Merlin was introvert. She and her mother's family came from Israel and she had served in the Israeli army. Her father, Martin, was English and had met her mother Yosheved at Ronnie Scott's nightclub in Soho. Merlin's secular marriage at Soho House was strictly in the Jewish tradition, even to the actions of the smashing of the plates by the groom. After the wedding, they spent their honeymoon in Spain in Cordoba and Seville and then settled in a small house in Brixton. As they were both highly intelligent, they got well paid jobs with Saatchi & Saatchi in advertising. Shula was always intrigued that when she had walked down Melchett Street in Tel Aviv, she little knew that she would later marry the stepson of the one-time Lady Melchett. Andrew and I became very fond of Shula, and she and Merlin always joined our family Christmas parties.

Another wedding which took place the same year was when my goddaughter Katya Galitzine married Nick Laing in St Petersburg. The day before they had arranged a vodka-fuelled yacht trip on the Neva for all their friends. We drifted past the Winter Palace, its golden spire glittering in the midsummer sunset. The marriage took place in St Nicholas, a gleaming cathedral, where the Tsars used to worship. Choirs chanted, candlelight wavered and priests intoned as Golden Crowns were held over the bride and groom's heads by four friends. Later there was a ball in the Pavilion of Roses at Pavlovsk, a magical place outside the city. We danced under the stars until a pale dawn lit up the skies and we were entertained by singers and dancers from the Mariinsky Theatre. Flying home the next day, Kerena and I reminisced on how much we loved St Petersburg, which I had visited before with Andrew.

Peter had left Greenpeace in 2000 to become a part-time Policy Director of the Soil Association. Before he left, Greenpeace had come to be seen by politicians, businessmen and the media as no longer a fringe organisation but as one of the most influential non-governmental organisations in the United Kingdom. Peter's time spent there had been totally fulfilling. His work involved many private and some secret meetings with senior politicians, including both Labour and Conservative Prime Ministers, and the heads of many companies.

But he found working for the Soil Association, as the main organic British food and farming organisation, just as rewarding. Peter was drafted to be a member of the Government's Organic Action Plan Group and later joined

270

the Rural Climate Change Forum. His work there brought him into contact with Prince Charles, whose views were much in sympathy with his own. He was often invited to meetings at Highgrove and also stayed with the Prince in Scotland several times.

Peter and Cassandra were very proud when their daughter Jessie became a barrister specialising in criminal law. Andrew and I went to the ceremony of calling to the bar at Lincoln's Inn, which I found a most impressive occasion. Jessie's partner Jonathan, who originally came from Zimbabwe, also became a barrister and they bought a small flat in Kentish Town near other members of the family.

While Paul Getty was alive, he and Victoria would ask us to the yearly cricket match played in the grounds of their beautiful home, Castle Maine House at Wormsley near High Wycombe. Victoria had virtually saved Sir Paul's life after he had been a serious drug addict. During a contest between Paul's team, led by Graham Gooch, and the Eton Ramblers, we lunched at round tables in a large marquee. Later Victoria suggested we visit a special lodge which was the library of Paul's priceless book collection. The illuminated medieval manuscripts were superb, but almost the best piece was a portrait by Francis Cotes of 'The Young Cricketer' holding his bat, while his stockings fell down below his green britches.

My family were very good about keeping in close touch, although because of Peter's busy life with the Soil Association and running the farm, I saw less of him than the girls. Kerena would join me in the Dolphin Square swimming pool once a week and lunch with me at the local Spanish bistro afterwards. I spoke on the phone every day to Pandora, who was busy in Devon with her oil painting and driving Ludo and Xan to their local schools and sporting activities. But not being a 'loner' like Andrew, I would have regular lunches with Jean Galitzine, Dominique de Borchgrave, Zelfa Olivier and Sandy Forsyth. Sandy and Freddie had a small farm in Hertford, so she was seldom in London, and Zelfa ran a travel company to Turkey, which kept her very busy. But I found that, if I didn't keep in close touch and kept to myself, depression was likely to steal into my life.

In 2002, we decided to take a villa in Corsica, which was to become our favourite summer holiday escape for the next few years, as we grew to love the rocky scene more and more. Known to be the most mountainous island in the Mediterranean, the oblong shapes were covered in scrub, known as the maquis – a dense jungle of evergreen aromatic plants spreading over more than half the island; arbutus and myrtle, lentiscus and rosemary, lavender and thyme. Made famous as the birthplace of Napoleon, Corsica was taken by the French from the Genoese, who had long held sway there. From his homeland, Bonaparte had come to rule France and most of Europe, too – a short genius from a small island with a great ambition to become an emperor. He was eventually exiled to St Helena, lost in the Atlantic Ocean. There it is said that his memories were not of his triumph or his policies, but of the aromas of his childhood.

We would fly to Ajaccio, the Corsican capital with its Napoleon museum, and hire a car and drive along the precipitous roads, to the port of Propriano, a blaze of whitewash with an endless main street, where the whole of life took place. Across the bay, our villa was perched on rocks above the sky-blue sea. With our friends and family staying, we would wander down a path to a small private beach. Sometimes I would swim round the rocks, to the next pink sandy beach and lie on my back, soaking in the sun and the perfumes of the wild herbs and flowers.

The children loved it, especially when Andrew wrote plays for them. We all took part, standing in the garden and ending down on the rocks on the beach, waving swords and swiping at knights and dragons in Beowulf and Ulysses and Robin Hood. Without television and laptops, we went back to games and charades in the happiest of evenings, when we were each other's entertainers. Sometimes we would drive to Propriano for dinner in our favourite restaurant Il Pescadori, overlooking the yachts anchored in the harbour. We would drink the aromatic *rosé* wine, while the children wandered down the long, narrow street, shopping for trinkets. Once we visited the inland village of Sartène to drink in a very upmarket restaurant and watch the residents sitting in the main square. Near us lay the Neolithic monuments of Filitosa with megaliths and primitive carvings and sacred caves. They transported us back in time to the long history of this granite island enduring in the turquoise sea.

As Andrew approached his seventieth birthday, he decided to celebrate by giving a dinner at the Garrick Club. This was also to honour our twenty years of marriage. My husband was always competitive about that fact that my marriage to Julian had lasted twenty-five years and so was determined to overtake him. As I write this memoir, we have been married for twenty-eight years, so he has succeeded in his ambition. But in giving the dinner at his club, he gave much pleasure to his closer friends. I will quote part of the speech he made at the end of the meal:

"I will speak a moment, I am afraid. Brevity, I think, is the soul of after-dinner speeches. So I'll keep it short. You will have more fun, chatting to your neighbour. And no replies please. I don't like being talked back to.

"That is a reason for why we are here. Old writers never die, they simply dine on china. We are met as old friends. And to mark me reaching an unlikely seventy years, and to herald my twenty years of love and marriage with Sonia – twice my previous record – and approaching hers.

"In my recklessness and waywardness and absorption in my books, I have neglected my old friends. Indeed, one of them said, 'Andrew, you know friendship is something to be *worked* at.'

"Yet you, my friends, have always been here, when I needed you. You have never forgotten our feeling, even the children of my friends, who are no longer here. You have put up with me and accepted me in my hazardous going on. I remember in the Army, the Adjutant wrote: 'I like Sinclair, but I find him rather quaint and eccentric.' What has changed?

"The other reason for being here is to celebrate my twenty years with Sonia, the love of my life. I cannot imagine how she has put up with me for so long. But the reasons of the heart are inscrutable. And without her love, I simply would *not* be here to talk to you. As Marlowe nearly wrote – in her 'are infinite treasures in a beauty rare.'

"If I have anything further to add, it is an adapted Auden's advice to his godchild:

And so I wish you keep a sense of wonder
     Only those who love that illusion
          Will go very far
For you will know of the confusion
Between what we do and say
          And who we really are.

"And so to the toast: *TO FRIENDSHIP AND LOVE FOR EVER.*"

Eighteen

My great sporting passion in life is tennis. Andrew and I are about the same standard. Apart from the grass court next door to our flat, we played regularly on the excellent hard courts at Battersea Park. But when I could, I would also watch all the main tennis tournaments on television, much to the amusement of my family. My first hero was the good-looking Tim Henman, who played with great style, but never quite made the Wimbledon finals, although the hill behind the Club House was named as Henman Hill. When Andy Murray took over from him as the only British player to reach the top ten, I would show him my allegiance in spite of his rather dour manner and lack of charm when being interviewed. Although perfectly acceptable for English men to be madly enthusiastic about football and their favourite teams, most people find it rather strange that women have the same passion for sport. But I must say, I rather draw the line at female boxing.

When Sir Patrick Sergeant started giving us tickets for the Number One or Centre Court at Wimbledon every July, we enjoyed it enormously. The atmosphere was typically British at its best. The traditional green and purple colour of umbrellas, the ties of the officials, and the hospitality marquees serving Pimms and champagne. We would lunch in the Members' dining-room with Patrick and his friends, and then, taking our padded cushions, find our numbered seats at the courtside. Watching live is so much more exciting than seeing the matches on television. When Julian was alive, we were once asked to the Royal Box and I was present at Wimbledon when rain stopped play and Cliff Richard rose to his feet and sang 'Living Doll' to the crowd, much to everyone's amusement if not total delight.

Andrew would watch cricket on television and, when not going out, we would often view our favourite programmes after dinner. But his chosen game was chess, at which he excelled, and he would play with his son Merlin, who was extremely competitive. He also taught my daughter Pandora's two boys Ludo and Xan how to play. When we stayed with them at Christmas, this and riding were their favourite pastimes.

In January 2006, Dominique de Borchgrave and I visited Syria for a week. How lucky it was that we decided to go when we did, six years before the terrible civil war broke out. While we were there, the atmosphere was tranquil and the people friendly. We had a charming guide called Amer Nadeem; he and our driver Mohammed took us to visit all the famous sites.

In Damascus, the hubbub never ceased, and the wailing through the loudspeakers from the minarets was as regular as clockwork. We first visited the museum enclosing the tiny synagogue and saw where the first alphabet was said to have been carved. Then to the impressive Umayyad Mosque, full of shoeless devout worshippers. We took the winding road for a panoramic view of Damascus and saw the marble tomb of Saladin, which had been funded by the Kaiser.

The next day was biting cold, but Amer took us to see the fabulous Krak des Chevaliers. Sited on a hilltop, it commands the route from the North into Lebanon. From behind, it is vulnerable because it is built not on the crest but on the saddle of its rise. Yet the perfection of the long fortress made it as intricate and great a testament to man-without-machine as any pyramid. As the east wind was blowing from China, Dominique and I were freezing as we walked up the endless steps to the tiny chapel of the Krak, where the minbar of a mosque now stands. But Amer had a surprise waiting for us – a feast of chicken and other delights set out on a table in the great inner hall. We tucked in hungrily before walking back down the edge of the battlement, thrilled with the day's magic.

Amer was determined to take us shopping the following day. As we walked down the market place known as The Street, the spices and scents were irresistible, and we made many purchases of clothes and scarves. I even bought a long embroidered coat, which seemed perfect there, but sadly was never to be worn again. Driving past the medieval Citadel of St Simeon and the giant Waterwheel at Hama, we eventually reached Palmyra. From the roof of the great Temple of Bel, we could see the palms of the oasis as green ruffles in the infinite desert. We walked down the main street, where Zenobia had briefly ruled after her triumph over Rome. Then down to the valley of the tombs where high marble pillars still remained, towering on one side of our path, and where grey desert foxes with white tails scavenged for dried bones. All around us lay the great shield of the desert running away flat to the rim of the world. That day, Amer laid on a true Bedouin lunch in an impromptu tent. Sitting on the earth and eating with our fingers, he tried to persuade us to finger the delicacies. I'm afraid I hid the testicles and eyes of the lamb in my bag, which later that evening in our hotel I flushed down the loo.

When our guide took us to see Aleppo, we were full of excitement as we had heard so much of its beauty and its ancient architecture. But when we arrived, Amer drove quickly through the streets past a row of high pillars and then southwards towards our final destination. Was it because there were things he wished us not to see in a divided city? As we now know, this was to become the centre of the future uprising against the Syrian Government and would be destroyed.

Driving on our final day towards Basra, we stopped at the Shabba Museum just outside the town, where we saw the exquisite third-century mosaics of Artemis and Acteon. In the city, we climbed up the steps of what is meant to be the largest basalt amphitheatre in the world. There we listened to our voices echoing round the empty vastness. Our visit to Syria was a never to be forgotten experience and the devastation to come was beyond our imaginings.

Dommy had been in love with Paddy Pakenham, the second son of the Lord Longford clan. He had been a brilliant lawyer until, for no apparent reason, he had a nervous breakdown and spent many years in a mental institution. There he met a nurse, whom he later married, and they produced three boys. When Dommy met him, he was living in a flat in Chelsea in the same block as his parents. His wife, whom he barely saw, lived in the country with the boys. Dommy remained in her Cadogan Square flat, and this slightly eccentric arrangement suited them admirably. Dommy became friendly with his wife and treated the boys as her own sons. They would visit her in London and she would give them extravagant presents and meals. Paddy was not an easy man and sometimes, when drunk, he could be extremely obnoxious and rude, but when sober he was witty and charming.

This knife-edge existence suited Dommy, and she never tired of describing his more exuberant activities – such as when staying with his friend Sir Algie Cluff. In Algie's absence one afternoon, Paddy decided to have a bath. Feeling like a drink, he went to the living room, leaving the bath overflowing. The water poured into the flat below much to the anger of the owners, who stormed up to Algie's flat. The naked Paddy ran away into the gardens outside and climbed up a tree, where the police found him. "I'm afraid I left the tap on," he said. This escapade, like many others, was forgiven by his host, who treated him rather like a court jester.

But soon after our return from Syria, Paddy was diagnosed with cancer, from which he died two years later. During this time my distraught friend drove him from one hospital to another and virtually became his nurse. The funeral took place at Brompton Oratory, organised with immaculate taste by Dommy and attended by his many friends and her two brothers who flew over from Brussels. With their usual

Catholic generosity, the Pakenham family took my friend under their wing, and she instinctively became part of the clan. This suited the two sides of her nature – her need to be with Paddy's Catholic peers and her snobbery, of which she had been in no way ashamed.

Three years later she herself had a serious brain tumour and died in the Cromwell Hospital. She had been so much part of my life that her loss was immeasurable, and I keep her photograph in my bedroom, together with those of my nearest and dearest.

In August 2006, Andrew and I charted a caique called *Cyri-hasan IV*, captained by a Turkish charmer called Yusef, and we spent a magnificent ten days touring round the coast south-east of Bodrum. We had various members of our family with us, including Andrew's son Merlin and his wife Shula. They had the next door cabin to mine, but unfortunately they decided to sleep on the deck, which happened to be just above my head. When they persuaded my grandchildren, Ludo and Xan, to join them, I got very little sleep with that thunder above. Yusef took us to some beautiful quiet bays, where we swam and water-skied. The chef Musifa produced delicious meals, which we ate round a table at the stern of the boat under the stars. We had one very rough crossing, but the crew took down the sails and we cruised slowly into a bay called Cleopatras. As before, I loved the timeless quality of sailing and was sad when our jaunt came to an end. At our last dinner, Yusef had a surprise for us. Apparently he was something of a conjurer and managed to tie himself up in a complicated tangle of ship's rope. He challenged us to set him free. After various unsuccessful attempts, we capitulated. How he performed the act remains his secret.

As our adventure came to an end, Andrew and I spent a quiet week by ourselves at a small hotel called the Atami, west of Bodrum. We swam from the beach nearby and recovered from family life. We visited Ephesus and the Temple of Apollo at Didyma. Andrew went on to the deserted hilltop city of Priene, where he found a timeless beauty. In the horseshoe theatre there, the lion thrones below the stone tiers were reaching up to the Temple of Demeter, the goddess of earth, and the green spikes of the pine trees were a fringe about the soar of the sacred rock spine beyond. For him, as he said, the spirit dissolved into sight. "I am what I see at Priene. Past is present is ever."

On our return to London, I found that Peter had become more deeply involved with his work at the Soil Association. He gave the annual City Ford Lecture in the Guildhall in January 2007, and he described the era of industrial intensive farming as a "brief blip. It will be seen as a wrong turn, from which we will hopefully recover fairly quickly." The event was run by the Food Standards Agency. He also pointed to the lower greenhouse emissions associated with organic food as "perhaps its greatest contribution to a healthier society." His views were challenged by speakers from the floor, rejecting the claim that organic production could feed the world. He replied that he believed that yield increases in the developing world from sustainable farming would outweigh any yield loss. "Organic farming does not have all the answers. But solar-powered, animal- and wildlife-friendly, pesticide-and-additive-free farming is where we're heading."

When a foot-and-mouth outbreak developed in the same year, Peter wrote a letter to *The Guardian* finishing: "The lesson we have to learn from the last outbreak is that Tony Blair was wrong to give in to threats of non-compliance with vaccination from the NFU, and that he was wrong to cave in to a multinational food company when it said that it would close a factory in the UK if we adopted a vaccination policy – that decision is now widely recognised. We can all help. Foot and mouth poses no risk to people. Vaccines against many serious diseases are widely used in farming (as they are in human health). Apart from vegans, all of us consume dairy products and meat from vaccinated animals. We should eat these products just as happily as we now eat produce vaccinated against many other diseases."

Peter had always been good at arguing his views, just as his father before him. I never got into a disagreement with him as, although I may have been in the right, I knew I would always lose. It is the other way round with Andrew, who says, "A man's place is always in the wrong."

Later that summer Andrew and I went to Surrey to lunch with Josephine Hart and Maurice Saatchi. This was a yearly event and took place in their garden with its fountains and multi-coloured herbaceous borders. Andrew sat next to the elegant wife of the vocal atheist and neo-Darwinist Richard Dawkins. Andrew pointed out to her that in the twentieth century, religious conflict had not killed more than ten million people, while materialist cults such as Communism and Fascism with their deranged leaders such as Hitler and Stalin and Mao, had killed ten times more people, over a hundred million. "The numbers of the dead," he said, "are a sort of moral choice in what you believe."

Andrew told me that later they went on to talk about religious faith. Andrew said that atheism had only spread from a small group of European intellectuals in the eighteenth century. After two hundred years, nine people in ten still believed in some sort of God or creative force. Even Russia had returned to the Orthodox Church, and Leningrad to St Petersburg. Surely it was democratic to respect religion in the majority. On the other side of the table I was praising Josephine's book *Damage* to my neighbour Maurice. I had thoroughly enjoyed it before it had become an international best-seller. Her last novel, *The Truth About Love* was, like all her books, about passion, but it was also about redemption, hinting at her own personal childhood tragedies. It brought together eight of the greatest poets in the English language and a selection of their poems. *Sin*, her second novel, was about a woman who was possessed by an obsessive envy and would stop at nothing to get what she wanted. The agent Ed Victor decided to get it reissued alongside *Damage*. This act gave Josephine huge pleasure. She wrote to the publisher, "I cannot tell you what it means to me that *Damage* and *Sin* will be Virago Modern Classics – my pride is profound. I think of it every single day." Sadly, she was to die before the publication of the books. But after her death, Maurice gave a party to celebrate the event and both Andrew and I found it moving and inspiring. She lived on. For as well as being a considerable author, she had revived the reading of classic texts by great actors in the British Library and for that, she will always be remembered.

Her memorial service at Westminster Abbey was filled to capacity, and during the service various actors read from some of her favourite poets. Instead of standing in the pulpit, they popped up in various places among the congregation, an informal touch which Josephine would have appreciated.

Nineteen

Now in my eighties, my thoughts turn towards my own longevity. I have lost so many close girlfriends and miss sharing thoughts and experiences over the telephone and the occasional lunch. Andrew is as loving as ever, but quite self-sufficient, writing daily in the next-door room, and we really get together only over our evening meal to exchange news and views.

I am not a deeply religious person, but nor am I an atheist. Both bible-bashing Fundamentalists and dogmatic atheists such as Richard Dawkins and Christopher Hitchens have a similar idea of what God means. They seem to think the word denotes a large, powerful man we can't see. The only difference between them is that one faith insists on God's existence while the other denies and tries to demolish the divine. In Karen Armstrong's book, *The Case for God: What Religion Really Means*, she writes, "For centuries, ideas of God and the Bible were far more subtle and profound than today's atheism or fundamentalism can conceive." She draws on 2000 years of Christian theology and mysticism to demonstrate rich, alternative ideas of the divine. God is by definition infinitely beyond human language. The fact that Dawkins and others think that pointing out the Bible's imperfections undermines Jewish or Christian belief only demonstrates their ignorance of the traditions they presume to subvert. Belief is not meant to be understood literally, as the early Christians seemed to understand. In the gospels, Jesus Himself sees God not as "an object of thought or speculation, but as an existential demand." In Islam, all speaking or theorising about the nature of Allah is mere *zanneh*, fanciful guesswork. Instead, try "Silence, reverence and awe," or music, ritual, the steady habit of compassion, and a graceful acceptance of mystery and 'unknowing'.

In his book *Afterdeath*, Andrew quoted Dr Jonathan Miller as "taking the extreme view of religion as a genetic folly, since the human race began," and went on to say that this ancestral irrationality had not been eradicated because of "the massive political institutions that are closely associated with religious beliefs, and the very elaborate system of religious-based education on children at an age when they are extremely susceptible." Dr Miller ended by citing the eighteenth-century Scottish philosopher David Hume on his own certain extinction. "I am no more puzzled by the darkness into which I am going than by the darkness from which I came." When Andrew had met Richard Dawkins and his wife while researching his book, they were amazed when he pointed out that only a tiny minority in the world, perhaps one in twenty human beings, did not believe in a proper burial or a soul or a spirit. Their reply was that most people needed to be educated. This level of faith in Western logic appeared to Andrew to be as superior as the attitude of Marie Antoinette. Let them eat the cake we have baked.

Many years ago, my deeply religious Catholic friend Nuala Allason, whose son Julian was a Knight of Malta, persuaded me to go with her to Lourdes. We set off to France by ferry and then hired a car for the six-hour drive to the shrine. The grotto was in a deep valley with a river running through it; water thundering down from the cascade above.

The Lourdes legend was started by Bernadette Soubirous, a shepherdess, fragile from having cholera as a child and semi-literate. One day she was gathering firewood by the banks of the river when she saw a beautiful small lady in white with a blue mantle, holding a rosary. At first nobody believed her but, as the lady kept appearing, the local priests told her to ask the lady who she was. When she did, the lady just smiled and looked down. But one day she told Bernadette to dig in the ground by a grotto. A spring would come up. Bernadette should drink from it and eat the surrounding plants. By now, the town people followed her each day, while she dug in the mud and tried to suck water from it. After several unsuccessful attempts in front of a jeering crowd, water began to pour from the spot where she had been digging. The spring has been active and miraculous ever since. Finally, the lady introduced herself to Bernadette. "I am the Immaculate Conception." Until that time the Mother of Jesus had been largely ignored by the Catholic Church. But only a few years before the Pope had issued new dogma concerning the Virgin Mary, claiming that she had been without sin so she was to be known henceforth as "the Immaculate Conception." How could an illiterate peasant girl know these words when few priests at the time were familiar with them?

The lady instructed Bernadette to tell the local priest to build a chapel over the grotto; people should come and drink from the spring and pray for forgiveness. And so a cult was born. Today Lourdes is the most popular pilgrims' destination in Christendom, and countless inexplicable cures have been scientifically witnessed there.

Bernadette herself took orders and retired to a faraway convent, for a life of contemplation, and finally died at the age of thirty-three years. Nuala and I stayed at an hotel called the St Francis of Assisi above the Basilica. That night we walked down the winding road towards the grotto. On either side were shops full of tasteless religious souvenirs and boxes of white sugared almonds. We reached the amphitheatre where pilgrims were preparing for the regular torchlight procession through the hill and singing 'Ave, Ave, Ave Maria,' as they went. As the evening darkened, we made our way to the grotto and joined the queue of people seeking a cure or salvation, rather like the queues for shelters in the London Blitz. The lame, the blind, people on crutches, parents carrying sick children, all hoping for a miraculous cure. As we arrived at the grotto – in reality a small pond – we touched the water and knelt briefly while we silently prayed. It was a deeply moving occasion but, as a doctor's daughter, it did not shake my disbelief in miracles.

Before going to sleep every night, I silently say the Lord's Prayer to myself. But when it comes to "Give us this day our daily bread", I try to imagine all the starving children in the Third World, and I pray to put food into their mouths. As I am an insomniac, I then pray for all the members of my extended family, imagining them all with their different needs. Then come the deep breathing techniques I have been taught and then, hopefully, the blissful sleep. Before I wake, I nearly always dream – usually irrational, frustrated or sometimes truly unpleasant ones. Once I talked to Jonathan Miller about a particularly weird dream I had. He told me, "Don't worry – dreaming is essential to sanity," which was very reassuring.

Dying is not what I worry about, but the gradual loss of my faculties. My dear friend, John Mortimer, wrote in an article, 'Clinging to the Wreckage': "Dying is a *métier* of slapstick and pitfalls. The ageing process is not gradual or gentle. It rushes up, pushes you over and runs off laughing. No one should grow old who isn't ready to appear ridiculous. The time will come when the voice of God will thunder at you from a cloud: 'From this day forth thou shalt not be able to put on thine own socks'."

Andrew and I have often talked of suicide, particularly if either of us had an incurable illness. We have said we would leave this world together, perhaps romantically walking out to sea until we could swim no more. I even bought a book called *Final Exit* by Derek Humphy, which tells one all one needs to know in great detail. He opens with the poem by John Keats:

> Darkling I listen, and for many a time
> I have been half in love with easeful death,
> Called him soft names in many a mused rhyme
>   To take into the air my quiet breath,
>   Now more than ever seems it rich to die,
> To ease upon the midnight with no pain …

When the writer Arthur Koestler was dying at the age of seventy-seven, Cynthia Koestler took her life rather than being left without him. Aged fifty-five, she was perfectly healthy, but in 1983 they were found dead in their living-room, seated on separate chairs. Beside them was a glass of whisky, two empty wine glasses containing a residue of white powder and an empty bottle of secobarbital. Arthur had already published an eloquent note, and Cynthia, whose death surprised her friends, left a few lines, saying "I cannot live without Arthur, despite certain inner resources."

I strongly believe suicide should be legalised as it is in Switzerland with their Dignitas clinic. In actual fact, I could not contemplate suicide unless, through illness, I had become an unbearable burden on my family. It would be a selfish act, causing much sadness. I would hopefully wish to be supportive and not to be supported by them until the end. In the meantime, I give death little thought until it thinks of me. I try and fill my days as fully as possible. I am a great believer in making short- and long-term plans for the days ahead, so that in turning the pages of my diary there are always events I wish to come.

In February 2009, Andrew and I took a winter break in Egypt, stopping at the Four Seasons Hotel at Sharm el-Sheikh. Such a vast, impersonal hotel, we were driven to our suite in a golf buggy. But the views over the Red Sea were superb, and we had some of the best winter swimming. To approach the ocean, one travelled in a tiny covered tram before taking the plunge. As usual, Andrew wrote for several hours every day – this time finishing his book, *Man*

and Horse: Four Thousand Years of the Mounted Warrior.
The drama was concentrated on the Scots Borders with
the Reivers and in the Wild West, with the homesteaders
fighting the cattlemen for the land. The finish was in the
First World War, when the cavalry were destroyed by the
machine gun and the tank.

The end of the year brought great sadness to me and my
family. Apart from his many admirers and friends, Mike
Richey died, aged ninety-two, in his flat in Brighton, of a
heart attack. He had had a couple of minor spasms before,
so his death did not come as a great surprise. Yet this did
not diminish the pain it brought me. He had been such
an important part of my life from our first meeting at his
brother Paul's house in Wilton Row. He had brought me
laughter and close companionship. He had shared his life
with mine after Julian's death, both in London and the Isle
of Wight. I had once thought myself in love with him – a
love which he was unable to return. He was adored and
admired by my children and, luckily, got on extremely well
with Andrew. In January, we all travelled to Brighton to a
memorial service in the Church of St Magdalene where there
was a Requiem Mass, an address by Libby Purves, a reading
by his nephew Peter from *Moby Dick* and some words from
Simon, his other nephew. Afterwards we all assembled for a
reception in the Garden Room of the Old Ship Hotel and
drank quite enough to remember Mike by.

Peter was as busy as ever, but he would lunch with me in
the flat when he could spare the time. As he was a vegetarian,
I would either try to cook an interesting meal or lazily buy
a pizza or a quiche. He was teetotal and liked drinking

lemonade, while I sipped my Chardonnay. One day he brought me a copy of a speech he made to the Norfolk Organic group, which summed up his beliefs. In the article he said, among many other things, that farming faced a 'perfect storm'. Fertilisers, like phosphates, were running out. About half the grain grown in Britain went to feed animals, not people. And now the new rich of China, India and Africa wanted meat and dairy products too. This was not sustainable. Organic farming was needed to grow more vegetable crops through solar power. Farming was a major source of productive and fulfilling jobs. It also protected natural beauty and wild life. "Along with saving the planet, we will have a better quality of life as a result."

Twenty

Kerena's children gave her a sixtieth birthday party at the cottage in Norfolk. A large marquee was erected in the garden with slides of her favourite volcanoes projected onto the canvas. We sat on straw bales and her three daughters served us a delicious dinner. They had all proved to be strong supports to their mother after her divorce from Adam Boulton. Since her days at the University at Aix-en-Provence, she had remained an avid Francophile. She enjoyed being close to another culture, feeling it provided her with a wider view of the world. She would often travel to France, sometimes alone and usually only for a couple of days, to visit exhibitions and towns of cultural and architectural interest. She returned to England happy and excited by what she had seen and the delicious meals she had eaten. I found these visits impressive. Since my marriage, I could never myself travel alone abroad or even have a meal by myself in a restaurant. I would always have Andrew or a friend by my side. Luckily Adam supported his family financially, so they had few worries on that score.

On the other hand, Pandora and Nick were always worried about money in spite of sending their two boys to state-run schools in nearby Exeter after their private prep schooling. Pandora often had to put her art on hold, but she and Nick were popular locally and would think nothing of driving twenty miles to attend dinner parties. Pandora was an excellent and rather relaxed cook, who would often shop in the morning and cook a gourmet dinner for twenty people that evening. She had also started breeding puppies from her Hungarian Vizslas to make some extra cash. She and Nick had stopped hunting, but they still loved going for long rides over the Devon moors. Damien Hirst and his partner were fairly close neighbours and gave lavish children's parties with enormous bouncy castles, while Ludo and Xan would leave with extravagant goodie bags. But when the Hirsts were separated, they only remained friendly with Damien's partner Mia, a lively American who would spend much of her time living in her river barge in London. At one time, Pandora had done some painting for Damien's dotted canvasses, but she left fairly soon, finding the work too demeaning.

When Harold Pinter died in 2008, it didn't come as a complete shock to anyone, as he had been diagnosed with cancer of the oesophagus six years earlier. After the diagnosis he had shown enormous courage, and in the latter months had taken to wearing a cap set at a jaunty angle. Andrew and I had known Antonia and Harold separately and later together for many years, but we would never consider ourselves close friends. Andrew had lived in the next door house to Harold in Hanover Terrace, when he was married to the celebrated actress, Vivien Merchant. Andrew was closer to Vivien and blamed Harold when she drank herself to death two years after he left her for Antonia. I had known

Antonia even before she was married to Hugh Fraser, and I had always admired her beauty and slim figure. We often attended the same parties during my marriage to Julian, and she would always appear the most beautiful girl in the room, attracting the best-looking men. Years later when I asked Hugh if he minded her flirting with other men, he replied, "No, she was so much younger than me and was still sowing her wild oats."

Harold's biographer, Michael Billington, recalled that the family origin was East European Ashkenazi rather than the Portuguese Sephardic Jews. In his review of Antonia's account of herself and Harold, he wrote of the passion and intensity of their marriage. "What may, initially, have seemed a problem was arguably the key to the relationship. If Harold was an irresistible force, Antonia could also on occasion be an immovable object." Sometimes they had tempestuous political disagreements. On the matter of Milosevic, Antonia argued that it was legitimate to try him as a war criminal, even if others were not similarly arraigned. And when Harold claimed that the United States was the world's most barbarous empire, Antonia reasonably argued that the Nazis or Pol Pot might have a superior claim.

Once at one of our parties in our flat overlooking the river, Harold saw a conservative politician he particularly disliked. "How could you have invited that bloody fascist?" he asked. I quickly introduced him to an attractive girl, who intrigued him until he simmered down. All through Harold and Antonia's life together, she kept a daily diary and then a month after his death, she decided to write a memoir. *Must You Go?* was an immediate success. When Frances Osborne interviewed her after the publication of the book, she wrote, "But her Pinter is not always easy to square with the better-known image of him as an irascible and confrontational left-wing writer." Then Antonia was quoted: "In private, he was rather a jolly fellow, not the public sort of brooding, enigmatic person. I don't like being bored – Harold was endlessly interesting. The things I missed most about him were that his reactions to everything were so individual – so you never knew how he was going to react."

Dylan Thomas had once again taken over my husband's life. It would be the centenary of the bard's birth in 2014, and already many events had been planned in his honour. Andrew's film *Under Milk Wood* was to be shown in cinemas and schools in Wales and all over the world. He was being asked by the British Council through diplomatic ties to present the film and speak at question-and-answer sessions afterwards. He liked to tell stories of the shenanigans between the stars, the tempestuous storms between Elizabeth Taylor and Richard Burton, the wit and charm of Peter O'Toole, and the beauty of Angharad Rees, who had become my great friend before she passed away. Like a fly trapped in amber, that time-capsule of life in an imaginary fishing village would sound for ever, the play of voices from a Wales that never really was and would always be so.

Dylan Thomas had rather obsessed Andrew for most of his life. His early Cambridge novel, *My Friend Judas*, was influenced by the Welsh poet. The play of *Adventures in the Skin Trade* was Andrew's search into Dylan's surrealism and nostalgia. His book, *Dylan the Bard*, was praised by the writer's wife Caitlin, who said that Andrew had captured the very essence of Dylan, and she did not know how. So when he was privileged to make the film of *Under Milk Wood* against long odds, he said at the end of that classic production, "I did not make that film nor the actors in it. Dylan's words were our incantation. His magic made our film."

That was true. Even the gods listened. Shot in a blustery February and March, the sun shone only over Fishguard, where the film was shot. All night in the town pub, the cast sang to harp and piano the old Welsh folksongs. The schoolchildren became the voices of the bard. As Richard Burton said, "All the Welsh are actors. Only the bad ones become professionals." In living, as in making movies, magic rarely happens. Andrew and I have found such touches in Scotland and India, New York and the Dordogne, Chelsea and Bali, and now on the river. What more can we ever have? Those treasured spells are cast in memory and last for ever.

One lasting memory was a holiday we spent in the summer of 2010 in Turkey. We rented a complex of three cottages surrounding a large swimming pool at Gümusluk, a short walk to the ocean. Kerena, Peter and Pandora came with their families and, counting boyfriends, we were sixteen in all. We shared our cottage with the Wesolowskis, while Kay and Peter settled in happily into the other two syringa-covered abodes. By day, after Kerena had given us a lesson in Pilates, we would all go our separate ways. Pandora and Nick would take their boys to a nearby beach, where they could water-ski and windsurf. Andrew and I wandered down to our local beach where the swimming was superb.

We'd eat lunch at the sea-side restaurant sitting in seclusion under an enormous spruce tree and later read our books on deckchairs. The routine suited everyone, and in the evening we would get together and dine at our cottage, sitting round joined-together tables lit by candlelight. Jessie's boyfriend Jon, the Zimbabwean lawyer, turned out to be a dab hand at the barbecue. Hannah had worked at Ruthie Rogers restaurant, The River Café and was a brilliant cook. With the others all giving a hand, each meal was a gourmet delight. One evening some of us drove to the local town where a concert was being given in the tiny whitewashed church. A dream of a holiday, which brought all of us even closer.

We were back in London for the Queen's Diamond Jubilee celebrations. Thousands of people lined the Mall, many having travelled from far and wide to watch the evening concert outside Buckingham Palace. Andrew and I are both staunch royalists, although all of my extended family tend to be Republicans. It didn't stop them coming to a champagne-fuelled afternoon fiesta to celebrate the occasion. We had family and close friends from the age of one to ninety, including my first great-grandchild. Peter's son Jay had married Blanca, a girl from Panama, and they soon had a son Nickolas. Our flat was the perfect venue from which to watch the procession of a thousand boats, as they proceeded with the gilded Royal Barge gliding down the river from Chelsea Harbour to the Tower of London. One hundred full-rigged ships sailed upriver until they reached Tower Bridge. What a regatta to end them all. Our friends Bamber Gascoigne and his wife Christina were part of the procession and had rowed all the way from Richmond in a skiff and back again. Talking to them later, they said it had been a lifetime experience, a unique imprint on memory, never to be erased.

A few months later, we woke one morning to see an enormous black cloud of smoke drifting on the far side of the river, above Nine Elms, the new Covent Garden. Then the shock on the news – a helicopter had hit the too-high crane on the top of one of the tall blocks rising on the South Bank near to where the new American Embassy was being built. Luckily, it was early morning and only one pedestrian and the pilot were killed. It made me feel that, in spite of personal minor disasters, one must always try and live for the moment – one never knows what disaster might be awaiting round the next bend of life.

The London Olympics proved a great triumph of the organisational skill possessed by the British for big occasions. From the bucolic opening pageant, directed by my old Royal Court directors Danny Boyle and Stephen Daldry, to the original finale, the Olympic Stadium had at last shown its worth. The best party trick was when our Queen was seen descending by parachute into the stadium as if in a James Bond movie. Daniel Craig had actually been to Buckingham Palace to ask her to take part in the spoof. Having a great sense of humour, Her Majesty was amused and agreed. In actual fact it was a doll dressed as the queen but fun all the same. Gold, silver and bronze medals were won in profusion. And when my personal sporting hero Andy Murray won both a gold and a bronze by beating the world's Number One at tennis and playing with his English partner in the Doubles, I cheered like a cricket or football fanatic. Our police, so often maligned, played their part and, thanks to the brilliant security arrangements, the Olympics proved a great morale booster to the British nation after all the economic gloom.

My children gave me a present of a computer several years ago. I had a few lessons on how to use it and then decided I would rather continue with my usual modes, the telephone and the human voice. I love talking to my daughters daily and Peter rings me regularly every Sunday. They all think I am crazy not to make use of the endlessly growing information that the internet has to offer. At the press of a button, I'm told that you go online to access untold facilities. I don't even carry my mobile with me, wherever I go. According to conventional wisdom, I should be permanently plugged in to all the newest versions of every available digital gadget, sifting all the latest data. But when would I ever get the chance to relax properly, to allow my body and mind to restore themselves and for my imagination to run riot? Yet whenever I try to explain this to anyone, I notice in their eyes a mixture of pity and non-comprehension. As the old poem goes, however, we must have time to stand and stare. And wonder and sift our memories and what we know.

Now an ally has emerged in Professor Paul Dolan, an expert in psychology at the London School of Economics. He was warned that the everyday stress of using mobile phones may be sending us mad. He argues that we'd all be much more content if we turned off our mobiles and concentrated on friends and family rather than impulsively checking emails and text messages. He further warns that unless people change their behaviour, they are putting themselves at risk of mental illness. This can develop, he believes, as a result of the constant nervous stress of checking our nagging digital input. Jeffrey Janata, the Director of Behavioural Medicine at University Hospital in Cleveland is also against the constant din of the mobiles. He argues that this can cause insomnia because of the disruption of the brainwaves during the incessant use of mobiles or computers before going to bed, worse than drinking cups of coffee in the evening.

Everything in the digital era has changed so dramatically since the mid-nineties, and this revolution will continue to mutate. But I'm afraid Andrew and I remain Luddites at heart, although if my television became redundant I would be devastated. We have each other, and if we want to chat we have our family and friends and no intruders. And we have time to think and be ourselves, with no stranger hacking into our private lives on Twitter. In actual fact, when I need an answer to some difficult question, I simply telephone one of my daughters who quickly obtains the information from her iPad.

As age catches up on us, life slows down. The post consists of endless catalogues and bills and only the rare invitation to a party or poetry reading or the launch of a friend's book. Strangely, I find this positive rather than negative. It means I have more time to spend either alone with Andrew or seeing more of my children and grandchildren, and I am able to keep in touch with their full-on lives. I still believe in living in the present and try to plan ahead to make sure there is something in my diary to look forward to. We go to the theatre and movies much less as time goes on, and often see again our favourite films. I used to be an avid reader of the latest cookery book and thought nothing of giving small dinners for eight or buffet parties for thirty. Cooking inventive dishes was a pleasure at which I excelled. But now our dinners for two are usually one-course affairs of a Spanish omelette and salad or plain grilled meat or fish and a green vegetable helped down by a glass or two of wine.

As life inevitably slows down, my thoughts turn to the unknown future. People are living to a much greater age due to the advance in medical treatment and the State's care of the elderly. Andrew addresses this in *Afterdeath: an Inquiry*. I will quote the penultimate paragraph:

If I may make a final statement in this inquiry – before any Last Judgement, of course, I would state this. The preference between those who believe in obliteration or an afterlife is weighted. Astronomy and mathematics, what Einstein called the cosmological constant, declare that the odds against the existence of human beings on this planet are several trillions to one. Although he rejected his hypothesis of a repulsive force that would balance gravity and stymie quantum physics, he is backed posthumously by recent string and quintessence and boson theories about the conversion of energy into mass, or one might poetically say, spirit into flesh. Or do we roll the dice, when Einstein said the job of God was not to do so? In terms of our cultures to date, the case for a creative principle is compelling. For who else may referee the chaos and quarks and black matter that underlie all? As for the soul, released at death from the body and the mind to seek a union with a primal source of energy, that is the belief of the faiths, held by most of humankind.

I feel there to be a great deal of truth in this theory. As Emily Dickinson wrote about our inevitable fate:

Because I could not stop for Death –
   He kindly stopped for me –
The carriage held but just ourselves –
And Immortality.
Since then – 'tis centuries – and yet
Feels shorter than the Day
I first surmised the Horses' Heads
Were Toward eternity.

But whatever the truth may be – and I would wish for a return to nothingness – I do admit to some feelings of dread. The thought of being a burden on Andrew or my family fills me with horror. A slow physical illness or a stroke or Alzheimer's, the need of hospitalisation or round-the-clock care, are conditions I would find it impossible to endure. But, of course, there would be nothing I could do about it, except suicide, if I was in my right mind. So, being an optimist at heart, death is something I rarely think about and take each day as it comes and make plans for enhancing our future life as much as our advancing years will allow.

I will never understand quite why people care for me. As Goethe said: "Know thyself? If I did I'd run away." Yet this is meant to be an autobiography. I have set down what I remember, from *suttee* as a child, to a kind of serenity as I approach my ending. Any readers of this record will have to judge me upon how I see myself and what I appear to have done.